How to Address the Loss? Forced Migrations, Lost Territories and the Politics of History

A Comparative Approach in Europe and at its Margins in the XXth Century

P.I.E. Peter Lang
Bruxelles · Bern · Berlin · New York · Oxford · Wien

Anne Bazin and Catherine Perron (eds.)

How to Address the Loss? Forced Migrations, Lost Territories and the Politics of History

A Comparative Approach in Europe and at its Margins in the XXth Century

L'Allemagne dans les relations internationales
Vol. 15

Cover image : Detail of the monument "To the unforgotten homeland and its dead", situated at the entrance of the Burghalden cemetery, Sindelfingen, Germany, 2017
© Catherine Perron

Financial support from : Centre de Recherches Internationales (CERI) - Sciences Po Paris, Sciences Po Lille, Centre d'Etude des Mondes Russe, Caucasien et Centre Européen (CERCEC)/EHESS, Centre d'Etudes et de Recherches Administratives, Politiques et Sociales (CERAPS-CNRS) and University of Lille.

Translation and editing: Malcom Green, Cynthia J. Johnson, Eunice Pelini Sanya, Roger Depledge, Charlotte Forfang.

Cette publication a fait l'objet d'une évaluation par les pairs.

Éditions scientifiques internationales
Brussels, 2018
1 avenue Maurice, B-1050 Bruxelles, Belgium
brussels@peterlang.com ; www.peterlang.com

ISSN 2034-4929
ISBN 978-2-8076-0580-0
ePDF 978-2-8076-0581-7
ePub 978-2-8076-0582-4
Mobi 978-2-8076-0583-1
DOI 10.3726/b14693
D/2018/5678/74

Imprimé en Allemagne

Information bibliographique publiée par « Die Deutsche Bibliothek »

« Die Deutsche Bibliothek » répertorie cette publication dans la « Deutsche Nationalbibliografie » ; les données bibliographiques détaillées sont disponibles sur le site <http://dnb.ddb.de>.

Editors' Acknowledgements

This book originated in a conference entitled "Penser la Perte/How to Address the Loss – Towards a New Approach to the Politics of History in Relation to Lost Territories and the Forced Transfers of Populations in Europe and at Its Borders", held at Sciences Po – CERI on 4 December 2015. Most of the papers published in the book were discussed during the conference.

We are grateful to the Centre de Recherches Internationales (CERI) – Sciences Po Paris and to Sciences Po Lille, as well as to the Centre d'Etude des Mondes Russe, Caucasien et Centre Européen (CERCEC)/EHESS and to the Centre d'Etudes et de Recherches Administratives, Politiques et Sociales (CERAPS-CNRS)/University of Lille for their financial support.

We would also like to express our gratitude to Malcom Green, Cynthia J. Johnson, Eunice Pelini Sanya, Roger Depledge, Charlotte Forfang, Michael Ayton and Annemarie Norman who helped with translating the texts into English and with editing, as well as to Dorian Ryser (CERI) and the Atelier de cartographie de Sciences Po who helped with the maps.

Contents

Methodological Considerations in Addressing the Issue of Forced Migrations, Lost Territories and the Related Politics of History: A Comparative Approach 11
Anne Bazin and Catherine Perron

The "German East": Myth? Reality? Lost Land of Dreams? 37
Eva Hahn and Hans Henning Hahn

Private versus Public: The Memorialization of the Exodus of the Istro-Dalmatians, 1945–2015 59
Gustavo Corni

The Politics of History of the Lost Land: Shifting European, National and Regional Approaches to the History of Karelia 81
Kimmo Katajala and Ilkka Liikanen

The *Kresy* in Polish Memory: Between a Lost Arcadia and the Bloodlands of East-Central Europe 109
Beata Halicka

The Ties of Greek and Turkish Refugees and "Exchangees" to their Lost Homelands: An Asymmetry of Memory 135
Michel Bruneau

Turkey's Guiding Light and Consolation in Addressing the Loss: Nationalism 167
Etienne Copeaux

Broken Lives, Silenced Memories and Reappropriations of the Past: The Jews of Egypt and Islamic Countries 179
Michèle Baussant

List of Abbreviations 199

List of Tables and List of Figures 201

Index 203

List of contributors 219

Abstracts 225

Methodological Considerations in Addressing the Issue of Forced Migrations, Lost Territories and the Related Politics of History: A Comparative Approach

Anne Bazin

Assistant Professor of Political Science, Sciences Po Lille and research fellow at CERAPS-CNRS, University of Lille, France

Catherine Perron

Assistant Research Professor of Political Science with tenure, Sciences Po, Center for International Studies (CERI), CNRS, Paris, France

A striking experience in the twentieth century, but only a small place in the European collective memory

The map of Europe has been redrawn many times during the twentieth century, because of several wars (two world wars and decolonization wars), the end of the Cold War and the disintegration of the USSR. This has been done in both peaceful and violent ways. Addressing and managing territorial loss or territorial changes is thus a phenomenon that Europe is accustomed to. One might even add that very few countries have been spared such a challenge at one moment or another in their recent history. Shifting borders, however, is not limited to the reconfiguration of space. It also implies rethinking and redefining the relationship with the territory, with the nation and with the state itself. This is particularly true when territorial transformations are accompanied by forced migrations such as those we focus on in this book.

We use the term "forced migrations"[1] to refer to the "population transfers" primarily used in the Greek–Turkish case (see Bruneau and Copeaux in this book), the "exodus" of Italians from Istria and Dalmatia (see Gustavo Corni in this book), the "expulsion" of Jews from Islamic countries (see Baussant in this book), the "expulsion" of Germans from Eastern Europe (see Hahn and Hahn in this book), the Finns' "flight" following the fate of the Karelians during the war (see Katajala and Liikanen in this book) and the "repatriation" of Poles from *Kresy* (see Halicka in this book). The vocabulary selected is quite important, and the choice of one term over another often has political connotations. We prefer to use the term "forced migrations", rather than "ethnic cleansing", because, as Antonio Ferrara argues: "security concerns, or social conflicts or enforcing repression and dispossession – have also prompted policies entailing (either as an instrument or as an outcome, sometimes unintended, but rarely unforeseen) the massive displacement and sometimes the killing of populations identified on grounds other than ethnic ones. In itself it is perhaps enough of a reason to speak about 'forced migrations' rather than ethnic cleansing."[2] Our use of the term is in line with the definition proposed by Krzysztof Ruchniewicz:

> Forced migrations are usually mass movements of people, which are carried out by direct (the order to leave a place is enforced with violence) or situational coercion (massive threat by violence), exercised by state power organs (independent or with international approval) or local actors (separatists, paramilitary groupings, etc.). The action of (understood in a broad sense) ruling powers is the impulse that triggers the population movement, which does not mean that these migrations would be organized, controlled or take place in a less violent form. Victims are mostly ethnic, social or religious/religiously defined groups, which are to be separated from the rest of the population of the given territories. These are often minorities or other groups which have been given a special status, often as a result of changes in national boundaries. They may be citizens of the former or of a state regarded as hostile, or also, as a result of the disintegration of a multinational state, that bears the necessity of the reconstitution of states – be stateless. Forced migrations usually take place in the context of a war with an external aggressor, a civil war and its domestic effects and/or of the implementation of an ideologically motivated, socio-political project such as the creation of a nationally united state or the totalitarian reconstruction of a society … Forced migrations are

---

1 "*Zwangsmigrationen*" in German, "*migrations forcées*" in French.

2 See Antonio Ferrara, "Eugene Kulischer, Joseph Schechtman and the Historiography of European Forced Migrations", *Journal of Contemporary History*, Vol. 46, No. 4, p. 739.

also characterized by the fact that the affected persons have no influence on the happening and usually cannot change the "top-down" assignment or categorization (national identity, race, class).[3]

In Europe and at its margins, especially during the first half of the twentieth century, entire populations – hundreds of thousands and even millions of people – have been expelled or have had to flee from territories conquered or taken over by another state, or because of the displacement of international borders, or in an exchange of population as part of a peace agreement. These populations were received as refugees, as expellees, or as repatriates and had to integrate (or reintegrate) within a state which was then considered as their homeland.

The purpose of this book is to analyse how hosting states and societies, as well as the groups that were forced to leave, dealt with the memory of forced migrations in the long term and how they addressed the different types of loss associated with these migrations. Given that many countries in Europe have experienced population transfers during the last century and a half, the issue remains deeply anchored in European memories. In an essay about "the seven circles of European memory", the German political scientist Claus Leggewie positions the memory of population transfers third in a series of seven concentric circles of supra- and transnational memory. The memory of the Holocaust is at the core of the disc, followed by Soviet communism. Third are "expulsions as a pan-European trauma".[4]

However, despite the fact that forced migrations have been the fate of many European people, expulsions and population transfers *per se* have never been addressed at the European level, and there has been no official recognition of them across Europe. The absence of debate at the European and European Union (EU) level is rather striking. Given that this trauma is shared by many European communities and by millions of people, forced migrations could have been used as a founding element to develop a European identity, for instance, in the same way that the memory of the Holocaust has been used as a negative founding myth. At the European and EU level, the memory of forced migrations is yet

3 Krzysztof Ruchniewicz, "Zwangsmigration" in online *Lexikon zur Kultur und Geschichte der Deutschen im östlichen Europa*, 2015. ome-lexikon.uni-oldenburg.de/p32750 (accessed 22 May 2015) [our translation].

4 Claus Leggewie, "A Tour of the Battleground: The Seven Circles of Pan-European Memory", *Social Research*, Vol. 75, No. 1, Spring 2008, pp. 217–234.

to be perceived as capable of promoting unity and a common identity; similarly, the capacity for division of this memory among neighbours has not been addressed. One can question the inability or unwillingness to address the loss in public debate. Is it linked to its proximity to genocidal acts, as Leggewie has argued?[5] Is it because the experience of forced migrations, though widely shared by Europeans, is mainly to be found in countries in South-Eastern and North-Eastern Europe which, with the exception of Germany, are not founding members of the EU? (In reality, this hypothesis is quite problematic because both Italy and France[6] have been affected by forced population transfers.) Or is it because the issue has long been ignored in societies because it was perceived as a divisive issue best avoided in public debate?

The frames within which the history of population transfers is usually narrated challenge mainstream Western historiography. As the American historian Benjamin Lieberman argues:

> There has been little place for the ethnically cleansed in standard histories of Europe because historians by custom tell the stories of nations. A focus on ethnic cleansing shifts perspective. The story of the rise of the nation state, often a triumph of self-determination, becomes a story of tragedy for those who were driven out. Moments of liberation and victory are also turning points for expulsion and ethnic cleansing. National heroes become champions of bigotry, aggression and exclusion. And in the case of ordinary people, the record of support for and participation in terror, violence and theft adds a profoundly pessimistic note to the story of modern European progress.[7]

The temporal frame is also challenged in the sense that, in Western historiography, World War I, for example, has until today mainly been thought of as a trench war and its time frame is identified as 1914–18. This frame does not apply in Europe's East, and especially not in the South-East, where the war is mainly remembered as a war of massive population displacements and is associated with the memory of the first genocide of the century, namely, the Armenian genocide.[8] The time

---

5 Claus Leggewie, *Der Kampf um die europäische Erinnerung. Ein Schlachtfeld wird besichtigt*, Munich, Verlag C. H. Beck, 2011, p. 27.

6 About this, see e.g. Philipp Ther, "Die 'Triage' im Elsass", in Philipp Ther, *Die dunkle Seite der Nationalstaaten. Ethnische Säuberungen im modernen Europa*, Göttingen, Vandenhoeck & Ruprecht, 2012, pp. 86–89.

7 Benjamin Lieberman, *Terrible Fate: Ethnic Cleansing in the Making of Modern Europe*, Lanham, Rowman & Littlefield, 2015 (2006), Preface, pp. xiv–xv.

8 Benjamin Lieberman, *Terrible Fate*, *op. cit.*, pp. 116–117.

frame thus extends to encompass the Balkan wars and even the Treaty of Lausanne in 1923 (and, even later, the Greek–Turkish friendship treaty of 1930). A comparative approach at a European level suggests to take into account these different frames and puts into question national historical narratives and representations.

The loss is rather easy to identify at the individual level. People have sometimes lost members of their family, often they have lost belongings, their social environment, connections to their ancestry, sometimes a language or a dialect, part of their traditions and customs, know-how … and ultimately a homeland (*Heimat*). At the group level, however, it is far more complex to define what has been lost. As Eva Hahn and Hans Henning Hahn note in their contribution to this book, what has been lost is often complex, ambiguous and historically challenged. The repeated shifting of borders and of sovereignty in some territories over a few decades has made it difficult to respond to the question of what belongs to whom and who belongs to what. The complexity of the issue also depends on what is referred to: land and landscapes, buildings, cemeteries or goods. It is quite easy to measure the loss of goods or even land. But what about the identity attached to a territory? This identity has to do with language (idioms), traditions and social relations within one's own group and/or among groups and communities. Is it possible to understand how the loss of interactions with other groups which once lived on the same territory impacts on one's identity? As the Czech historian and politician František Palacký wrote in the middle of the nineteenth century, "The Czech course of history is the interaction and the permanent conflict with the Germans".[9] How can the loss resulting from the destruction of the relationship with the other be measured? Eva Hahn and Hans-Henning Hahn have studied these issues concerning what has long been referred to as the "German East" in Germany. Their questions correspond perfectly with most cases of forced migrations, as several contributions in this book show. For these reasons, we suggest rethinking the patterns of national and group memories by placing them within a wider frame. Indeed, for far too long, these memories have been assessed only as part of national and/or local/group narratives.

9 František Palacký, *Dějiny národu českého v Čechach a na Moravě* (History of the Czech Nation in Bohemia and in Moravia), Prague, 1848, pp. 12–13.

Forced migrations: a political tool recently reshaped to fit within the current pattern of human rights norms

"Population transfers" have been used for centuries as part of domestic and international policies. In the first half of the twentieth century, these transfers were still considered a legitimate means for solving minority or security problems (see e.g. the end of the Balkans wars, the Lausanne Treaty of 1923 or the transfer of the German populations from the East after World War II mentioned in the Potsdam Agreement, art. 13).[10]

Today, forced migrations are denounced as a violation of human rights: they are perceived as a violation of fundamental as well as economic, political and social rights. Population displacement is no longer accepted as a long-term solution to a conflict, at least not by the so-called international community. It might be tolerated as a transitory state before the return of the population and is often presented as such, even though the period of transition may sometimes be rather long. The UN's recognition of a "right to return" of the Palestinian people in 1974 helped change how forced migrations were perceived both at the international level and in international law.[11] Ever since, groups of expellees such as the German *Vertriebene(n)* have repeatedly referred to the UN resolution concerning the Palestinians to reinforce their claims to a right of return (*Heimatrecht*).[12] In addition, Western societies began to pay new attention to victims (of forced migrations) in the 1980s. The public recognition of their suffering led to the idea that they could play a central role in addressing post-conflict situations. Listening to victims and hearing them tell their own narratives became a moral duty.[13] The Austrian historian Philipp Ther highlights a "decisive difference" between the international attitude to the Yugoslav Wars of the 1990s and the attitude to the aftermath of World War II. He writes about a "shock effect and the unanimous international rejection". Ther points out that

---

10 See Philipp Ther, *Die dunkle Seite der Nationalstaaten*, *op. cit.*, pp. 69–108.

11 UN General Assembly Resolution 3236, passed on 22 November 1974, declared the right of return to be an "inalienable right".

12 See the petition sent to the UN by the *Sudetendeutsche Landsmannschaft* on 2 December 1975, in which there is an explicit reference to the UN General Assembly Resolution 3236, passed on 22 November 1974, which mentions a right of return for the Palestinians.

13 See, *Raisons politiques*, "Les victimes écrivent leur histoire", No. 30, 2008. Elazar Barkan, Alexander Karn (eds.), *Taking Wrongs Seriously: Apologies and Reconciliation*, Stanford UP, 2006.

during the Yugoslav wars "the lack of consent of the great powers and neighbouring states contained the ethnic cleansing and led to the Dayton Peace Agreement and even to the return of refugees".[14] However, the question remains complex, since this unanimous rejection of population transfers, at least by Western democracies, is accompanied by the refusal to reconsider the European post-war order, which is characterized by the recognition of the intangibility of borders and the absence of legal, material or territorial claims linked to it. One can add a will to peaceful cooperation as a fundamental dimension of the European integration.

Today, forced migrations are not only morally condemned but are also outlawed, at least by the signatories to the Rome Statute of the International Criminal Court, which lists, in Article 7 §1 (d), "Deportation or forcible transfer of population" among the crimes against humanity.[15] The current international norm considers population transfers a crime against peace or humanity. However, as the German historian Michael Schwarz argues, it is still not as clear as that in the case of internationally organized and supervised "population transfers", especially when those are seen as the last option in an apparently insoluble conflict.[16]

Yet, in academic literature as well as in popular representations, population transfers are perceived as belonging to a history of violence.[17] Even though there is a widespread consensus among academics[18] for

---

14 Philipp Ther, *Die Dunkle Seite der Nationalstaaten*, *op. cit.*, p. 240 [our translation].

15 The condemnation of forced migrations (ethnic cleansing), though almost unanimous among academics as well as in the international community of states, is fairly recent and still debated on some points (especially the expulsion of the Germans from East-Central Europe after World War II). See Michael Schwarz, "Questions de point de vue: une perspective nationale, européenne et globale sur les 'purifications' ethniques modernes", in Carola Hähnel-Mesnard, Dominique Herbet (dir.), *Fuite et expulsions des Allemands. Transnationalité et représentations 19è–21è siècle*, Villeneuve d'Ascq, Presses du Septentrion, 2016, pp. 38–39. The change of attitude towards using these means in international relations has occurred rather slowly after World War II. It was during the wars in Yugoslavia at the beginning of the 1990s that international condemnation became clear and almost unanimous.

16 See Michael Schwarz, "Questions de point de vue", *op. cit.*, p. 38.

17 In his latest book, *The Killing Compartments: The Mentality of Mass Murder*, New Haven, Yale University Press 2015, Abram de Swaan places "forced migrations" under the title "Mass Pogroms".

18 This is not the case among the associations of victims of ethnic cleansing or forced migrations, which often draw outspoken or inferred parallels between these two forms of mass violence – with the aim of gaining the same status as victims as those of genocide – one of the crimes that internationally receives the highest opprobrium.

a need to distinguish them from genocides,[19] forced migrations are considered highly traumatic. Put differently, they are thought to have long-lasting consequences which can be felt even after the disappearance of the generation that experienced them. These migrations are in fact often accompanied by a process of impoverishment and social downgrading of expelled populations, which have to endure the loss of most of their property and therefore the loss of their capacity to make a living. Unlike refugees, expellees cannot return, even in the long term. Furthermore, open wounds often persist among expellees and transcend generations. These include feelings of being uprooted, individual psychological suffering, hate and a desire for revenge. These perceptions usually shift from feelings of injustice to openly revisionist attitudes. As Ernest Renan pointed out, not only is the relation to the past fundamental for creating a common feeling of belonging, but moreover, shared sufferings unite far more than shared joys. And, "as far as national memories are concerned, mourning is better than triumph, because it imposes duties, it commands common efforts"[20] such as, for instance, the restoration of the nation's

---

19 See Michael MANN, *The Dark Side of Democracy. Explaining Ethnic Cleansing*, Cambridge, Cambridge University Press, 2005, pp. 7–8 and p. 17, or Benjamin LIEBERMANN, *Terrible Fate, op. cit.*, p. XIV, or Stephane ROSIÈRE, *Le nettoyage ethnique. Tereur et peuplement*, Paris, Ellipses, 2006, p. 6, or Norman NAIMARK, "Ethnic Cleansing", *Online Encyclopedia of Mass Violence* [online], published 4 November 2007 (accessed 9 March 2016), http://www.massviolence.org/Ethnic-Cleansing, ISSN 1961–9898, or Philipp THER, *Die Dunkle Seite der Nationalstaaten, op. cit.*, pp. 8–9 and Michael SCHWARZ, *Ethnische "Säuberungen" in der Moderne. Globale Wechselwirkungen nationalistischer und rassistischer Gewaltpolitik im 19. und 20. Jahrhundert*, Munich, Oldenbourg Verlag, 2013, pp. 2–3, who place forced migrations on a continuum of mass violence that runs from pogroms to genocide, all of them insisting nevertheless on the necessity to analytically distinguish forced migrations/ethnic cleansing from the latter. As Philipp Ther puts it: "Ethnic cleansing and genocides differ in several respects, in terms of objectives, results and in their spatial dimensions. In the case of a genocide, the destruction of a certain population group is the goal, for which a specific intent (*dolus specialis*) is assumed in international law. The primary goal of ethnic cleansing, on the other hand, is the systematic removal of a population group from a certain territory." He continues: "another argument for a differentiation between ethnic cleansing and genocide is based on the – for the historian – inevitable consideration of spatial dimensions of history. Expulsions and forced relocations were always associated with spatial conceptions of target and receiving areas, usually a co-ethnic state. Accordingly, most of the ethnic cleansing was transborder … Genocides are at best based on a deportation to nowhere, symbolized by the end of the railway tracks in Auschwitz-Birkenau." Philipp THER, *Die Dunkle Seite der Nationalstaaten, op. cit.*, pp. 8–9 [our translation].

20 Ernest RENAN, *Qu'est-ce qu'une Nation?* 1882, p. 51; http://classiques.uqac.ca/classiques/renan_ernest/qu_est_ce_une_nation/renan_quest_ce_une_nation.pdf.

greatness or pride after a dark episode.[21] It is thus easy to politically instrumentalize the memory of sufferings endured. For all these reasons, the persistence of such negative memories has become a challenge for peace and stability in Europe and at its margins.[22]

The role of the past in international relations: how and why does the memory of forced migrations count today within the European integration context?

The past interferes with international relations in different ways. As the Belgian political scientist Valérie Rosoux pointed out quoting Marie Claire Lavabre, one must distinguish between the weight of the past and the choice of the past, two concepts which in reality are in constant interaction.[23] The choice of history refers to how actors choose (or not) to use references to the past. How they interpret history and choose their references depends on their present preoccupations. In many cases, the past is used as a keystone argument within both national and international contexts. It is a tool that helps legitimize one's position and claims, and it is a political issue as well. The weight of the past can be understood across different levels: when the memory of a past event shapes the perception of the current reality; when the consequences of the past weigh on current policies; and, ultimately, through actors' personal histories.

Interpretations of the past often diverge. The same event can be interpreted differently and take on a greater or lesser role in the following period[24] or a different meaning depending on the periodization in history. For instance, did the expulsion of Germans from Eastern Europe in 1945–7 occur during the last period of the war or, on the contrary, during

---

21 Benjamin Lieberman, *Terrible Fate, op. cit.*, p. 34.

22 Catherine Perron, "§96 Bundesvertriebenengestez. Ein Instrument der Versöhnung Deutschlands mit seinen mittel-und osteuropäischen Nachbarn?" in Corine Defrance, Ulrich Pfeil (Hg.) *Verständingung und Versöhnung nach dem „Zivilisationsbruch"? Deutschland und Europa nach 1945*, Bruxelles, P.I.E Peter Lang, 2016, pp. 499–518.

23 Valérie Rosoux, *Les usages de la mémoire dans les relations internationales. Le recours au passé dans la politique étrangère de la France à l'égard de l'Allemagne et de l'Algérie de 1962 à nos jours*, Brussels, Etablissements Emile Bruylant, 2001.

24 For example, the History of the Teutonic Order, which is presented in Polish textbooks as part of German expansionism towards the East, while German textbooks focus on the civilizing dimension of these conquests. For further details, see the work of the Polish historian Jerzy Holzer, who was a member of the German–Polish Historian commission.

the first post-war period? These two interpretations have quite different political consequences. The choice of terms relating to population transfers also illustrates divergent interpretations of the phenomenon.[25] These divergences are not *per se* a problem in international relations; they are normal, often necessary, and they offer a constructive basis for dialogue. They cannot, however, be ignored. On numerous occasions, conflicts from the past associated with forced migrations have poisoned bilateral relations. A recent example is the conditionality linked to the abolition of the Beneš Decrees which a few German politicians tried to impose on the Czech Republic during the European integration process. Until 2004, the Sudeten German question had been repeatedly instrumentalized in the debate about the expansion of the EU, both at the European level (European Commission, European Parliament) and at the national level in Austria, Hungary or Germany.[26]

Dealing with the memory of the loss and of forced migrations

In addition to historians, other kinds of stakeholders are likely to take an interest in the memory of the loss, and of forced migrations. These may include the displaced persons themselves – individually or in groups – as well as states and governments. While these actors are quite independent, they interact at different levels. For instance, a state can relay claims internationally, and a government can financially support associations of expellees or, on the contrary, denounce their actions. Shifts across categories and even positions are not uncommon. Leaders of associations may engage in politics to defend their cause. In the German case, for instance, many historians dealing with these issues from the 1960s to the 1990s were expellees themselves and often members of the *Landsmannschaften*. Moreover, leaders of these associations were active

---

25 See Eva Hahnová (Hahn), *Sudetoněmecký problém: obtížné loučení s minulostí* (The Sudeto–German Issue: A Difficult Farewell to the Past), Prague 1996. Chapter 7 is entirely dedicated to this aspect "Our history: the Czech–German past, a problem of interpretation", pp. 174–199.

26 Anne Bazin, "Les décrets Beneš. De l'usage du passé dans le débat européen", *Critique Internationale*, No. 21, October 2003, pp. 42–51.

In Germany, however, this was not the case at the government level. See Gerhard Schroeder, *Rede anläßlich des 50. Jahrestages der Charta der deutschen Heimatvertriebenen am Tag der Heimat*, 3 September 2000, in Berlin.

politicians in Bavaria or at the federal level.[27] These stakeholders certainly cannot be placed in a unified and homogeneous category. The distinction between historians and memory entrepreneurs is often blurred. As the Italian historian Enzo Traverso has rightly pointed out concerning the politics of history, "In exile, borders between the scholar and the activist become porous, unstable".[28] Two reasons could explain this: the first is the marginal position of the exiled in the hosting society, and the second is their status as losers. The same is true in the case of forced migrations, in the sense that expellees often had to endure a double defeat. In the German, Italian, Finnish and Greek cases, not only did expellees become part of a defeated nation, they also had to endure their loss. This outsider position may have nourished a critical attitude towards mainstream national history writing. Furthermore, these stakeholders (professional or amateur historians, editorialists, leaders of associations, politicians, artists ...) have their own rationality and are pursuing their own objectives. They can either oppose each other in their use of the past for political, personal or very pragmatic reasons, or they can cooperate.

To examine how this troublesome past has been addressed in different countries, we will draw on the concept of "politics of history" (*Geschichtspolitik*). According to Edgar Wolfrum, politics of history is "a field of action and politics on which actors load history with their specific interests and try to politically use it. The politics of history aims at publicity and seeks legitimizing, mobilizing, politicizing, scandalizing and defaming effects in the political dispute".[29] The politics of history can be addressed in two ways. The first pays attention to actors competing to impose their narratives and interpretations of the past (e.g. by promoting a specific aspect of the past or focusing on one period in particular, thereby silencing other moments or downplaying some events) on their actions, on the interactions they share, and on national and international (normative) contexts. The

---

27 See the debate about the *Ostforschung* in the late 1990s in Germany: Anne Bazin, "Dědictví studené války v přístupu k sudetské otázce v Německu a v České republice" (The Cold War Legacy on the Treatment of the Sudete Issue in Germany and the Czech Republic), in Muriel Blaive, Georges Mink (eds.): *Benešovy dekrety. Budoucnost Evropy a vyrovnávání s minulostí* (The Benes' Decrees. The Future of Europe and the Politics of the Past), Prague, Dokořán, 2003, pp. 40–52.

28 Enzo Traverso, *L'histoire comme champ de bataille*, Paris, La Découverte, 2012, p. 216 [our translation].

29 Edgar Wolfrum, *Geschichtspolitik in der Bundesrepublik Deutschland. Der Weg zur bundesrepublikanischen Erinnerung 1948–1990*, Darmstadt, Wissenschaftliche Buchgesellschaft, 1999, pp. 25-26.

second focuses on how the past is remembered and memories kept alive: celebrations, memorial days, rituals and the performance of these rituals, building of memorials; the establishment of institutions dealing with the past (commissions of historians, academic or political institutions dealing with the past), exhibitions, museums, archives, and so on. Naturally, this dimension also focuses on any type of memory-related activity undertaken by civil society in an attempt to create or transmit historical consciousness, that is, media productions dealing with history (films, documentaries, witness interviews), or individual production of narratives about the past such as novels, autobiographies or artworks.

The concept of the politics of history makes it possible to overcome the binary and somewhat static vision opposing the influence of institutionalized forms of memory of the past on the one hand, and, on the other, the resistance of individual, family or group memories to a vision of the past imposed from above. By highlighting the polity dimensions (forms, actors, institutions), the political aspects (processes and structuring) and the policies (understood as the content promoted), the concept allows us to examine how actors occupying multiple positions, that is, political, administrative, academic and/or militant positions, are struggling to make sense of the past, shape public memory and, in so doing, impose their vision of the future. Focusing on the politics of history dealing with the burdensome past of lost territories and forced migrations enables us to identify the legacy of these experiences in societies, in public memory, and within domestic and foreign (neighbouring) politics and policies. It also makes it possible to analyse the competition relative to the interpretation of past events and to address the interaction between official memory, history as a science and primary experiences through individual memories. By comparing different case studies of politics of history related to the loss in Europe and at its margins, this book aims to contribute to a comparative research analysing the emergence of a new approach to collective memory and memory culture that includes all forms of public representations of the past.

State of the art: addressing the loss in academic literature

The origins, uses and history of the loss of territories and of forced migrations have been extensively addressed in academic literature. The first studies about forced migrations before World War II focused on the Greek–Turkish population exchange and on South-Eastern European cases.[30] During and immediately after World War II, the main studies on the subject were conducted in the USA by Joseph Schechtman and Eugene Kulischer, two Jews born in Russia who had themselves fled their home country.[31] Schechtman first studied "all possible aspects of population transfers in Europe during World War Two", the majority of which concerned the resettlement of German minorities from Eastern Europe implemented by the Third Reich.[32] During the war and in its immediate wake, Schechtman and Kulischer pursued their research on population transfers not only in Europe[33] but also in the Middle East (Arab refugees)[34] and Asia (population transfers between India and Pakistan). Kulischer coined the term "displaced person", and was also "the author of many estimates of the population losses caused by the Second World War".[35]

Over the next three decades, no further global research on forced migrations was conducted. Only case studies were undertaken, and they were often carried out by directly concerned individuals or governments, mostly focusing on the German *Vertriebene(n)*.[36] The subject began to

---

30 Stellio Séfériades, "L'échange des populations", Académie de droit Internationnal, *Recueil des cours*, 1928, IV; André Wurfbain, *L'échange Gréco–Bulgare des minorités ethniques*, Lausanne, 1930; Stephen Ladas, *The Exchange of Minorities. Bulgaria, Greece and Turkey*, New York, 1932; André Rodoconarchi, *Les finances de la Grèce et l'établissement des réfugiés*, Paris, 1934; G. Streit, *Der Lausanner Vertrag und der griechisch–türkische Bevölkerungsaustausch*, Berlin, 1929.

31 Antonio Ferrara, "Eugene Kulischer, Joseph Schechtman and the Historiography of European Forced Migrations", *op. cit.*, pp. 715–740.

32 Joseph Schechtman, *European population transfers 1939–1945*, New York, Oxford University Press, 1946, p. ix.

33 Eugene Kulischer, *The Displacement of Population in Europe*, Montreal, 1943; Joseph Schechtman, *European Population Transfers, op. cit.*; Eugene Kulischer, *Europe on the Move: War and Population Changes 1917–1947*, New York, Columbia University Press, 1948; Joseph Schechtman, *Postwar Population Transfers in Europe 1945–1955*, Philadelphia: University of Pennsylvania Press, 1962.

34 Joseph Schechtman, *The Arab Refugee Problem*, New York, Oxford University Press, 1952.

35 Antonio Ferrara, "Eugene Kulischer, Joseph Schechtman and the Historiography of European Forced Migrations", *op. cit.*, p. 723.

36 Bundesministerium für Vertriebene, Theodor Schieder (ed.), *Die Dokumentation der Vertreibung der Deutschen aus Ost-Mitteleuropa* (1953–1962) (See the analysis of Mathias Beer about the genesis and development of this project in Mathias Beer, "Im Spannungsfeld von Politik und Zeitgeschichte. Das Großforschungsprojekt 'Dokumentation der Vertreibung der Deutschen aus Ost-Mitteleuropa'", *Vierteljahreshefte für Zeitgeschichte*, 46, 1998, pp. 345–389); Johann W. Bruegel, "Die Aussiedlung der Deutschen aus der Tschechoslowakei, Versuch einer Darstellung

attract renewed interest after the breakdown of the Communist regimes in Eastern Europe and the end of Cold War.[37] Archives became widely accessible and national history began to be reassessed at the same time when the wars in former Yugoslavia showed the European people that forced migrations were also a European tragedy.[38] Population transfers and ethnic cleansing became a subject of academic debate, mostly in Anglo-Saxon publications.[39] In the same period, drawing on the studies

---

der Vorgeschichte", *Vierteljahreshefte für Zeitgeschichte*, 2. Heft, April 1960, pp. 134–164; Alfred DE ZAYAS, *Nemesis at Potsdam: the Anglo-Americans and the Expulsion of the Germans. Background, Execution, Consequences*, London/Boston, Routledge & K. Paul, 1977; Wolfgang BENZ, *Die Vertreibung der Deutschen aus dem Osten: Ursachen, Ereignisse, Folgen*, Frankfurt am Main, Fischer Taschenbuch, 1985.

See also Renée HIRSCHON, *Heirs of the Greek Catastrophe. The Social Life of Asia Minor Refugees in Piraeus*, Oxford, Clarendon Press, 1989.

37 Rogers BRUBAKER, "Aftermaths of Empires and the Unmixing of Peoples: Historical and Comparative Perspectives", *Ethnic and Racial Studies*, Vol. 18, No. 2, April 1995, pp. 189–218.

38 Benjamin KOSTRUBIEC, "Bouleversements territoriaux et migrations forcées au 20e siècle en Pologne", *Espace populations sociétés*, No. 2, 1992, pp. 203–214; Alexandre TOURMAKINE, *Les migrations des populations musulmanes balkaniques en Anatolie*, Istanbul, Beylerbeyi, 1995; Detlef BRANDES, Edita IVANICKOVÁ, Jiří PEŠEK, *Erzwungene Trennung: Vertreibungen und Aussiedlungen in und aus der Tschechoslowakei 1938–1947 im Vergleich mit Polen, Ungarn und Jugoslawien*, Essen, Klartext Verlag, 1999.

39 Dariusz STOLA, "Forced Migrations in Central European History", *International Migration Review*, Vol. 26, No. 2, 1992, pp. 324–341; Christopher GOEBEL, "A Unified Concept of Population Transfer (revised)", *Denver Journal of International Law and Policy*, No. 22 (1), aut. 1993, pp. 1–27: Joseph SCHECHLA, "Ideological Roots of Population Tranfer", *Third World Quarterly*, Vol. 14, No. 2, 1993, pp. 239–275; Bill FRELICK, "Faultlines of Nationality Conflict: Refugees and Displaced Persons from Armenia and Azerbaijan" *International Journal of Refugee Law*, Vol. 6, No.4, 1 January 1994, pp. 581–619; John MCGARRY, Brendan O'LEARY, "The Political Regulation of National and Ethnic Conflict", *Parliamentary Affairs*, Vol. 47, No. 1, 1994, pp. 94–115; Akbar S. AHMED "'Ethnic Cleanising': A Metaphor for Our Time?", *Ethnic and Racial Studies*, Vol. 18, No. 1, January 1995, pp. 1–25; Rogers BRUBAKER, "Aftermaths of Empires and the Unmixing of Peoples", *op. cit.*; Chaim KAUFMANN, "Possible and Impossible Solutions to Ethnic Civil Wars", *International Security*, No. 4, Spring 1996, pp. 136–175; Christa MEINDERSMA, "Population Exchanges: International Law and State Practice. I", *International Journal of Refugee Law*, Vol. 9, No. 3, 1997, pp. 335–364; Chaim KAUFMANN, "When All Else Fails: Ethnic Population Transfers and Partitions in the Twentieth Century", *International Security*, Vol. 23, No. 2, Fall 1998, pp. 120–156; John MCGARRY, "'Demographic Engineering': The State-Directed Movement of Ethnic Groups as a Technique of Conflict Regulation", *Ethnic and Racial Studies*, Vol. 21, No. 4, July 1998, pp. 613–638; Arthur HELTON, "What Is Forced Migration?" *Georgetown Immigration Law Journal*, Summer, No. 4, 1999, pp. 521–532.

undertaken by Schechtmann and Kulischer, the American sociologist Andrew Bell-Fialkoff attempted to renew – though in a quite controversial manner – a global reflection on forced migrations.[40] However, it was not until the turn of the millennium and the first decade of the twenty-first century that the number of publications on the subject reached a peak.[41]

Up until the end of the 1990s, territorial losses and forced migrations were predominantly examined within national frames. In the German case, for instance, most publications were either dedicated to analysis of the historical and political dimension of the loss (establishing facts and figures,[42] understanding causes and identifying mechanisms that forced people to leave,[43] looking at how borders were drawn and redrawn), or

---

40 Andrew Bell-Fialkoff, *Ethnic Cleansing*, New York, St Martin's Press, 1996.

41 Norman Naimark, *Fires of Hatred: Ethnic Cleansing in XXth Century Europe*, Cambridge MA, Harvard University Press, 2001; Philipp Ther, Ana Siljak (eds) *Redrawing Nations. Ethnic cleansing in East-Central Europe, 1944–1948*, Lanham, Boulder, New York, Oxford, Rowman & Littlefield, 2001; Michael Mann, *The Dark Side of Democracy, op. cit.*; Wolfgang Benz, *Ausgrenzung, Vertreibung, Völkermord. Genozid im 20. Jahrhundert*, Munich, dtv, 2006; Stéphane Rosière, *Le nettoyage ethnique, op. cit*; Benjamin Lieberman, *Terrible Fate, op. cit.*; Pertti Ahonen, Gustavo Corni, Jerzy Kochanowski, Rainer Schulze, Tamás Stark, Barbara Stelzl-Marx, *People on the Move. Forced Population Movements in Europe in the Second World War and its Aftermath*, Oxford, 2008; Ralph Melville, Jiří Pešek, Claus Scharf (eds.) *Zwangsmigrationen im mittleren und östlichen Europa. Völkerrecht – Konzeptionen – Praxis (1938–1950)*, Mainz 2008; Witold Sienkiewicz, Grzegorz Hryciuk (ed.), *Wysiedlenia, wypędzenia i ucieczki 1939–1959: atlas ziem Polski: Polacy, Żydzi, Niemcy, Ukraińcy*, Warszawa, Demart, 2008 (Translated into German: Witold Sienkiewicz, Grzegorz Hryciuk (eds.); *Zwangsumsiedlung, Flucht und Vertreibung, 1939–1959, Atlas zur Geschichte Ostmitteleuropas*; Warszawa, Demart S. A. 2010, Bonn, Bundeszentrale für politische Bildung, 2010); Richard Bessel, Claudia Haake (eds), *Removing Peoples. Forced Removal in the Modern World*, Oxford, Oxford University Press, 2009; Jessica Reinisch; Elizabeth White (eds) *The Disentanglement of Populations. Migration, Expulsion, and Displacement in Post-War Europe, 1944–9*, Basingstoke, New York, Palgrave Macmillan, 2011; Philipp Ther, *Die dunkle Seite der Nationalstaaten, op. cit.*; Antonio Ferrara, Niccolo Pianciola, *L'Età delle Migrazioni Forzate. Esodi e Deportazioni in Europa 1853–1953*, Bologna, Il Mulino, 2012; Michael Schwarz, *Ethnische "Säuberungen" in der Moderne, op. cit.*; Jan Pikorski, *Die Verjagten, Flucht und Vertreibung im Europa des 20. Jahrhunderts*, München, Siedler, 2013; Michel Bruneau, *De l'Asie mineure à la Turquie. Minorités, homogénéisation ethno-nationale, diaspora*, Paris CNRS Editions, 2015; Bulutgil, Zeynep. *The Roots of Ethnic Cleansing in Europe*, Cambridge, Cambridge University Press, 2016.

42 Tomáš Staněk, *Odsun Němcu z Československa 1945–47* (The transfer of the Germans from Czechoslovakia 1945–47), Praha, 1991.

43 Ferdinand Seibt, *Deutschland und die Tschechen, Geschichte einer Nachbarschaft in der Mitte Europas*, Munich, Piper, 1993; Walter Ziegler (ed.), *Die Vertriebenen vor der Vertreibung. Die Heimatländer der deutschen Vertriebenen im 19. und*

they dealt with its legal, psychological, sociological or cultural dimensions (investigating traumas, and analysing the integration of displaced populations into their host society, which sometimes was supposedly their own former community,[44] and their specific customs, traditions, language and beliefs).[45] Interestingly, other issues were neglected. For instance, no attention was paid to the question of the repopulation of vacant territories in the countries of departure or to the global and transnational dimensions of the phenomenon.

In the last two decades, the research framework has considerably evolved. The approach to the loss of territories and forced population movements has shifted in an attempt to overcome national-centredness. This evolution is partly due to the internationalization and Europeanization of the issue, as well as to a new space dedicated to victims, as mentioned earlier. In Western societies, individual suffering seems to have overcome collective prejudices. What is now denounced is no longer the damage inflicted on a state, a social class or an ethnic group, but rather the consequences for an individual's physical and moral integrity as well as his or her dignity. At the same time, how memories are recalled today has also changed and has shifted from national frames to social groups, families and individual victims.[46] This new approach mirrors the new focus on victims in war studies, which can be (only)

20. Jahrhundert: Strukturen, Entwicklungen, Erfahrungen, Munich: Iudicium, 1999; Volker ZIMMERMANN, *Die Sudetendeutschen im NS-Staat. Politik und Stimmung der Bevölkerung im Reichsgau Sudetenland (1938–1945)*, Essen, Klartext, 1999.

44 Renée HIRSCHON, *Heirs of the Greek Catastrophe*, *op. cit.*; Elisabeth KONTOGIORGI, *Population exchanges in Greek Macedonia. The Forced Resettlement of Refugees*, 1922–1930, Basingstoke, New York, 2006; Olivier FORCADE, Philippe NIVET (eds.), *Les réfugiés en Europe. Du XVI au Xxème siècle.* Paris, Nouveaux monde éditions, 2008; Andreas KOSSERT, *Kalte Heimat, Die Geschichte der deutschen Vertriebenen nach 1945*, Munich, Siedler Verlag, 2008; Karin POHL, *Zwischen Integration un Isolation: Zur kulturellen Dimension der Vertriebenenpolitik, in Bayern (1945–1975)*, München, Iudicium Verlag, 2009.

45 This has, for instance, very much been the case in Germany, where in the 1950s the ethnologists were very keen to collect dialects, folk songs, clothing, cooking, customs and traditions from the expellees, in order to save what was in their eyes in danger of disappearing. See Hermann BAUSINGER's analysis of the phenomenon in *Volkskunde. Von der Alterturmsforschung zur Kulturanalyse*, Tübingen, Tübinger Vereinigung für Volkskunde, *1971*.

46 Sandrine LEFRANC, Lilian MATHIEU, Johanna SIMÉANT, "Les victimes écrivent leur histoire", *Raisons politiques*, No. 30, 2008/2, and also Didier FASSIN, Richard RECHTMAN, *L'empire du traumatisme. Enquête sur la condition de victime*, Paris, Flammarion, 2007.

partly explained by the fact that in the twentieth century, a new way of conducting war emerged in which civilians became more substantially involved in conflicts in different ways.

In this respect, the end of the 1990s was a turning point in Germany, for instance, following the initiation of a debate about German victims of World War II. The debate concerned German civilian victims of the war, including those who had died under Allied bombings, women raped by Allied soldiers at the end of the war, and expellees from Eastern Europe.[47] The success of the novel *Im Krebsgang*, written by the Nobel Prize winner Günter Grass in 2002, is a good illustration of this. Moreover, numerous novels, TV documentaries and media investigations dealing with this issue were published or broadcast in the early 2000s.[48] The debate in Germany raised new questions about the contextualization of events and the need to promote a broader approach to the issue, especially because the political context had changed. Indeed, the Eastern neighbours (Poland, the Czech Republic), the *Heimat* of millions of German expellees, had become democracies and were more open to dialogue, even on difficult issues such as the forced transfer of populations. In the early 2000s, there was a rather tense debate about the proposal of the German Federation of Expellees (*Bund der Vertriebenen*) to create a "Centre against Expulsions" (*Zentrum gegen Vertreibungen*) in Berlin. The reaction of the Eastern neighbours – namely Poland[49] – led numerous historians in both Germany and Poland

47 See the documentaries on TV about the bombing of Dresden, and the success of the book by the historian Jörg FRIEDRICH, *Der Brand. Deutschland im Bombenkrieg 1940–45*, München, Propyläen Verlag, 2002, about the Allied bombing of Germany during and at the end of the war; Brigitte RAUSCHENBACH, "L'ambiguïté des sémantiques de la victime en Allemagne", *Critique internationale*, No. 38, 2008, pp. 177–189; and from the same author a book review about *Luftkrieg und Literatur* from Wilhelm SEBALD, "L'absence de la parole et sa traduction", *Critique internationale*, No.24, 2004, pp. 195–199.

48 See the documentary series, *Die große Flucht*, broadcast on *ZDF* in November and December 2001; the news magazine *Der Spiegel* (Nos 13–14–15, March and April 2002) published a series of reportages about the German expulsion titled "*Die Deutschen als Opfer*". The front page of *Der Spiegel* for 4 February 2002 was about the shipwreck of the *Wilhelm-Gustloff* (a boat full of expellees who were trying to flee on the Baltic Sea when they were torpedoed by the Soviets and sunk).

49 See Dieter LANGEWIESCHE, Edita IVANIČKOVÁ und Alena MÍŠKOVÁ (eds.), *Mythen und Politik im 20. Jahrhundert, Deutsche – Tschechen – Slowaken*, Veröffentlichungen der Deutsch–Tschechischen und Deutsch–Slowakischen Historikerkommission Bd. 18; zugleich: Veröffentlichungen zur Kultur und Geschichte im östlichen Europa Bd. 42, Essen 2013; Detlef BRANDES, Dušan KOVÁČ und Jiří PEŠEK (eds), *Wendepunkte in den Beziehungen zwischen Deutschen, Tschechen und Slowaken*

to not only take part in the debate but also to engage in common research projects in order to overcome national frames.[50]

The perspective of EU accession for Central European States in 2004 was clearly a major incentive for trans-Europeanizing the issue. It brought new insights, such as the interest in a transnational historiography of a phenomenon as intertwined as forced migrations.[51] It also gave way to a focus on scale variations, that is, variations on a local, national and supranational level, in order to enable a better grasp of the complexity of the phenomenon.[52] The frequently changing patterns between perpetrators and victims according to power constellations[53] have been addressed, as has, closely related to this, the fact that repatriation

---

1848–1989, Veröffentlichungen der Deutsch–Tschechischen und Deutsch–Slowakischen Historikerkommission Bd. 14; zugleich: Veröffentlichungen zur Kultur und Geschichte im östlichen Europa Bd. 2, Essen 2007; Christoph CORNELISSEN, Roman HOLEC und Jiří PEŠEK (eds), *Diktatur – Krieg – Vertreibung. Erinnerungskulturen in Tschechien, der Slowakei und Deutschland seit 1945*, Veröffentlichungen der Deutsch–Tschechischen und Deutsch–Slowakischen Historikerkommission Bd. 13; zugleich: Veröffentlichungen zur Kultur und Geschichte im östlichen Europa Bd. 26, Essen 2005; Thomas STROBEL, Dariusz WOJTASZYN, "Das Deutsch–Polnische Geschichtsbuch – ein neues Element im historischen Dialog zwischen Polen und Deutschen" in Elżbieta OPIŁOWSKA, Krzysztof RUCHNIEWICZ, Marek ZYBURA (eds) *"Das Friedenszeichen von Kreisau" und "Der Händedruck von Verdun": Wege zur deutsch–polnischen und deutsch–französischen Versöhnung und ihre Symbole im kollektiven Gedächtnis der Gesellschaften*, Wrocław, 2000, pp. 179–189.

50 The *Lexikon der Vertreibungen* is one of the attempts to Europeanize the question of forced migrations. See Detlef BRANDES, Holm SUNDHAUSSEN, Stefan TROEBST (eds), *Lexikon der Vertreibungen. Deportation, Zwangsaussiedlung und ethnische Säuberung im Europa des 20. Jahrhunderts*, Wien, Böhlau, 2010. See also. Martin SCHULZE-WESSEL et al., 9. September 2010; URL: http://www.dt-ds-historikerkommission.de/konzept.pdf.

51 Keith S. BROWN (ed.), "Homelands in Question: Paradoxes of Memory and Exile in South-Eastern Europe", *Balkanologie*, Vol. 5, Nos 1–2, 2001.

52 In chronological order: Philipp THER, Ana SILJAK (eds) *Redrawing Nations, op. cit.*; Michael MANN, *The Dark Side of Democracy, op. cit.*, Anja KRUKE (ed.) *Zwangsmigration und Vertreibung. Europa im 20. Jahrhundert*, Bonn, Verlag Dietz, 2006; Benjamin LIEBERMANN, *Terrible Fate, op. cit.*; Stéphane ROSIÈRE, *Le nettoyage ethnique, op. cit.*; Richard BESSEL, Claudia HAAKE (eds.), *Removing People, op. cit.*; Detlef BRANDES, Holm SUNDHAUSSEN, Stefan TROEBST (eds.), *Lexikon der Vertreibungen, op. cit.*; Jessica REINISCH, Elizabeth WHITE (eds.) *The Disentanglement of Populations, op. cit.*

53 As Michael SCHWARZ writes, the necessity of becoming cautious and of a great discernment because of the frequent changing of roles between victims and perpetrators depending on the power constellations demands that we "become cautious about the risk of sacralization of the victims of a particular policy of violence" [our translation], in Michael Schwarz, "Questions de point de vue", *op. cit.*, p. 27.

also frequently became a way of colonizing marginal territories.[54] For instance, the massive resettlement of Greek refugees from Asia Minor in Macedonia among Slavic-speaking populations significantly transformed the demographic character of the territory; likewise, the Poles who were forced to leave the former Eastern part of Poland (*Kresy*) were transferred to the German-vacated region in the new Western Poland;[55] and the Italians from Istria and Dalmatia were resettled in the Trentino-Alto-Adige region, where a German-speaking minority was living.

In this context, little attention has been paid to an important question: how would these issues interfere with the present, and how would they evolve according to the political constraints of good neighbourhood and European/international standards that have emerged since the end of the Cold War? As a matter of fact, the analysis carried out in the field of memory studies, that is, distinct from history, are rare. This may reflect the difficulty in dealing with the memory of the Communist terror and totalitarianism in Western European countries.[56] Comparative analyses have so far been rare, because they are perceived as problematic in the sense that comparativism may lead to relativism. In Germany, the public debate about the "Centre against Expulsions" and its strong politicization stood in stark contrast with the progress of historical research.[57] This discrepancy suggests that it is necessary to pay even greater attention to historical representations (*Geschichtsbilder*), myths and memory frames and to their evolution. It was only towards the end of the 2000s that the first studies dealing with these questions were published.[58]

---

54 Keith S. Brown (ed.), "Homelands in Question ", *op. cit.*, p. 5.

55 Catherine Gousseff, *Échanger les peuples – Le déplacement des minorités aux confins polono–soviétiques (1944–1947)*, Paris, Fayard, 2015.

56 See debates in the European Parliament before the adoption of the resolution of 2 April 2009 on European conscience and totalitarianism.

57 Philipp Ther, Jürgen Danyel (eds.), "Nach der Vertreibung: Geschichte und Gegenwart einer kontroversen Erinnerung", (Introduction) *Zeitschrift für Geschichtswissenschaft*, 2005, Vol. 10, p. 867.

58 Concerning the German case, one can cite for instance: Andrew Demshuk, *The Lost German East: Forced Migration and the Politics of Memory, 1945–1970*, Cambridge, Cambridge University Press, 2012; Christian Lotz, *Die Deutung des Verlusts: Erinnerungspolitische Kontroversen im geteilten Deutschland um Flucht, Vertreibung und die Ostgebiete (1948–1972)*, Köln Weimar, Böhlau Verlag, 2007; Philipp Ther, Jürgen Danyel (eds) "Nach der Vertreibung", *op. cit.* Concerning other national cases such as Italy, see Marina Cattaruzza, *L'Italia e il confine orientale*, Bologna, Il Mulino, 2007.

How can the loss be addressed? The objective of our research project

Drawing on the available literature, our collaborative book attempts to help close the gaps outlined above by addressing the issue of loss by focusing on memory issues and on the politics of history. Unlike the studies cited above, its objective is not to further the analysis of forced migrations, but rather to shed light on the conflicts of memory concerning loss as well as on latent conflicts. To this end, it analyses the historical and memorial constructions that nourish them. We believe that this dimension is extremely important, because memory is a fundamental aspect when addressing forced migrations. Most of the states/governments which expelled populations – or carried out "transfers", as they have called them – have worked at erasing, as much as they can, anything that might recall the presence of these populations. At the same time, the populations collectively forced to leave consider their duty to remember a high priority, enabling them to maintain the identity of the group. Refusing to forget was, in some cases, a means of maintaining possible claims on lost land and property, or even a right to return.

Figure 1: *Monument situated at the entrance of the Burghalden cemetery in Sindelfingen, Germany*

"To the unforgotten homeland and its dead - The Federation of Expellees"
© Catherine Perron, 2017

Figure 2: *Reverse side of the monument*

© Catherine Perron, 2017

With regard to those who forced the departure of entire groups, history has been rewritten (for communist regimes, for instance, see Beata Halicka's chapter on the Polish case in this book) or silenced (see Etienne Copeaux's analysis in this book of how Turkey addressed the loss). Symbols or monuments inherited from expelled groups (churches or mosques, cemeteries, architectural testimonies, street names, inscriptions on buildings, etc.) were destroyed, erased or transformed. New historical narratives were released in an attempt to relegitimize the expulsion *ex post*. This held true even when the regime had changed from an authoritarian one to a democratic one, as was the case in Central Europe after 1989, and even after original justifications (such as collective guilt) for population transfers were no longer accurate or morally acceptable. After regime changes, new arguments were found to maintain a fragile stability and to avoid paving the way for any claims of restitution, compensation, right of return or even debates about the role of the former government, the army and/or elites in the process of forced transfer.[59]

[59] See, in the Czechoslovakian case, how this debate about expulsion, which was initiated among dissidents (Charta 77), never reached the rest of the society. In Czechoslovakia and Poland during the Cold War there were debates about the recent past, but these took place in the very restricted circles of the dissidents. In these countries, the expulsion of Germans was presented by the communist governments as a necessary and just act which would provide a solution to the German problem.

This book addresses these issues using a comparative approach. Our objective is to go beyond a simple identification of similarities and common issues. We have thus deliberately decided to base the comparison on a diachronic approach from the Greek–Turkish population exchange in the 1920s (see Bruneau and Copeaux in this book) to the departure of the Jews from Egypt and from Islamic countries up until the end of the 1960s (see Baussant in this book). This approach allows us to analyse historical and memorial processes over the long term. The available academic literature[60] on modern forced migrations reveals a clear consensus neither on periodization nor on the spatial dimension of the phenomenon. Some authors, such as Andrew Bell-Fialkoff, have traced back the practice of

---

After 1945/1948, neither intellectuals nor politicians publicly questioned the principle of expulsion in the two countries. Any statement diverging from the official interpretation would have been accused of supporting West-German revanchism. The German question reappeared in the Czechoslovak dissidence at the end of the 1970s in a debate on totalitarianism; this was actually the common denominator of the political writings of the dissidents. It was first addressed by questioning the expulsion of the Sudeten Germans after the war and it revolved around three main issues. A moral question: by subscribing to the theory of "collective guilt", did President Beneš and the post-war Czechoslovak political elite break with the humanist principles on which democratic Czechoslovakia had been based in 1918? A political question: the expulsion of the Germans from Czechoslovakia had, to a large extent, sealed the alliance of President Beneš (in exile) with the communists, under Stalin's patronage. Because transfers of populations had been the privilege of the two totalitarianisms of the twentieth century, had the barely restored Czechoslovak democracy made a first step towards the establishment of a totalitarian regime by depriving the non-Slavic minorities of their civil rights on the basis of ethnic criteria? And lastly, an identity question: the disappearance of the German minority had profoundly transformed the nature of Czech society. Should the expulsion of the Germans, which had deprived the Czechs of an essential interlocutor, be considered as a "Pyrrhic victory" for the Czechs? The debate on the question of the transfer of the Sudeten Germans was highly controversial and raised numerous and difficult questions of the recent past in Czechoslovakia. However, it remained confined to the very limited circles of the dissidence and never reached the rest of society. While the people no longer subscribed to communist propaganda concerning German revanchism, their position on transfers did not shift from a national(-ist) approach: the expulsion was a historic fact and one could not and did not have to look back. There was no reason to discuss it. See Bohumil Černý, Jan Křen, Václav Kural, Milan Otáhal (eds.), *Češi, Němci, odsun, Diskuse nezávislých historiku* (Czechs, Germans, transfert, discussion among independent historians), Prague, Academia, 1990; Jacques Rupnik, *The Other Europe. Rise and Fall of Communism of East Central Europe*, London, Weidenfeld and Nicolson, 1988; Anne Bazin, "Vaclav Havel et la question allemande", *op. cit.*

60 See e.g. Philipp Ther, *Die Dunkle Seite der Nationalstaaten*, *op. cit.* For an in-depth discussion about "times and spaces" of ethnic cleansing, see Michael Schwartz, *Etnische Säuberungen in der Moderne*, *op. cit.*, pp. 16–20.

"ethnic cleansing" to antiquity (to the Assyrians), when conquered people were forced to move, or to medieval forms of religious cleansing.[61] As far as Europe is concerned, the debate has largely focused on the question of whether forced migrations are a phenomenon typical of the twentieth century[62] or whether they can be traced back to the beginning of the nineteenth century (in Greece and, later, in the Ottoman and Russian Empires).[63] Three to four periods are usually distinguished in the twentieth century. These can roughly be summed up as follows:

(1) 1912–1923. Territorial losses and forced migrations linked to the end of the Ottoman Empire (Balkan wars and Greek–Turkish population exchange) with a focus on South-Eastern Europe that often overlooks the fact that forced migrations also took place elsewhere in Europe at that time (e.g. in the French region of Alsace).

(2) 1938–1944. Forced migrations and territorial rearrangements linked to the German occupation of Europe and Nazi visions of a new European order (this period has sometimes been extended to the 1930s and comprises the Soviet mass deportations as a result of totalitarian rule).

(3) 1944/5–1948. Forced migrations linked to the end of World War II and the reorganization of Eastern Europe (change of borders, but not only these). This period also includes population displacements within the USSR. Little attention is given to cases of forced migrations in the rest of the world as a result of the post-World War II new world order and of decolonization. It must be said, however, that these population displacements also affected Europe, either because of the arrival of citizens of other European countries (e.g. the Italians or French from lost overseas colonies or Jews from Muslim countries) or because European colonial powers shared responsibility for events such as the Palestinian Nakba, population exchanges following the Indian partition, or the departure of Jews from Muslim countries (see Michele Baussant's chapter in this book).

(4) 1988/91–1999. The re-emergence of the phenomenon of forced migrations during the Yugoslav wars, as well as in South Caucasus.

---

61 Andrew Bell Fialkoff, *Ethnic Cleansing*, *op. cit.*

62 Norman Naimark, *Fires of Hatred*, *op. cit.*, and Philipp Ther *Die Dunkle Seite der Nationalstaaten*, *op. cit.*

63 Argument of Benjamin Liebermann, *Terrible Fate*, *op. cit.*, p. xi, and Michael Schwartz, *Etnische Säuberungen in der Moderne*, *op. cit.*

The spatial delimitation of the phenomenon is hardly more consensual. While most studies have focused on Europe in one way or another, Europe has been defined in widely varying ways (e.g. the inclusion of the Ottoman Empire, the Caucasus and Russia). We have therefore chosen to go beyond a chronological and/or regional approach and to address the issue thematically. This allows us to bring together case studies from Europe (from North to South: Finland, Poland, Germany, Italy, Greece) and its margins (Turkey and Israel). We are aware, however, that our study is far from comprehensive given the number of cases of forced migrations recorded in history.

We assume that both the politics of history and the politics of the past, which we understand in their practical dimension, that is, from the perspective of legislative, executive and judicial decisions,[64] have strongly evolved over time because of various constraints or opportunities: regime changes, European integration and the pressure of international standards (the emergence of human rights, a focus on victims in post-conflict studies, a European approach to international relations and good neighbour policies).

Assumptions and guidelines for a comparative approach

We have identified three main constraints or opportunities whose impact should be evaluated in order to address the issue of forced migrations, lost territories and the politics of history:

(1) *European integration.* This is a political project which, since its initiation, has sought to reconcile the people of Europe, overcome the poison of nationalism responsible for two disastrous wars in Europe, and, last but not least, promote a common European identity. The process of strengthening European identity is closely connected to the recognition and building of a shared memory (see the projects of European museums or the European heritage label).[65] In this

64 Edgar Wolfrum, *Geschichtspolitik in der Bundesrepublik Deutschland*, *op. cit.*

65 Etienne François, Kornelia Kończal, Robert Traba, Stefan Troebst (eds.) *Geschichtspolitik in Europa seit 1989, Deutschland, Frankreich und Polen im internationalen Vergleich*, Göttingen, Wallsteinverlag, 2013; Aleida Assmann, "Europe: A Community of Memory?", *Twentieth Annual Lecture of the GHI*, 16 November 2006; from the same author, *Auf dem Weg zu einer europäischen Gedächtniskultur?*, Wien, Picus Verlag, 2012; Valérie Rosoux, "Mémoire(s) européenne(s)? Forces et limites de l'intervention politique dans la mise en scène de l'histoire", *Politique et*

context, the memory of population transfer, although still barely addressed at the European level, represents a common base on which a common identity may be developed. Since its origins, European integration has also been based on the principle of the intangibility of borders and on the idea of overcoming these borders. Through a process of increasingly deeper exchanges of goods, people and ideas, borders have now become areas of exchange and they are no longer perceived as frontlines within the EU. Within a few decades, Europeans have developed an international relations approach that promotes trans-border cooperation and the establishment of good neighbourhood relations, with a special focus on the protection of minorities across borders. This approach has had an impact on how the question of forced migrations associated with loss of territories has been dealt with within Europe.

(2) *An evolution in historiographical practices.* After World War II, Western countries broke with the promotion of national narratives based on heroic myths which were specific to the nineteenth century and to the first half of the twentieth century in Europe.[66] This approach was then characterized by an apologetic vision of the nation. Narratives of the past were likely to fuel warmongering or revisionist ambitions in the same way as history directly or indirectly endorsed nationalist ideologies. Many aspects of national grand narratives have been criticized because of their disregard for regional particularities, their minimization of social tensions, and, also, for their only presenting the winners' point of view. Progressively – and notably since the end of the Cold War[67] – an important fragmentation occurred with the emergence of previously silenced pages of history often linked to victims' memories. The growing publicization of counter-histories as well as the breaking up of post-war myths promoted a renewed interest in memory studies, challenging the vision carried by official narratives often presenting their own people as "victims".[68] A new

---

sociétés, Vol. 22, No. 2, 2003, pp. 17–34; Oriane Calligaro, François Foret "La mémoire européenne en action", *Politique européenne*, No. 37, 2012, pp. 18–43.

66 Gérard Noiriel, *Sur la "crise" de l'histoire*, Paris, Gallimard, 2005.

67 Tony Judt, "The Past is Another Country: Myth and Memory in Postwar Europe", *Daedalus*, Vol. 1, No. 4, fall 1991.

68 Heidemarie Uhl, "Vom Nachkriegsmythos zur Ethik der Erinnerung. Transformationen der Erinnerungskultur in Europa von 1945 bis zur Gegenwart", *Revue d'Allemagne et des Pays de langue allemande*, Vol. 44, No. 2, 2012, p. 191.

culture of memory has developed, based on a "duty to remember". For the first time in centuries, one began to commemorate and lament not only one's own victims but also "the victims of one's own crimes".[69]

(3) *Largely linked to point 2 above, the emergence of the figure of the victim as a central figure of the policies of the past.* Linked to the memory boom which started in the late 1970s in Western Europe, new attention has been paid to victims, making it morally difficult, if not impossible, to promote what was for long considered the best guarantee of lasting peace: "prescriptive forgetting"[70] or silence. This pacification approach goes back to Ancient Greece.[71] Today, in opposition to this practice, long advocated in Europe (see France after World War II or Spain in the 1970s), a "duty of remembrance" increasingly appears the new norm in dealing with the past. A significant consequence of how the memory of the Holocaust has been built in the West, this approach is, among other things, presented as a moral duty towards the victims. The duty of remembrance is now accompanied by a right for victims to be heard, to have their own narrative and therefore to participate in the writing of history.[72] This evolution has led to a multi-perspective approach to historical narrative, which has become increasingly fragmented and has lost its inclusive dimension (a great national unifying narrative) as well as its faculty of historically situating facts and events.[73] It is thus important to at least analyse the interactions between the different actors and their productions.

The different contributions in this book all examine the interactions between actors (social groups, state institutions, political parties, interest groups, media) engaged in the politics of history and the politics of the past, their motivations, their resources in different European countries, and the public they seek to address. They examine the ideological as well as the political, scientific and social contexts in which these actors evolve. They also assess how these politics change when new norms develop over the course of time.

---

69 Aleida Assmann, *Das neue Unbehagen an der Erinnerungskultur. Eine Intervention*, Munich, C. H. Beck, 2013.

70 Paul Connerton, "Seven Types of Forgetting", *Memory Studies*, 1, 2008, pp. 59–71.

71 Christian Meier, *Das Gebot zu vergessen und die Unabweisbarkeit des Erinnerns. Vom öffentlichen Umgang mit schlimmer Vergangenheit*, Munich, Siedler Verlag, 2010.

72 Sandrine Lefranc, Lilian Mathieu, Johanna Siméant, "Les victimes écrivent leur histoire", *op. cit.*, p. 6.

73 Tony Judt, "Introduction", *Reappraisals. Reflections on the Forgotten Twentieth Century*, New York, Penguin, 2008.

The "German East": Myth? Reality? Lost Land of Dreams?*

Eva HAHN

Independent historian and author specialized in Czech History and Czech–German relations

Hans Henning HAHN

Professor Emeritus of Modern East European History, University of Oldenburg

"An overwhelming disaster for 'Germany's existence'"

In a call in 2003 to view the problems of expulsion on a European level, Karl Schlögel, Professor of East European Studies at Frankfurt/Oder, stated: "I have always felt that the loss of the German East was an overwhelming disaster for 'Germany's existence'".[1] These words prompt a number of observations which should each be concluded by a question mark leading to a further insight:

- Which territory was Karl Schlögel referring to exactly? What is the "German East", where is it, and how can it be located concretely?
- This "German East" has apparently been lost. What is this loss exactly – who lost what?

---

* This chapter has previously been published in German under the title of "Der 'deutsche Osten' – Mythos? Realität? Verlorenes Traumland?" in Izabela SURYNT, Marek ZYBURA (Hg.), *Narrative des Nationalen. Deutsche und polnische Nationsdiskurse im 19. und 20. Jahrhundert*, Osnabrück, fibre Verlag, 2010. We would like to thank the publisher and editors for their permission to reprint.

1. Karl SCHLÖGEL, "Nach der Rechthaberei Umsiedlung und Vertreibung als europäisches Problem", in Dieter BINGEN, Włodzimierz BORODZIEJ, Stefan TROEBST (eds): *Vertreibungen europäisch erinnern? Historische Erfahrungen – Vergangenheitspolitik – Zukunftskonzeptionen*, Wiesbaden, Harrassowitz Verlag, 2003, pp. 11–33, p. 15.

- The loss of the "German East" was regarded by Schlögel not merely as a disaster, but indeed as an "overwhelming disaster", one moreover for "Germany's existence". So this "German East" must have a very special relevance to German national identity. Assuming that by "identity" we are referring not to a pre-designated and objectively describable fact, but rather to the outcome of a discourse among a large social group that sees itself as a "we group", in this case a nation, and thus as a construct undergoing constant change, two further questions arise:
- When was the "German East" construed as having a bearing on German national identity?; and:
- Can this identity construct still claim to be relevant today, in the first decades of the twenty-first century?

Where is the "German East"?

If one examines the specialist literature, one rarely finds the "German East" spoken of as the territories which at a certain time constituted Germany's national territory, and which thus can be defined quite concretely by constitutional law. The designation aims, in fact, at something else. Here are three examples penned by well-known historians from the Federal Republic:

- Hans-Ulrich Wehler, 2002: "These territories, which were inhabited for centuries by Germans, have been lost to us. That is the price when a country risks all-out war twice over."[2]
- Heinrich August Winkler, 2002: "Of the territories that became German during the medieval Eastward expansion, all that remained was the section West of the Oder–Neisse line."[3]
- Hagen Schulze, 1996: "The German settlement area was cast back to its boundaries from the late Middle Ages, five hundred years of culture in the German East were wiped out, the social fabric in the remaining territories was churned up, atomised, and the normal social milieux destroyed."[4]

---

2 Hans-Ulrich WEHLER in "Die Debatte wirkt befreiend". The historian Hans-Ulrich Wehler on the belated treatment of the suffering and misery of the displaced persons, in *Der Spiegel* 13/2002, pp. 61–64.

3 Heinrich August WINKLER, *Der lange Weg nach Westen*, Vol. II, Deutsche Geschichte vom "Dritten Reich" bis zur Wiedervereinigung, Munich, C. H. Beck, 2000 (cited from the 4th edition. 2002, p. 117).

4 Hagen SCHULZE, *Kleine deutsche Geschichte*, Munich, C. H. Beck, 1996, pp. 227.

All three authors emphasize the loss here (Hagen Schulze goes further when he says "wiped out"), although ownership – one can only lose something one had owned – is clearly not something anchored in the constitution, but stems from the fact of settlement, which rendered the territory "German". They also emphasize the long period involved; Hagen Schulze uses here the term "settlement area" and talks of the "culture of the German East".

This has scarcely helped clarify which territories are actually meant. One may assume that the former Prussian provinces of East Prussia, Farther Pomerania and Silesia are meant. But should Austrian Silesia also be included under the "German East"? Does the present Czech Republic as a result belong to the "German East"? Or the city of Lviv (Polish Lwów, Russian Lvov, Latin Leopolis, German Lemberg), once situated in the Habsburg Kingdom of Galicia and Lodomeria? And what about Vienna, from which Bohemia, Moravia and also Lemberg were ruled, and which, all said and done, was still regarded as the capital of the Eastern March during World War II? Does Transylvania also belong here, together with Hermannstadt?

Since the 1950s, it has become the habit to start out from the borders of Germany in 1937, and for a long time it was these borders on which revisionist demands were based in Federal Germany. At the same time it was overlooked, or passed over in embarrassed silence, that neither the German government of that time nor large sections of German society saw these borders from 1937 as the rightful German Eastern border. So it is scarcely surprising that for a long while the term "German East" could not be localized in this restricting way. This also left its stamp on education in Federal Germany – as shown in an excerpt from the *Grundsätze(n) für die Behandlung des deutschen Ostens im Unterricht* (Principles for Treating the German East in School Lessons) from 1955. Point 1 of the principles for geography described the "German East" as follows:

Figure. 3 – *Germany's Eastern borders in 1945*

> The German East is still a part of Germany. The land inhabited and shaped by the Germans must, as German territory, be distinguished from the German Reich, as the core German state. The days in which the German East territories were negated in the text books now seem to be over, and happily a growing willingness to include issues concerning the German East in course material has recently been observed. It seems though that the individual German peoples in territories outside the borders of 1937 have received too little attention, so there is still much to be done. A thorough grasp of "Germany's destined realm" [*Schicksalsraum*] must be part of an adolescent's indispensable equipment today.[5]

Some peers of Hans Henning Hahn (co-author of the present chapter) may remember their history and geography teachers giving such lessons on "Germany's destined realm" in the East, thus arming us with the "indispensable equipment" mentioned here. Not that it helped us gain a clearer idea of Eastern Europe. On the contrary: the "German East" remained hazy, evidently located somewhere between the Baltic, the Adriatic and the Black Sea.[6] Nor do present-day notions seem a lot more concrete. The oft-cited "German settlement areas in Eastern (Central) Europe" remained curiously placeless, while suggesting through the contraction to "German East" – particularly in people's recollections – a compactness that remains to be questioned.

If the "German East" cannot be distinguished either by the constitution or by geography, what do ethnic aspects tell us about the term? Since it was mainly used during the inter-war years, an overview of the population of Eastern Central Europe in the 1920s may provide more clarity (Table 1).

---

5 *Der Deutsche Osten im Unterricht. Vortrag, Gesetzesauszüge, Erlasse, Unterrichts-Grundsätze, Schriften-, Film- und Lichtbildverzeichnis*, published by the Arbeits- und Sozialminister des Landes Nordrhein-Westfalen. *Der Wegweiser, Zeitschrift für das Vertriebenenwesen*, Vortragsheft 8, Düsseldorf 1955 (= Schriftenreihe für die Begegnung der deutschen Stämme 8), p. 29.

6 The website of the Bundesinstitut für Kultur und Geschichte der Deutschen im östlichen Europa (BKGE) in Oldenburg talks of the "regions between the Baltic and the Adriatic" – the term 'deutscher Osten' is consciously avoided and the emphasis placed on the cultural and ethnic diversity (http://www.bkge.de/5838.html).

Table 1: Overview of the population of Eastern Central Europe in the 1920s

State	*Overall population of the state/nation*	*Germans*[7]
Poland 1921[8]	27.1 million / 69 %	1 million / 3.9 % (2.3 %[9])
Czechoslovakia 1921[10]	13.6 million / 65.5 %	3.1 million / 23.4 % (22.3 %[11])
Hungary 1920[12]	7.98 million / 89.6 %	551,211 / 6.9 % (5.5 %[13])
Estonia 1922[14]	1.1 million / 87.7 %	18,319 / 1.7 %
Latvia 1930[15]	1.9 million / 73.5 %	69,855 / 3.7 %
Lithuania 1923[16]	2 million / 84.2 %	29,231 / 1.4 %
Yugoslavia 1921[17]	12 million / 82.9 %[18]	513,472 / 4.3 % (3.59 %[19])
Romania 1920[20]	16 million / 71.9%	713,564 / 4.5 % (4.1 %[21])

7 The designation 'German(s)' has been used in various censuses and statistical estimates with regard to subjective statements on linguistic affiliation or averred nationality, so the details could only be approximate in nature and fluctuated with time. The nationalistic (*völkisch*) racists were alone in inventing the fiction that national affiliation can be read from objectively measurable traits that are independent of the person's own wishes.

8 Wilhelm Winkler, *Statistisches Handbuch der europäischen Nationalitäten*, Vienna and Leipzig, Wilhelm Braumüller, 1931, p. 180.

9 Joseph Rothschild, *East Central Europe between the Two World Wars*, Seattle and London, University of Washington Press, 1974, p. 36 gives the number of 740, 992 Polish citizens who stated in 1931 that German was their native tongue.

10 Wilhelm Winkler, *Statistisches Handbuch der europäischen Nationalitäten*, *op. cit.*, p. 93.

11 Joseph Rothschild, *East Central Europe between the Two World Wars*, *op. cit.*, refers to the figures for 1930, p. 89.

12 Wilhelm Winkler, *Statistisches Handbuch der europäischen Nationalitäten*, *op. cit.*, p. 115.

13 Joseph Rothschild, *East Central Europe between the Two World Wars*, *op. cit.*, refers to the figure for 1930, p. 192.

14 Wilhelm Winkler, *Statistisches Handbuch der europäischen Nationalitäten*, *op. cit.*, p. 166.

15 ibid., p. 154.

16 ibid., p. 137.

17 ibid., p. 209.

18 Serbs, Croatians and Slovenians.

19 Joseph Rothschild, *East Central Europe between the Two World Wars*, *op. cit.*, refers to the figures for 1931, p. 203.

20 Wilhelm Winkler, *Statistisches Handbuch der europäischen Nationalitäten*, *op. cit.*, p. 229.

21 Joseph Rothschild, *East Central Europe between the Two World Wars*, *op. cit.*, refers to the figures for 1930, p. 284.

State	*Overall population of the state/nation*	*Germans*
Bulgaria 1926[22]	5.4 million / 81.3 %	4,000 / 0.1 %
USSR 1926[23] USSR 1938[24]	146.6 million / 53.1 % Russians 158.5 million / 66 % Russians	1.2 million / 0.8 %) 1 million[25] / (1.4 %[26])
Total	c. 233.68 million	7,199,652

In the states of Eastern Europe in the 1920s, there were – if one ignores the Free City of Danzig and the Memel Territory, which enjoyed a special status – around 7 million people who professed to be ethnic Germans or spoke German. If we ignore the Soviet Union, we are looking at nine states with a total population of around 87 million, in which c. 6 million Germans lived. Which is to say: together, the German minorities made up around 6.9% of the total population. A more realistic estimate of this figure is arrived at if one compares the fact that according to the Federal Statistical Office in Germany, in 2005 some 7.3 million non-naturalized aliens were living in a total population of 82.4 million. With the exception of Czechoslovakia (around 23% Germans), the percentage of German-speaking people during the inter-war period was in all parts appreciably lower than the percentage of aliens in present-day Germany. The idea of a "German East" somewhere between the Baltic, the Adriatic and the Black Sea, or even of compact German settlement areas, lacks any hard, statistically demonstrable basis.

Germans had lived in Eastern Europe in different social and cultural-historical contexts for different lengths of time – in some cases for several centuries, in others for only one or two generations. Outside the Soviet Union, almost half of them lived in Czechoslovakia, with the remainder scattered across the other Eastern Central European states. There can be no talk of a "struggle between the peoples" (*Volkstumskampf*), to cite

22 Wilhelm Winkler, *Statistisches Handbuch der europäischen Nationalitäten, op. cit.*, p. 220.

23 ibid., p. 198.

24 *Der Neue Brockhaus*, Vol. 4, Leipzig, 1938, p. 250.

25 ibid.: "Apart from small urban colonies, the approx. 1 million Germans are peasants who were settled on the Volga, in the region of the Black Sea, Volhynia, the Caucasus and Siberia."

26 *Volk auf dem Weg. Geschichte und Gegenwart der Deutschen aus Rußland. Eine Ausstellung der Landsmannschaft der Deutschen aus Rußland*, Berlin, 2006, p. 62.

a word still readily used after 1945 – political problems outside of the normal everyday conflicts in multicultural societies were only seen in Czechoslovakia and Poland, and even there they were mostly driven by the Reich. There is little to suggest that the European order that arose after World War I would have become unstable had the German Reich not intervened. But above all: the question of where to look for the "five hundred years of culture in the German East", whose loss Hagen Schulz bemoans, outside the borders (*Reichsgrenzen*) of 1937, remains open – not to mention Schlögel's "overwhelming disaster for 'Germany's existence'".

Attempts at a definition

Images of history are tenacious, and even resist empirical study and realistic consideration. Thus it is not surprising that the recent publication on the "German East" finds Gregor Thum opening his article on "Mythic Landscapes" with the somewhat apologetic observation: "The 'German East' really did exist."[27]

Evidently, the concept must be defended against the doubting Thomases. And our curiosity is awakened concerning the definition, which gives itself an air of originality:

> The "German East" really did exist. It was the setting for the transition from German culture to the cultures of the eastern neighbours: a space in which various cultures existed side by side, responded to one another and flowed together, it was the site of bitter conflicts and immense creativity. Its reality eluded the *clichés* of German cultural missionising in Eastern Europe or of the German "urge to move east". It was more complex, more complicated, more confused. It had less to do with the encounter between peoples and states than with the interactions of countless individuals. Its sudden end in the middle of the last century, when the German attempt at the total subjugation and violent Germanisation of Eastern Europe during World War II led to the expulsion of the Germans from Eastern Central Europe, gave a taste of things to come. The expunging of the "German East" was not the result of fate descending like a bolt from the blue. But nor was it the end of some inevitable or even necessary development.

27 Gregor THUM, "Mythische Landschaften. Das Bild vom 'deutschen Osten' und die Zäsuren des 20. Jahrhunderts", in Gregor THUM (ed.), *Traumland Osten. Deutsche Bilder vom östlichen Europa im 20. Jahrhundert*, Göttingen, Vandenhoeck & Ruprecht, 2006, pp. 181–211, here p. 181.

Bravo! That is a very remarkable synopsis of the multicultural situation in Eastern Central Europe, but – what is German about it? What justifies us or anyone else in labelling this quite realistically described East as a "German East"? The "interaction of countless individuals" involved not only Germans, but also Jews, Armenians, Poles, Ukrainians, Romanis, Czechs, Slovakians, Romanians, etc., without distinction. So should we speak just as equally of a "Jewish East", an "Armenian East", and so on? And by analogy, would it be justified to speak today of the Federal Republic as the "Turkish West"?

Gregor Thum allows for this in some respects. Without eschewing the term "German East", he points out, at the end of his article,

> that a mere reactivation of the old notions of the East has become impossible. With the change in perspective, the "German East" as a past reality calls less for rediscovery than new discovery. How the Germans of today discover their own new East from yesteryear, and whether they learn to comprehend it as a historical phenomenon without any new myths, instrumentalisation and clichés, will be seen in years to come.[28]

Do we comprehend the "German East" as a myth? Not only does Thum's attempt at a definition and description point to this, but the title of the anthology he has edited, *Traumland Osten* (Dreamland East), suggests so, as does a new book by Wolfgang Wippermann titled *Die Deutschen und der Osten. Feindbild und Traumland*[29] (The Germans and the East. Enemy Image and Dreamland). Dreams seem to be "in" among German historians. But the question is whether this does not tend – inadvertently – to defuse the issue.

It may be taken as a truism that the "East", unlike the other points of the compass, is freighted with highly evaluative and metaphorical generalizations, and scores of pertinent images of the East or Orient already came from Antiquity and assumed a highly emotionalized stereotype during the Middle Ages.[30] The ambivalent, but mostly negative, threatening stereotypes changed focus during the course of the eighteenth and nineteenth centuries from the Orient to Eastern Europe,

---

[28] ibid., p. 209.

[29] Wolfgang Wippermann, *Die Deutschen und der Osten. Feindbild und Traumland*, Darmstadt, Primus Verlag, 2007.

[30] Uta Bellmann, *"ORIENTierungen". Über die Entstehung europäischer Bilder vom Orient und von Arabien in der Antike – Einflußfaktoren und stereotype Fortführung im Mittelalter*, Berlin, Klaus Schwarz Verlag, 2009.

which consequently changed from a Northern to an Eastern Europe.[31] Some aspects of the old picture of the Orient are then to be found in the images of East Europe. After 1989, we saw that no one outside of Russian society wished to remain "Eastern"; everyone as far as the Ukraine rushed to underline their "westernness". A saying in Cologne "*In Deutz bejinnt Asien*" – Asia begins in (the suburb of) Deutz – can be found in fitting versions all over Europe.

Originally, the disdain for the "East" corresponded with a fear of it, and this fear spawned the image of the "German East" as a bulwark or antemural.[32] The nationalistic (*völkische*) discourse has been full of this ever since the mid-nineteenth century. The menacing East European, if not Asiatic, steppe and the stereotyped dichotomy between European (= Occidental) culture and Eastern, Asiatic savagery and despotism can be traced to the present from Wilhelm Jordan's notorious Poland Speech in 1848, and not only in nationalistic writings. Friedrich Engels, for instance, was by no means free of the image of the East and Slaves.[33] In the aforementioned *Grundsätze(n) für die Behandlung des deutschen Ostens im Unterricht* from 1955 we read, for instance:

> In religious instruction, the difference in the values attributed to human life by Occidentals and Asians must also be underscored as the chief cause of the crime of expulsion from the homeland, and as the decisive reason for the solidarity in the West.[34]

The loss of the East produced the idyllic picture of a purely agrarian "German East" in which the world was still fine. The East is remembered as an Arcadia, and now a lost paradise, just as the narrative of the expulsion after 1945 was based on and elaborated from the Biblical expulsion, as

31 See in particular Larry Wolff, *Inventing Eastern Europe. The Map of Civilization on the Mind of the Enlightment*, Stanford CA, Stanford University Press, 1995.

32 This has been worked out very impressively for East Prussia by Robert Traba, *"Wschodniopruskość". Tożsamość regionalna i narodowa w kulturze politycznej Niemiec* ("Eastern Prussia". Regional and National Identity in German Political Culture), Poznań-Warszawa, Poznańskie Towarzystwo Przyjaciół Nauk, 2005, in particular pp. 180–244.

33 See Roman Rosdolsky, *Zur nationalen Frage. Friedrich Engels und das Problem der 'geschichtslosen' Völker*, Berlin 1979 (revised dissertation, Vienna 1929; excerpted in *Archiv für Sozialgeschichte*, IV/1964, pp. 87–282).

34 *Der Deutsche Osten im Unterricht, op. cit.*, p. 24.

has already been examined elsewhere.[35] So the loss of the "German East" produced the myth of "paradise lost", and also actually works with those religious associations.

All of these motifs – the East with its negative connotations, the disdain and fear shown towards it, the image of the bulwark/antemural and the lost *heimat* idyll – are motifs from the mythical narrative of the 'German East', but they are not specific to the latter because we also encounter them in other mythical contexts, such as in the Polish *Kresy* myth, or in Polish and other antemural tales. This also applies to the East as the mirror society of Christian Europe, as we know since the fictional travelogues of John Mandeville from the second half of the fourteenth century, or Montesquieu's *Lettres persanes* and Voltaire's *Zadig*.

Even though these motifs are likewise all to be found in the German nationalistic discourse since the nineteenth century, they are not specific to it, for they are also present in other Western discourses (including those of Poland). To repeat the question that was already posed: what is the connection between this mythical East, which is shared by many European nations and has everywhere much the same structure, and the "German East"? Is the "German East" just one version of a "European East", as some cultural historians would like us to believe as they Europeanize our history books? Or is there – likewise as a myth – a specifically "German East"? It seems important here to distinguish between the German myth of the East and the myth of the "German East". The concern is evidently not only with the same mythicized object, but above all with highly differing mythical contents.

This can be demonstrated by the antemural motif: the antemural or bulwark implies something defensive, at back of which is a fear of attack and invasion from which one seeks protection for one's world and values. Already with the first appearance of the nationalistic discourse in the Poland debate at the Paulskirche in Frankfurt, it was evident that the "German East" was not about defence but about seizing the "East":

> I admit this without beating about the bush: our justice is none other than the right of the strongest, the right to conquer. Yes, we have conquered. The Germans have conquered Polish lands, but these conquests were made such that they cannot be handed back. As has so often been said, they are not

[35] Hans Henning Hahn, Eva Hahn, "Mythos 'Vertreibung'" in Heidi Hein-Kircher, Hans Henning Hahn (eds) *Politische Mythen im 19. und 20. Jahrhundert in Mittel- und Osteuropa*, Marburg, Verlag Herder Institut, 2006, pp. 167–188.

> conquests by both the sword as well as by the ploughshare. In the West we have only ever been conquered; in the East we have had the great misfortune to be conquerors ourselves, and with that we provided hosts of German poets with the occasion for touching jeremiads on the various nationalities that had to fall to the inexorable force of the German race.[36]

The blatant aggression in these words has not always been preserved like this, but later, during World War I and then with even more force in World War II, was unleashed – heaven knows, not only on paper or from public platforms. The claim to appropriate, whether – to keep to the terminology from then – by the sword or by the ploughshare, or by "civilized German behaviour" or culture, turned the "acquired" territories in the "East" into the "German East".

Which is to say: the German myth of the "East" differs from other myths of the "East" by the – put positively now – aspect of duty, the civilizing mission. Much the same applies to the myth of the "German East", to which comes, additionally, the claim to ownership.

In a word: we are dealing here with a *colonial myth* that is directed to its own continent, and which in keeping with this also envelops the whole of medieval history. This dynamic aspect is much more than simply the bulwark and antemural ideology that is to be found elsewhere.

Just as today we conceive of anti-Semitism not as a Jewish problem but as a problem of the society in which anti-Semitism raises its head, an explanation for the myth of the "German East" should not be sought in the East but rather among the Germans, or more precisely in the German discourse. The developments in this discourse over the last 200 years have been too complex to be sketched out here in a few pages. Instead of coming up with a new narrative, the rest of this chapter will concentrate on four key questions that arise from the discourse on the "German East" and the myth of the same. These questions should in some ways constitute analytical probes by which the confusing terrain of this discourse can be fathomed.

---

36 Speech by parliamentarian Wilhelm Jordan on 24 July 1848, in Franz Wigard (ed.), *Stenographischer Bericht über die Verhandlungen der deutschen constituirenden Nationalversammlung zu Frankfurt am Main*, Frankfurt am Main, 1848, Vol. 2, pp. 1,143–1,154, here p. 1,146.

First probe: the open border

As is well-known, the beginning of the German national discourse was marked by Ernst Moritz Arndt's rhyming catalogue of questions *Was ist des Deutschen Vaterland?* (*What is the German's Fatherland?*), which sought to establish the size and location of the Fatherland. The lack of clarity about Germany's place in Europe already became overly clear through the difficulties in which the Paulskirche became entangled during all the political debates concerning Germany and the exterior on the question of what borders a newly founded German National State should have in an already existing Europe.[37] After the founding of the Reich in 1871, the nationalist discourse focused more and more on what actually should be Germany's Eastern border. While the German borders in the West were deemed by some as needing correction, already since Gustav Freytag it had become increasingly normal to speak of a 'border zone' in the East, as if the act of abstraction required to envisage the border as a line did not apply in the East and could be rescinded. This border zone was then progressively thought of more as a mission, as a civilizing task, as "our wild East", and with that the medieval expansion drive was recast according to what purportedly was the modern colonial idea. The popular image of the East as a steppe justified the idea of an unbounded land which thus was void of culture. The German border in the East was seen as open, and the behaviour of imperial Germany, especially in the last year of World War I, up to and including the Treaty of Brest-Litovsk on 3 March 1918, made this all too clear.

---

37 Still unsurpassed: Günter WOLLSTEIN, *Das "Großdeutschland" der Paulskirche. Nationale Ziele in der bürgerlichen Revolution 1848/49*, Düsseldorf, Droste Verlag, 1977; regarding the Polish aspect see Hans Henning HAHN, "Wolność polska czy jedność niemiecka? Zgromadzenie Narodowe w kościele św. Pawła i stosunki polsko-niemieckie w roku 1848 " (Polish Freedom or German Unity? The National Assembly in the Church of St. Paul and Polish–German Relations in 1848), in Roman BÄCKER, Marek CHAMOT, Zbigniew KARPUS (eds), *Społeczeństwo w dobie modernizacji. Polacy i Niemcy w XIX wieku. Studia ofiarowane Profesorowi Kazimierzowi Wajdzie w siedemdziesiątą rocznicę urodzin* (Society in the Age of Modernization. Poles and Germans in the 19th century. Studies offered to Professor Kazimierz Wajda on the seventieth anniversary of his birthday), Toruń, Wydawnictwo Uniwersytetu Mikołaja Kopernika, 2000, pp. 203–218.

Bernhard Struck, in a commendable article,[38] has pointed to the amount of influence the division of Poland had on the cartographic depiction of the German–Polish border region in the nineteenth century. He, too, pinpoints 1848 as the watershed in the cartographic portrayal of the East, in which various means of graphic representation, statistical data, place names and the construction of linguistic enclaves aided a gradual Germanization.

Second probe: myths of loss

The typology of modern myths includes the myth of loss,[39] and the German discourse similarly evinces a long tradition of lamenting territorial losses. *Meyers Lexikon* from 1875 offered an interesting variant of this shortly after the founding of the German Reich: after first evoking an empire, including Italy, stretching from the Rhône to the Weichsel, it then bemoaned its many losses. This culminated in the sentence:

> G.[Germany] has in part made up for losses in the W.[West] by replacements in the E.[East], where with its dominion over the Slavs, who once extended to the Elbe and Thuringian Saale and Upper Franconia, it could spread its language.[40]

The idea of compensating in the East for losses in the West was fully in line with the citation above from Wilhelm Jordan in the Paulskirche: "In the West we have only ever been conquered; in the East we have had the great misfortune to be conquerors ourselves." At the same time he notes that the focus of nationalistic thinking has swung progressively from West to East.

The alleged "Disgrace of Versailles" provided the next occasion to bewail losses. And much was bewailed – the loss of the prestige

38 Bernhard Struck, "Farben, Sprachen, Territorien. Die deutsch–polnische Grenzregion auf Karten des 19. Jahrhunderts", in Christof Dipper, Ute Schneider (eds), *Kartenwelten. Der Raum und seine Repräsentation in der Neuzeit*, Darmstadt, Primus Verlag, 2006, pp. 177–192.

39 Heidi Hein-Kircher, "Überlegungen zu einer Typologisierung von politischen Mythen aus historiographischer Sicht – ein Versuch", in Heidi Hein-Kircher, Hans Henning Hahn (eds), *Politische Mythen im 19. und 20. Jahrhundert op. cit.*, pp. 407–424, here p. 414.

40 *Meyers Konversations-Lexikon. Eine Encyklopädie des allgemeinen Wissens*, 3rd edition, Vol. 5, Leipzig 1875, p. 257.

Germany aspired to as a world power, the loss of its hegemonic position in Europe, the disappointment that all its sweet Pan-German dreams in the debates about the war goals during World War I, above all in Eastern Europe, had been dashed, and ultimately the loss of territories, with the losses in the East evidently being far more painful than those in the West and North. One contemporary commentator, the *Volksforscher*[41] Max Hildebert Boehm (1891–1968), summed up the losses in 1936 as follows:

> A debacle, such as Germanity has not seen for hundreds of years in the East, has become reality. And indeed it was now the entire German East that succumbed to this fate and was made aware of the inner community of fate [*Schicksalsgemeinschaft*] and its vital link with its people and the Reich.[42]

The continuation of this rhetoric of loss after 1945 to the remarks from the early twenty-first century cited at the beginning no longer needs to be spelt out.

Third probe: images of history and of Eastern Europe

The "German East" primarily consists of a hodge-podge of images of history, and it is even tempting to regard it as a product of these images. German "*Ostpolitik*", which is to say political action directed towards and in relation to Eastern Europe, throughout the entire twentieth century cannot be understood without the images of history that were used. It is enough, in fact, to read the pertinent chapter in Hitler's *Mein Kampf*, or diverse texts by Rosenberg, to grasp the relevance of these conceptions. Scholarship has never denied that the Nazis worked with such images so as to convey their politics through their propaganda. That they themselves not only adopted nationalistic conceptions of history, honed them and created new ones, but above all believed in them themselves is often put aside as unimportant. Any irrelevance attributed to nationalistic conceptions of history can only be explained on a superficial level, along the lines of historical scholarship with positivist foundations. But on a closer examination of, for instance, their genesis, contents and impact, they

41 The German term for a person who studies the sociological, anthropological and cultural aspects of humanity from a nationalist and racist perspective.

42 Max Hildebert Boehm, "Der deutsche Osten und das Reich", in Karl C. Thalheim, A. Hillen Ziegfeld (eds), *Der Deutsche Osten. Seine Geschichte, sein Wesen und seine Aufgabe*, Berlin, Propyläen-Verlag, 1936, pp. 1–18, here p. 16.

prove to be spurs to action and means of legitimation. As they gradually dominated the discourse, they greatly diminished the field of alternative conceptions and rapidly determined what was deemed expressible and thus thinkable. This can be observed on the one hand in the persistence of nationalistic elements in the discourse after 1945. On the other hand, it turns out that, in the main, these images of history were not Nazi inventions, but had steadily become part of the nationalistic discourse during the nineteenth century, with a particularly wide-ranging effect on the German elites. It suffices here to cite the bestseller by ex-*Reichskanzler* Bernhard von Bülow from World War I:

> The work of colonising the German East, which began almost a thousand years ago and is still unfinished, is not only the greatest but the sole thing that we Germans have accomplished to date. Never in the history of the world has colonisation been carried out on such a scale with so little spilt blood and as little violence as here.[43]

The history of the first half of the twentieth century has shown that nothing cost as much blood as the German project to colonize Eastern Europe. All the more appalling in our view is that still, at the beginning of the twenty-first century, the idea that German national identity is tightly connected with the "German East" is still alive and kicking.

The nationalistic conceptions of history contained not only genuinely racist ideas, but also, in particular, images of Eastern Europe – whether in stereotypical form or in posturings of cultural superiority or in historical justifications of the Penckian paradigms of *Volksboden* (soil of the people) and *Kulturboden* (soil of the culture),[44] or, ultimately, in legitimizations of the concept of a German mission to the East created by predictions of the future based on past matters. On which levels of the discourse the images were produced and treated is of less importance here. Key elements of the Sybel–Ficker dispute from 1859/61[45] crop up again in Hitler's arguments for the conquest

---

43 Fürst von Bülow, *Deutsche Politik*, Berlin, Verlag von Reimar Hobbing, 1916, p. 259.

44 Albrecht Penck, "Deutscher Volks- und Kulturboden", in *Volk unter Völkern. Bücher des Deutschtums*, Vol. 1, edited for the Deutscher Schutzbund by K. C. von Loesch together with A. Hillen Ziegfeld, Breslau, Hirt, 1925, p. 62–73.

45 The dispute between the two historians Heinrich von Sybel (1817–95) and Julius Ficker (1826–1902) was ostensibly about an interpretation of the policies of the medieval emperors (Eastward expansion vs Italian policies), which, however, concealed the option of "lesser German" or "pan-German". For sources see Friedrich Schneider

of a German colonial empire in Eastern Europe. The continuity of this discourse is obvious – just as every discourse develops, it is not and cannot be imperative, and yet the knowledge that there can be no such thing as discursive determinism cannot prevent such significant continuities from being detected. The images of history that construct the "German East" clearly number among them.

Fourth probe: colonial war?

The fourth probe follows on from the Bülow citation above. Since the latter half of the nineteenth century, the line of action largely known by Medieval Studies today as the "medieval settlement process" has until the 1960s been understood – not only in academic circles but also by the broad public – as the German colonization of the East. Before the acquisition of overseas colonies by the German Reich, this had a compensatory function, because it was regarded as one of the marks of a "proper" European cultural nation that it should possess colonies and disseminate European culture, religion and "civilized behaviour" in the world outside Europe. Soon the imaginary of Eastern Europe and above all of Poland as a German colonial mission was no longer regarded as a past achievement in this field, but as a mission for the future.[46]

This raises the question: should the two World Wars be qualified as colonial wars on European soil – at least those parts of them that took

---

(ed.), *Universalstaat oder Nationalstaat. Macht und Ende des Ersten deutschen Reiches. Die Streitschriften von Heinrich von Sybel und Julius Ficker zur deutschen Kaiserpolitik des Mittelalters*, Innsbruck, Universitäts Verlag – Wagner, 1941; cf. also in this context Friedrich Schneider, *Die neueren Anschauungen der deutschen Historiker über die deutsche Kaiserpolitik des Mittelalters und die mit ihr verbundene Ostpolitik*, 4th augmented edition, Weimar, Verlag Hermann Böhlaus, 1940; a more recent analysis of the dispute is given in Thomas Brechenmacher, "Wieviel Gegenwart verträgt historisches Urteilen? Die Kontroverse zwischen Heinrich von Sybel und Julius Ficker über die Bewertung der Kaiserpolitik des Mittelalters (1859–1862)", in Ulrich Muhlack (ed.), *Historisierung und gesellschaftlicher Wandel in Deutschland im 19. Jahrhundert*, Berlin, De Gruyter, 2003, pp. 87–112.

46 See the very useful anthology of quotations with its analytic introduction – Eva Hahn "Oldenburger HistoArt Gruppe: Ostkolonisation. Archäologische Sondierung einer deutschen 'Kulturleistung'. Eine Text- und Bildcollage ... als HistoArt Beitrag zur Erforschung von Deutschlands östlichen Nachbarschaften", in Edmund Dmitrów, Tobias Weger (eds), *Deutschlands östliche Nachbarschaften. Eine Sammlung von historischen Essays für Hans Henning Hahn*, Frankfurt am Main et al., Peter Lang, 2009, pp. 324–362.

place in East Europe? The evidence of the discourse seems to speak for the thesis, and this applies to a far greater extent to World War II than to World War I. But caution is advised. If we maintain that World War II was the last major colonial war in global history to date, we run the risk of comparing mountains with molehills, because it is far from enough to point out that the one case involves continental colonialism while the other cases concern overseas colonialism. A tempting categorization by labels has evidently brought about this misapprehension – because comparisons between World War II and other colonial wars would downplay the former on a colossal scale. Although the colonial wars or colonial conquests of the sixteenth to nineteenth centuries doubtless had racist motives and a concomitant impact, they cannot be compared with either the racial theories of the Nazis or their appalling implementation in World War II. Just how far colonial practices during the German empire, such as the quashing of the Herero uprising in South-West Africa (today Namibia) with its clearly genocidal intent and upshot, already pointed to the programmatic realization of mass genocide as the avowed practice of German politics during World War II remains undecided. A continuity can perhaps be evidenced here, but it would be no more compelling than the discursive continuity from Sybel to Hitler mentioned above.

Should the occurrences that are generally summed up in Germany under the term "expulsion" thus be viewed as an accompaniment to the processes of decolonization that are seemingly "normal" in global history? This label is also a tempting possibility for making universal historical categorizations, but does not stand up, first of all, to detailed inspection. What has been called systematic expulsion already began in 1939 with Hitler's "*Heim-ins-Reich*" (Back home to the Reich) policies, so that at least half of the people later designated as expellees had either been evacuated by the Nazi authorities, very often under coercion, or had fled. Above all, the expulsion from Eastern and East Central Europe in the years 1945–8 by no means encompassed all the Germans in these regions – only those who lived in the Eastern states adjoining Germany, to wit Poland and Czechoslovakia. This was directly linked with the initiation of the war by the Third Reich because, as the Allies saw it, this was done by deliberately instrumentalizing the German minorities in the neighbouring countries. The aim was thus to put a stop, once and for all, to any repetition of this political manoeuvre in the neighbour states. Neither Romania nor the Soviet Union saw any form of forced migration or indeed any such thing as 'ethnic cleansing', to use a fashionable if ill-suited term. The fact that, since the 1950s, voluntary migrants have come in an almost unbroken stream from Eastern Europe to the Federal Republic may be taken to indicate that nothing like all Germans were 'expelled', and that no one thought of doing such a thing, or, thus, of ethnic decolonialization.

In other words: although there can be no mistaking the fact that World War II had strong colonial aspects, there is no comparing it to earlier colonial wars, either in its magnitude or its outcome. Hitler's words "What India was for England will be the Eastern area for us!"[47] tell us about Hitler's view of the world and his colonial intentions, but also prove that the Nazis failed to understand the ideological image European colonial policies had of themselves as missions for spreading European culture, along with Christianity; moreover, with their version of colonial politics in the European East, they abandoned *de facto* the European consensus here – not only with regard to the fact that, since the beginning of the modern era, Europe had not been viewed as a place for colonial expansion and subjugation, but also regarding the concrete forms whereby colonial war was realized in practice. Nazi policy in Eastern Europe was, for its protagonists, a logically consistent colonial policy motivated by racism – but for the historian performing an a posteriori analysis, the differences from what had previously marked classic European colonial politics command attention. The by no means complete expulsion of Germans from Eastern Central Europe as an upshot of World War II can in turn only be regarded as decolonization if as a result one focuses on the dismantling, or indeed demolition, of the claims to German cultural superiority, along with the traditional, ethnically derived concepts of moral value and order that come with them.

Conclusions: Eastern policies

Over the first half of the twentieth century, especially in the inter-war years, the "German East" underwent a fairly successful discursive build-up as an essential part of German identity. Erika Steinbach's efforts not only to gain respect for the memories of those affected by expulsion, which no one of course begrudges her, but also to raise the

---

47 Adolf Hitler between 8 and 11 August 1941, cited here from *Adolf Hitler: Monologe im Führer Hauptquartier 1941–1944. Die Aufzeichnungen Heinrich Heims*, Werner Jochmann (ed.), Hamburg, 1980, p. 55.

expulsion to a cornerstone of national memory and thus of German national identity, along with Karl Schlögel's "overwhelming disaster for 'Germany's existence'" mentioned at the beginning, indicate that debate on this point is still ongoing.

Questions about collective identity and its elements are rated by many historians as a kind of 'software' that is of minor importance when one is faced with the hard facts of political and economic reality. Is that really so? A possible consequence of the thoughts presented here is of course the question of the role played by the way in which the "German East" was construed in the twentieth century as a major component of German identity, which played and still plays an important part in drafting and realizing German foreign policy vis-à-vis Eastern Europe in what has come to be known as *Ostpolitik*.

Just how far foreign policy can be part of a collective identity may be answered both descriptively and normatively. Generally, we understand foreign policy to mean political action in relations with partners viewed as equals, in the normal case with subjects of international law, in order to represent one's own interests and with the aim – when it is a matter of peaceable foreign policy – of coordinating everyone's interests. The strategic goals of German *Ostpolitik*, during the two World Wars and their prior history, stood in a direct reciprocal relationship to the identity discourse about the "German East". The phraseological continuities up into the first decade of the twenty-first century are plain to see.

As regards the normative dimension of these issues today, we can note the following.

The Czech foreign minister of the time, Karel Schwarzenberg, noted, at a panel discussion at the Robert Bosch-Stiftung in Berlin on 31 March 2007, that he did not like the term "*Ostpolitik*", and preferred "neighbourhood policy".[48] As this remark came in the context of his efforts to counter the demonization of Russia and its president, Vladimir Putin, he clearly wished to avoid the usual negative connotation of the term "East".

An analysis of the nationalistic concepts of history shows that nationalistic *Ostpolitik* was regarded and understood as having the greatest relevance for identity. This is without doubt the key characteristic of German *Ostpolitik* in the first half of the twentieth century. Not that

48 For the panel discussion see http://www.bosch-stiftung.de/content/language1/html/13527.asp (accessed 20 June 2009); Karel Schwarzenberg's utterances reported here, heard first-hand by Hans Henning Hahn.

the finding necessarily says anything about German *Ostpolitik* in other periods, but it does permit the following concluding remark, worded in a somewhat normative way.

Every national society is personally responsible for the formulation of its national identity. Foreign policies – and thus also *Ostpolitik* – are clearly not the field of politics in which national identity, which in the final analysis is only for the domestic audience, should find its expression. For this reason, German foreign policies, together with a foreign cultural policy, that depend, to whatever degree, on mythical notions of the "loss of the German East" would encounter scant acceptance in Europe; they would be regarded by all the neighbouring countries as quite incomprehensible to the rational mind, and would lead to isolation.

Translated from German by Malcolm Green

Private versus Public: The Memorialization of the Exodus of the Istro-Dalmatians, 1945–2015

Gustavo Corni
Professor of Contemporary History, University of Trento

Italy 1945: winner or loser?

The twenty-fifth of April 1945 was the date chosen in Italy in the immediate post-war period as a symbolic moment to celebrate the end of hostilities and the role played by the Resistance movement. More specifically, this date marked the liberation of (the major urban centres in) Central and Northern Italy by the partisans. In fact, in the following years, owing to the split in the Resistance coalition between Communist and Socialist partisans on one side and the moderates (predominantly Catholics) on the other, the institutionalization of this celebration was slow and disputed among the major political parties; this is a consequence of the incipient Cold War, in which Italy found itself in a neuralgic position.[1]

However, above and beyond the political differences regarding the interpretation of 25 April, what must be emphasized is that after World War II, the idea that Italy had won the war spread rapidly and became established in internal Italian public opinion. This view then became embedded in a public narrative of the war, which focused at length on the key role played by the partisan movement and its liberating actions. This was considered decisive in this collective account in bringing the war to an end and establishing Italy's status after the war.[2]

---

1 Filippo Focardi, *La guerra della memoria. La Resistenza nel dibattito pubblico italiano del 1945 a oggi* (The War of Memory. Resistance in Italian Public Debate from 1945 to Today), Roma–Bari, Laterza, 2005.

2 Gustavo Corni, "Italy after 1945: War and Peace, Defeat and Liberation", in Lothar Kettenacker –Torsten Riotte (eds), *The Legacies of two World Wars. European*

A few months after 25 April, there was a bitter realization: Italy, which had in the meantime become a democratic republic (after the narrow victory of the republican option over the monarchist one in a referendum on 2 June 1946) was required by the Allies to abide by a punitive peace treaty. The peace treaty's harshness came as a surprise to the new Republican ruling class, who were convinced instead that Italy, thanks to the partisan movement, deserved to be recognized as an equal ally along with the other victors.[3]

Putting the Liberation at the centre of the public debate, of the collective memory, meant among other things downplaying – indeed silencing – for several decades the role that Italy played during the first part of the war (1940–3) as an ally of Germany, from the campaigns for military conquest to the tough policies enforced during the military occupation in Greece and in the Balkans.[4] More generally, the accounts made of the Fascist regime have often been sugar-coated, with emphasis placed particularly on the allegedly radical differences with National-Socialist Germany, its ally; and even the final stage of Fascism under the guise of the Italian Social Republic, in 1943–5, was mostly downgraded to a puppet manoeuvred by the German occupying forces.[5] Within the context of the discrepancies between the public account of the war and post-war period and the reality of the situation of a defeated country on which a harsh peace treaty had been imposed, there arises the dramatic human vicissitudes of those people, Italian by citizenship, language and culture, living in the colonies now lost (Libya and Oriental Africa) as well as in the territories on the Eastern border of the peninsula, at the Eastern shores of the Adriatic sea, who found themselves at the centre of a tough political and diplomatic dispute during a decade after the

Societies in the Twentieth Century, Oxford, Berghahn, 2011, pp. 257ff.

3 Sara Lorenzini, *L'Italia e il trattato di pace del 1947* (Italy and the Peace Treaty of 1947), Bologna, Il Mulino, 2007.

4 In general, Giorgio Rochat, *Le guerre italiane 1935–1943. Dall'impero d'Etiopia alla disfatta* (Italian Wars: From Aethiopian Empire to the Defeat), Turin, Einaudi, 2005. Among the most recent empirical studies, which revise in depth the minimising and rosy interpretation of the "Italians good guys", see Eric Gobetti, *L'occupazione allegra. Gli italiani in Jugoslavia (1941–1943)* (The Joyful Occupation. Italians in Yugoslavia), Roma, Carocci, 2007.

5 For a historiographic outline of interpretations of Fascism in the post-war period, see my own *Fascismo. Condanne e revisioni* (Fascism. Condemnations and Revisions), Rothe ma, Salerno, 2011.

war with Communist Yugoslavia, resurrected under the surge of the victorious Communist partisan movement created and led by Josip Tito.

The historical context

The Istrian and Dalmatian exodus is not the only case of the collective displacement of Italians in the immediate post-war period. In fact, between the war and the early 1970s, for many different reasons and in many different situations, hundreds of thousands of Italian men and women were forced to abandon their homes and properties, which in many cases had been in their possession for many years.[6] I am referring to those who lived in colonies such as Libya, the Dodecanese and Ethiopia – some of which had already been evacuated during the war – and to the Italians residing in Tunisia and Egypt. This was a long and complex process, brought about primarily by the events of the war, then by the loss of the colonies as a result of the peace treaty and lastly – as in the case of Libya – by the expropriation perpetrated in 1970 by the nationalist government of Muammar Gaddafi. Out of the roughly 650,000 Italians estimated to have been residing in these territories in the early 1940s, we can calculate that at the end of 1949 over 200,000 residents in the colonies (half of these in Libya alone) had already been repatriated, plus several hundreds of thousands of Italians residing in Tunisia who were repatriated halfway through the following decade. The last were the 13,000 Italian colonists and residents in Libya, expelled and expropriated in July 1970 by Gaddafi without any compensation. This complex series of population shifts, though traumatic and fraught with negative consequences for those directly involved, remained on the whole completely sidelined in the Italian collective memory of the post-war period, unlike the Istrian and Dalmatian Exodus between 1945 and 1956.[7]

Therefore, let us focus on this last historic event. Between 1945 and the mid-1950s, around 250,000 Italians were forced to leave cities and villages that their families had inhabited for generations. These cities and villages were situated along the Eastern coast of the Adriatic

6 Patrizia AUDENINO, *La casa perduta. La memoria dei profughi nell'Europa del Novecento* (The Lost Home. Memory of Refugees in Twentieth-Century Europe), Roma, Carocci, pp. 53ff.

7 On the Libyan case see the recent research of Luigi SCOPPOLA IACOPINI, *I "dimenticati". Da colonizzatori a profughi, gli italiani in Libia 1943–1974* (The "Forgotten". From Colonizers to Refugees. Italians in Libya), Foligno, I Quaderni del Museo dell'Emigrazione, 2015.

Sea, from the Gulf of Trieste and down to Istria and Dalmatia. These people were to a large extent Italian in terms of culture and language, and their presence in these areas dated back as far as the early modern period, when the Republic of Venice had colonized the Eastern Adriatic coast, down to Greece, installing merchants, officials and soldiers.

The expulsive dynamic taking place in the first decade after the end of hostilities is defined as an "exodus", and the denomination was coined at the very time of the events by its protagonists. The exodus of the Istrians and Dalmatians from their homeland fits in with the broader context of the forced displacement of populations that affected the European continent in the aftermath of the two twentieth-century World Wars.[8] It is of course a minor page of this history, and is in fact much less widely known and studied than others, for example the expulsion of 11–12 million Germans and German speakers from the Eastern regions of the continent between 1944 and 1947.

The issue of the exodus, however, is of interest to us because it left a dramatic mark on the history of post-war republican Italy. It also affected public and private memory. But first, we must put forward a concise reconstruction of the events.

To place the exodus in its historical context, it is necessary to consider Fascist Italy's policy towards its 'alien' population in the inter-war period, as well as the political and military events that occurred in the Balkans during the World War II. The exodus was a direct consequence of these developments. At the end of World War I, an active and radicalized "border" fascism gained ground in the territories recently annexed by Italy: Trieste, Gorizia, Istria and the Northern part of the Dalmatian coast with Zara/Zadar.[9]

After the seizure of power in late October 1922 Mussolini and the Fascists, acting on behalf of the wealthy bourgeois elites and presenting themselves as the defenders of the Italian nation, carried out a series of measures, particularly in the important harbour and commercial centre of Trieste. They included the closure of Slovenian and Croatian schools (completed in 1928–9), the forced Italianization of names and a rigid policy

---

8 See in general Antonio Ferrara e Niccolò Pianciola, *L'età delle migrazioni forzate. Esodi e deportazioni in Europa 1853–1953* (The Age of Forced Migrations. Exodus and Deportations in Europe), Bologna, Il Mulino, 2012, as well as Pertti Ahonen et alii, *People on the Move. Forced Population Movements in Europe in the Second World War and its Aftermath*, Oxford, Berg, 2008.

9 Anna Maria Vinci, *Le sentinelle della patria. Il fascismo al confine orientale* (The Sentinels of the Homeland. Fascism at the Eastern Border), Rome–Bari, Laterza, 2001.

towards the Slovenian and Croatian clergy, considered the bulwark of the national identity of the Slavic minorities. Even more drastic measures were planned, such as an extensive colonization programme in the countryside, where there was a particularly significant presence of Slavs.

The denationalization policies of the Fascist regime were not particularly successful, also owing to a lack of financial resources; as the historian Raoul Pupo noted, "the efforts to wipe out Slovenian and Croatian national identity were not even close to successful".[10] They did, however, speed up the emigration to Yugoslavia of around 50,000 to 100,000 Slovenes and Croats. They also sparked the formation of underground groups of Slavic anti-fascists, who were severely persecuted by Italian police. In general, these policies brought out tensions and divisions within the social fabric of Dalmatia and Venezia Giulia, leading to what the historian Elio Apih has called a "degeneration of civic living".[11]

The second contextual element to be considered is the occupation policy of defeated Yugoslavia following the short military campaign of spring 1941 implemented by Germany, Italy and their allies. The winners subjected the area to a process of radical 'Balkanization', with the aim of stirring up national tensions so as to reduce the costs of occupation and the danger represented by the partisans. Yugoslavia was divided among the Axis powers, satisfying respective expansionist or nationalistic ambitions. Mussolini in particular got control of the so-called Province of Ljubljana (central and Southern Slovenia), the Dalmatian coast and Montenegro. A satellite state was set up in Croatia under a double and disputed hegemony of both Germany and Italy, and was assigned to the leadership of the ultra-nationalistic and anti-Semitic group of the *ustaša* led by Ante Pavelić. They established a repressive regime that grasped onto the most atavistic instincts of Croatian nationalism, while at the same time becoming a useful tool of the occupiers.

Italian policy in Yugoslavia, executed by a mixed military and civilian apparatus, was in general very severe.[12] Civilians were interned en masse and populations were uprooted in order to weaken their connections with the partisan movement, in the main communist. In the concentration camp on the Dalmatian island of Arbe/Rab, built in the summer of 1941,

10 Raoul Pupo, *Il lungo esodo. Istria: Le persecuzioni, le foibe, l'esilio* (The Long Exodus. Istria: Persecutions, Foibe, Exile) Milan, Rizzoli, 2005, p. 33.

11 Elio Apih, *Trieste*, Rome–Bari, Laterza, 1988, p. 138.

12 Marco Cuzzi, *L'occupazione italiana della Slovenia (1941–1943)* (The Italian Occupation of Slovenia), Rome, Ufficio Storico Stato Maggiore Esercito, 1998.

almost 10,000 people were detained in harsh conditions (at least one tenth of them died of starvation) and Ljubljana was closed off with barbed wire.[13]

However, the annexation, denationalization and colonization plans drawn up by the Italian military and civilian authorities remained mostly on paper, owing to lack of time and resources. In the most in-depth study on the subject, Davide Rodogno notes that "the reality of the occupations was very different from the regime's projects and ambitions, and almost nothing of the post-war new order was accomplished".[14]

It is against this background of ethnic tensions and occupation policies performed by the Italians (and Germans) that the subsequent massacres and the post-war exodus have to be understood.

The "*foibe* massacres"

On 8 September 1943, the Italian armistice with the Allies created a power vacuum in the Yugoslav territories that Italy had occupied previously. The Italian occupation structure, both civilian and military, underwent an early phase of violence by Slovenes and Croats in this period, associated with the *foibe*. *Foibe* are subterranean cavities of the karst territory of Istria, which had traditionally been used by the local peasants as dumps. Over a short number of weeks, in September 1943, groups of partisans and ordinary citizens initiated a series of brutal attacks that resulted in around 500–700 victims, mostly Italians. Recent research, drawing mainly on Slovenian and Croatian archives, stresses the absence of any genocidal plan in this first phase of murders. Italians undeniably were the predominant victims because they represented the arrogant state power: *carabinieri*, public officials, local fascist party leaders, but also middle-class representatives. "Several threads of logic seem to be intertwined: summary, turbulent and extreme application of the law, nationalist outbursts, social rivalry and rural vendettas, as well as a plan to uproot Italian power."[15]

After the Italian armistice, the Germans established the so-called Adriatic Littoral Operation Zone (*Operationszone Adriatisches Küstenland*)

13 Carlo Spartaco Capogreco, *I campi del duce. L'internamento civile nell'Italia fascista (1940–1943)* (The Camps of the Duce. Civilian Internment in Facist Italy), Turin, Einaudi, 2004.

14 Davide Rodogno, *Fascism's European Empire. Italian Occupation during the Second World War*, Cambridge, Cambridge University Press, 2006, p. 412.

15 Raoul Pupo, *Il lungo esodo*, *op. cit.*, p. 75.

in the Eastern border area, in order to stabilize communications with the Austrian part of the Reich and to have better control over partisan activities. The German and other Slavic collaborationist units' repressive actions became even harsher, which consequently led to the strengthening of the Yugoslav communist partisan movement.

Relations with the small groups of Italian partisans in the border area, whether communist or not, were highly complex. Tito managed to incorporate a number of groups of Italian Communists into his well-organized army, many of whom favoured the plan to annex the Eastern part of Northern Italy to Communist Yugoslavia, in the immediate post-war period. The leaders of the *Partito Comunista Italiano* (Italian Communist Party – PCI), headed by Palmiro Togliatti, moved with caution (ambiguously, according to their critics) when faced with Tito's territorial requests that the Isonzo river should be the future border between Italy and Yugoslavia. This request implied that Trieste and Gorizia, as well as the important industrial centre of Monfalcone, would become part of the future Yugoslav state.[16] The Communists of Venezia Giulia and Istria had a different attitude. They were under great pressure (after all, Tito's partisan army could be considered a positive model of a successful national war of liberation), and as a result accepted the Yugoslav position entirely. The race for Trieste (between the Allied forces and the Yugoslav partisan units)[17] ended with the liberation/occupation of Trieste and surroundings by the latter, on 30 April 1945.

Just a few weeks later, pressure from the USA led to the withdrawal of Yugoslav troops from the port city, after a bloody phase of purges and violence. The agreement, signed in Belgrade on 9 June 1945, divided Venezia Giulia into two zones: Zone A, which included Trieste and its immediate *hinterland*, under Allied administration, and Zone B, which included Northern Istria (but not the city of Pola/Pula, assigned to Zone A), under Yugoslav administration. Trieste and the Eastern border area of Italy assumed, therefore, a crucial role in the unfolding Cold War.[18]

---

16 Roberto Gualtieri, *Toglatti e la politica estera italiana. Dalla Resistenza al trattato di pace 1943–1947* (Togliatti and Italian Foreign Policy. From Resistance to the Peace Treaty), Rome, Editori Riuniti, 1995.

17 Geoffrey Cox, *The Race for Trieste*, London, Kimber, 1977.

18 Giampaolo Valdevit, *La questione di Trieste 1941–1954. Politica internazionale e contesto locale* (*The Trieste Question. International Politics and Local Context*), Milano, Franco Angeli, 1986.

It is within this regional and global context that the second and more radical wave of violence against Italians must be interpreted, although only a minority of the victims were actually dumped in *foibe*. This went on for several months and took many different forms: summary courts, spontaneous executions, planned deportations in concentration camps (from which the majority never returned), a mixture of actions from below and policies performed by the new local communist authorities. The victims of this second phase of the *foibe* were mostly Italians; however, we do not have reliable statistics about nationalities. A certain percentage were Slovenian and Croatian (alleged) collaborators (*domobrani* and *ustaša*). Again, following these findings recent historiography rejects the interpretation that it was in fact an Italian genocide. Across the whole of Yugoslavia, the Titoist regime launched bloody purges of entire national, social and professional groups that were considered politically dangerous. In Venezia Giulia the enemies ended up coinciding to a great extent with the Italians.

It is very difficult to quantify the victims of this second wave, who surely number several thousand, but not quite as large a figure as that suggested by some Italian historians of 15,000–20,000, which is undoubtedly an exaggeration.[19] A cause-and-effect link between the *foibe* and the following exodus established by subsequent interpretations seems too artificial and disguises the complexity of the immediate post-war situation. The archival documentation recently scrutinized by historiography suggests that it is more likely that these waves of violence, and the subsequent administrative and economic measures enacted by the Yugoslav regime at the local level, left in the Italian communities a deep fear made up of anguish and uncertainty about the future. As a provisional conclusion, we may sum up with the words of the Italian historian Raoul Pupo: "The critical turbulent transition of the authority from the Nazi-Fascist power to the Yugoslav Communist one took place without determining per se large scale population transfers."[20]

19 Marina Cattaruzza, *L'Italia e il confine orientale* (Italy and the Eastern Border), Bologna, Il Mulino, 2007, p. 294.

20 Raoul Pupo, "L'esodo degli italiani da Zara, da Fiume e dall'Istria. Un quadro fattuale" (The Exodus of Italians from Zara, Fiume and Istria. A Factual Framework), in Marina Cattaruzza, Marco Dogo, Raoul Pupo (eds), *Esodi. Trasferimenti forzati di popolazione nel Novecento europeo* (Exodus. Forced Population Transfers in the European Twentieth Century), Naples, Edizioni Scientifiche Italiane, 2000, p. 186.

The Exodus

It appears that no official, explicit and overarching decision to expel all Italians was taken by the new Communist Yugoslavian government.[21] But, precisely this assumption was the interpretation given by the Italian side for many years and passed on through collective memory. It is also doubtful whether the political will of the new Communist Yugoslav government was actually to rid itself of the Italian minority. This doubt can only be clarified if Yugoslavia makes the archival documentation fully accessible to research. The way the exodus was actually carried out is in fact fraught with contradictory behaviour: on the one hand, the local communist authorities hindered the exodus by threatening the supposed instigators; on the other, the Italian inhabitants of the area were pressured into quickly leaving cities and villages en masse. This marks a clear difference from the policy implemented towards the German-speaking minorities in Vojvodina and Banat, who were collectively dispossessed of their properties and deprived of their civil rights. Their complete expulsion took place quickly and involved more than 250,000 people.[22] Instead, a series of "national rights" had to be granted to the Italians, according to the official slogan of the "Italian-Slav brotherhood", evoking the widest possible collaboration in the construction of socialism; obviously this project excluded all those who were regarded as *a priori* hostile. There was, however, a crucial precondition: the Italians would have to accept the ideology of the new regime. According to the dogmatic Stalinist ideology, this could not be an individual acceptance, established on a voluntary basis, but had to be based on objective class criteria. Hence, a clear distinction was drawn up by the new communist ruling elite between "honest anti-fascist" Italians and Italians who were "reactionary" or "enemies of the people". Italians living in the region were mostly urban dwellers of lower-middle-class or middle-class descent. They were in general property owners, who only stood to lose from the policies of nationalization and social redistribution advocated by Tito.

In October 1945, the Yugoslav authorities carried out an ethnic census in the area. They manipulated the census by scaling down the share of

---

21 This interpretation has been maintained in the pioneering study by Cristiana Colummi, Liliana Ferrari, Gianna Nassisi, Germano Trani, *Storia di un esodo. Istria 1945–1956* (History of an Exodus. Istria 1945–1956), Trieste, ISRMLFVG, 1980.

22 Hans-Ulrich Wehler, *Nationalitätenpolitik in Jugoslawien. Die deutsche Minderheit 1918–1978*, Göttingen, Vandenhoeck & Ruprecht, 1980.

the Italian-speaking population (the same had been done by the previous Italian authorities), in order to instrumentalize these figures in the forthcoming Paris Peace Conference. Consequently, the majority of Italian speakers were *ex officio* defined as "denationalized" Slavs (owing to Italian pressure in the preceding decades) and counted as Slav speakers. According to this manipulated census, Italians in Istria, Venetia Giulia and Dalmatia accounted for 24.3% of the total population, down from 45.3% in the previous Habsburg census of 1910. The peace conference in Paris 1946/7 ratified the existing post-war borders: all the territories in which Italians were counted as a minority were to be assigned to Yugoslavia, a victorious state backed by the victorious Stalin. The areas in which Italians had the majority were to be given to Italy. The proposal of the Italian government to set up an internationally monitored plebiscite in the contested territories (as in the Istrian peninsula) came to nothing.[23] All individuals had the right to opt freely for one solution or the other. Opting meant leaving their homes, their jobs and all of their belongings for a new homeland. This was the case also for some hundreds of Italian industrial workers, mostly Communists, who decided to leave Trieste and Monfalcone and move to the new socialist state, in which they saw the realization of their ideological dreams. They soon were heavily disappointed. Tito's split from Moscow in 1948 upset the Italian immigrants, who were in general loyal to the Soviet Union. Under the label of "deviationism" most of them were deported in camps, while others were expelled. Only a small minority adapted with great difficulty to the new trend.[24]

The exodus, often described in a single model, should in fact be split into territorial cases with their own specific characteristics. In Zadar/Zara, the first area involved in the process, the majority of the population was Italian in terms of language and culture. Still before the end of hostilities, they deserted their hometown, not because of pressure by the Yugoslav authorities, as an initial step in a plan aimed at expelling all Italians from the area. More plausibly, they were forced to abandon their houses owing to the tremendous air raids carried out by British and American bombers

---

23 Some experts, such as the historian Ernesto Sestan, himself of Istrian origin, were convinced that in the event of a plebiscite the majority, feeling nationally Slavic, would vote to remain in Yugoslavia. See his *Venezia Giulia. Lineamenti di storia etnica e culturale* (Venetia Julia. Outline of Ethnic and Cultural History), Udine, Del Bianco, 1997, originally published in 1947.

24 See Alfredo Bonelli, *Fra Stalin e Tito. Cominformisti a Fiume 1948–1956* (Between Stalin and Tito. Cominformists in Fiume), Trieste, ISRMLFVG, 1994.

on that strategically important harbour. When the Communist partisans entered the city in early May 1945, there were just a few thousand people left, a minority of whom were Italians.[25]

In Rijeka/Fiume, inhabited by a clear Italian majority, the arrival of the Yugoslav liberators gave way to a series of repressive actions to disrupt the strong Italian autonomist movement, whose anti-fascist (but not communist) credentials were no longer important. The liberators set out a policy of intense Croatization in order to oust the Italian elites predominant in commerce and industry for good. In 1946–7 a policy of confiscation and dispossession was put into practice under various pretexts. However, the inadequate preparation of the new Communist ruling elite ended up worsening the material conditions of the whole population of the city and the countryside. Accused generically of being "enemies of the people", Italians in Fiume soon found themselves in an unbearable situation. In 1946 a stream of emigration began, eventually involving around 20,000 people. The Yugoslav authorities reacted by criticizing those leaving and attacking the ecclesiastic hierarchy, which was accused of instigating the exodus.[26] However, they did nothing to reduce the flow. The exodus continued over the next two years, under the form of individual free option, which – as we have already seen – was provided by the clauses of the Paris Peace Treaty of February 1947.

While the flows of Italians from Zara and Fiume happened mostly without being noticed by a larger public, it was not the same in Pola/Pula, as they took place under the gaze of Italian and international public opinion. At the end of the war the coastal city had been assigned to Zone A, under the military administration of the Western Allies. But with the passing of time the eventuality became concrete that the city would be assigned to Yugoslavia. This threw the Italian-speaking inhabitants into a panic. Moreover, the city was completely isolated in Zone B, encircled by a majoritarian Croatian rural population. The economic situation of the Italians continued to deteriorate. After a period of uncertainty, the news from Paris in the summer of 1946 caused a traumatic change in

25 Cristiana Colummi, "Guerra, occupazione nazista e resistenza" (War, Nazi Occupation and Resistance), in *Storia di un esodo*, *op. cit.*, p. 47f.

26 There was great support for Bishop Ugo Comozzo, including by the shipyard workers; Orietta Moscarda, "La giustizia del popolo. Sequestri e confische a Fiume nel secondo dopoguerra" (People's Justice. Seizures and Confiscation in Rijeka after the Second World War), in *Qualestoria*, 1997, p. 83.

the Italian community's attitude, as all hopes crumbled. A committee began to collect individual options for emigration. Out of the 32,000 Italian residents in Pula, more than 28,000 chose to leave. The exodus was initially improvised and only belatedly did the Italian government provide shipping and assistance for the evacuees. Many people took with them the coffins of their relatives, exhumed from the city cemetery. It was the sign of a definitive parting. Once in Trieste, some set off for further destinations outside Europe.

Istria had been the centre of the *foibe* both in September 1943 and at the end of the war. In this area, the Yugoslav authorities enacted property confiscations and forced labour against the Italian-speaking inhabitants, in the context of an "overall denationalization plan", which also entailed highly symbolic actions, such as the removal of the San Marco lion from city gates and public buildings.[27] After February 1947, the possibility of an option was introduced in Istria. Those choosing to opt for Italy were obliged to leave, thereby automatically losing their property. Not only did a large percentage of the Italians living in the coastal towns take the option (as was expected) but many inland inhabitants did too. For example, 90% of the population of inland town of Pisino/Pazin opted for Italy. The Yugoslav authorities attempted to block in any way they could this unexpected mass flow, which endangered the social and economic fabric of the area, but emerged unsuccessful. The exodus reached its peak between 1947 and 1949, but the options were reopened in 1950. In total, over 50,000 Italians were involved in this region.

The last act of these complex dynamics occurred at the beginning of the 1950s in the Northern part of Istria (nowadays Slovenian territory), assigned by the Paris Peace Conference to Zone B.[28] The pattern enacted by the Yugoslav authorities was the same: processes, summary violence, confiscations, pressure by the administration and the media. In this case, similarly to what happened in Pula, the Italian working class, largely close to the Communist Party, reacted with protests and strikes. This demonstrates the gap that existed between Yugoslav policies and the prevailing attitude of the Italian public, though it was often ideologically

[27] *Storia di un esodo, op. cit.*, p. 121.

[28] See Katja Hrobat Virloget, Catherine Gousseff, Gustavo Corni (eds), *At home but foreigners. Population Transfers in 20th Century Istria*, Koper, Annales University Press, 2015.

sympathetic. The protest was against the Yugoslav economic policy, which by cutting off all traditional commercial and work contacts with Trieste obviously damaged the Italians. The regime's reaction was to encourage rural Slovenes to move into the towns (Capodistria/Koper in particular), thereby applying a characteristic pattern of Yugoslav nationalism: the Slav countryside against the Italian city.

The main reason why the exodus began so late in the Capodistria/Koper area is connected to its proximity to Trieste and the Italian residents' hope that the territory would be definitively returned to Italy. However, the Yugoslav authorities stayed. They put the Italian population under increasing pressure, branding them as "fascists", while the Italian Communists were disparagingly labelled "extremists". Italian schools were closed and teachers were forced to leave. There was also heavy pressure on the Italian-speaking clergy, culminating in an assault on the Archbishop of Trieste and Koper Antonio Santin during his visit to the diocese in June 1947.

In April 1950, the Yugoslav authorities organized local elections in Zone B as a reaction to elections held in Trieste, which had seen the triumph of moderate Italian parties.[29] The Communist Party gained a clear victory in an atmosphere of intimidation, which had convinced many Italians to desert the polls. This provided another incentive for them to abandon a radically transformed territory that many no longer saw as their own.

The definitive assignation of Zone A to Italy by the Western powers in October 1953 was the ultimate drive for the Italian exodus from Istria. In the first wave of apparently spontaneous violence, thousands of people were forced to abandon their homes and properties. They were followed by the vast majority of Italians living in Northern Istria. Between October 1953 and August 1956 around 25,000 people fled from the Zone. They were joined by around 3,000 autochthonous Croats and Slovenes from Istria.

---

29 ibid., pp. 355ff.

Figure 4 – *Borders of Trieste / Istria (1937-1954)*

Source: https://it.wikipedia.org/wiki/File:Confini_Trieste-Istria2.jpg

It is difficult to give accurate numbers of those involved in the exodus, partly because 'militant' historiography has often proposed preposterous figures. The total number given by refugee associations is 350,000, which was accepted in particular by Italian historians and journalists in the first decades after the events. A general census by the Italian government in 1956 estimated a total of 270,000; other estimates give slightly lower figures, and the figure of 250,000 seems to be accepted as a "realistic estimate of the migratory flow" by the most recent studies.[30]

Slovene and Croatian researchers have recently suggested a much lower number, 190,000 refugees, reflecting a long-established tendency to downscale the phenomenon. In general, they deny that it has to be evaluated as an exceptional event, caused by conscious policies carried out by new rulers, and place it as a "normal" voluntary migration, connected mainly to economic reasons.[31] In this respect, the Slovene and Croatian interpretation differs dramatically from the long-established interpretation provided by nationalist historiography in Italy, which regards the exodus as an attempt at genocide aimed at the Italians living on the Eastern border. Leaving aside quantitative differences, the crucial fact is that a whole community, in its entire social structure, abandoned its homeland under heavy pressure.

According to new research, we have to reconsider the crucial question of what were the main driving forces for those who left. The most prominent force was fear, fuelled by the initial brutal waves of violence. Then, it was the repressive and inquisitional atmosphere established by the Yugoslav Communist regime. There were also other reasons, such as the sudden subversion of social and cultural hierarchies and the fading of tight networks of habits and customs, such as religious practices. These factors have been underestimated, because the dominant nationalist historiography on both sides emphasizes the interaction between Yugoslavia's "ethnic cleansing" project and the reaction of the Italians. Social and economic factors were therefore placed second; the most recent Italian historiography is inclined to contrast this lack underlying the increasingly difficult material conditions in earning a living base.[32] In a short period of time the Italians in Yugoslavia experienced a dramatic

---

30 Raoul Pupo, *Il lungo esodo, op. cit.*, p. 510.

31 Recent developments in Slovene and Croatian historiograhpy are exemplified in the papers by Marta Verginella and Luciano Giuricin, in *Esodi, op. cit.*, pp. 269–285.

32 Paolo Purini, *Metamorfosi etniche. I cambiamenti di popolazione a Trieste, Gorizia, Fiume e in Istria, 1914 – 1975* (*Ethnic Metamorphoses. Population Changes in Trieste,*

change in living conditions, which contributed to an increase in psychological illness and estrangement. We may interpret the exodus as a consequence of a deep identity crisis, connected to the modernization processes that the new Communist regime was energetically enforcing. Feeling "out of place" in their own country became the main reason for the decision of the Italians in the area to leave. Although, in many cases, from a formal point of view it looked like a "free option", a voluntary decision, in general the exodus can "without a doubt be included in the category of forced migration, even if they are the only ones in which the decision to migrate, taken by individuals or households, had an active role in the population movement".[33]

No memory in the new "homeland"

In the aftermath of the evacuation, as well as later, several associations were founded in order to offer the evacuees a network of relations and, at least to some degree, ways to concretize their requests to the state and to the political parties. The first association to be founded was the largest one: the *Associazione Nazionale Venezia Giulia e Dalmazia* (National Association for Julian Venetia and Dalmatia), founded in Trieste in 1947 and diffused in a great number of local sections all over Italy. In its first years the association had around 100,000 members. It has nowadays around 8,000. Another smaller association, founded in 1954, pretends to represent and reproduce in exile the traditions and culture of Istria. It is named *Unione degli Istriani* (Union of Istrians) and its core aim is well presented in the subheading *Libera provincia dell'Istria in esilio* (Free province of Istria in exile). Another important representative association is the *Associazione dei Giuliani nel mondo* (Association of the Julians of the world), whose aim is to give a voice to the large number of Julians, evacuees or not, who live scattered as a result of the emigration worldwide.[34]

These and other similar associations, focusing on cultural and linguistic aspects, cannot in be compared, as their political influence is considered, with the expellee organizations from the German Eastern

Gorizia, Fiume and Istria), Udine, Kappa Vu, 2010 and Marta Verginella, *Il confine degli altri* (*The Border of Others*), Rome, Donzelli, 2008.

33 Antonio Ferrara, Niccolò Pianciola, *Migrazioni forzate*, *op. cit.*, p. 18.

34 For an overview of the different associations and their aims cf. www.leganazionale.it (last entry 15 September 2016)

provinces, since the latter have played an important role in domestic and foreign policy during the Adenauer era.[35] The protest of the Italian evacuee associations was sometimes loud, but mostly in vain, in particular in the wake of the signing of the Treaty of Osimo between Italy and Yugoslavia on 10 November 1975. The treaty not only resolved once and for all the question of the inter-state borders, but silenced also every claim in the field of properties, patrimony and pensions. The influence of these associations, although scattered in all Italian regions and abroad, has remained weak and limited to the local level, in particular Trieste and the nearby region. But even here, the associations' influence in representing the interests of the evacuees has to be considered small. For example, in 1983 the Autonomous Region Friuli-Venezia Giulia gave birth to a regional institution to preserve and disseminate the cultural traditions of the lost territories: the *Istituto regionale per la cultura istriano-fiumano-dalmata* (Regional Institute for Istrian-Fiuman and Dalmatian Culture). One of the major aims of this institution was to create a new museum, organized according to the most modern technologies. The museum was in fact opened in a central alley of Trieste, but only in June 2015.

For a long time, the memory of this painful episode remained circumscribed at the level of the associations, families and individuals, and was important only for the survivors and their heirs. They still remain largely uninterested in exchanging opinions with historians and in telling their story to larger audiences. Neither the refugees from the Eastern borders nor the colonizers and Italian residents in Africa (who in those same years left the former colonies or other overseas territories) experienced a particularly warm welcome when they returned to Italy. Their presence was disturbing, and at the political level they were a reminder of the endeavours of Fascism (or at least could be interpreted as such). The colonizers had in the past been chosen to play a leading role in the regime's propaganda – even though it probably did not reflect their personal points of view. The attraction of colonies played an important role in late nineteenth and early twentieth-century Italian culture.[36] After 1945, however, a new leaf was turned, and all questions concerning colonies and Italian presence in the Balkans were shelved.

---

35 Pertti Ahonen, *After the Expulsion. West Germany and Eastern Europe 1945–1990*, New York–Oxford, Oxford University Press, 2003.

36 Nicola Labanca, *Oltremare. Storia dell'espansione coloniale italiana* (Overseas. History of Italian Colonial Expansion), Bologna, Il Mulino, 2002, pp. 448ff.

It was easy to brand those returning with their burden of suffering and with considerable material and non-material damage as "fascists". Similarly – with the crucial addition of a war lost in the worst way – the soldiers who returned from prison camps had been greeted with indifference and even hostility.[37] This contributed to mutual attitudes of indifference, which took root in particular in the memory of the refugees' associations.

The reasons for collective repression can be traced back to Italian post-war politics. In the new political climax of the "Berlusconi era" (dating from the early 1990s) there emerged a strong tendency to stress the fact that the *Partito Comunista Italiano* (PCI) had tried to draw a veil of silence over its ambiguous behaviour in Trieste in the final phase of the war and the early post-war years. In 1944–5 the regional party was openly pro-Tito. The links to the Yugoslav Communists were reinforced during the Resistance, when Italian communist partisans had enrolled in large numbers in the well-organized partisan army of Tito. The party leaders in Rome also adopted an ambiguous position regarding the Eastern border. On the other hand, even the Italian government (monopolized for the four decades following the end of the war by the moderate, pro-Western *Democrazia Cristiana* – Christian Democratic Party) had plausible reasons not to emphasize controversies with Yugoslavia. After 1948 (following the rupture with Moscow), Yugoslavia became an increasingly important political and economic partner for Italy and for Western Europe. It quickly changed from being Italy's historical and most dangerous enemy to a potential ally, a crucial factor for *détente* in Europe. Even regarding the Trieste question, which had remained open for a decade until 1954 when the port city was definitively and formally returned to Italy, this forced all the Italian political parties to act with caution towards Yugoslavia.

Only belatedly were response plans implemented by the government to give the incoming refugees homes and jobs; however, the resources allocated for this purpose were totally inadequate. This took place in Trieste and its surroundings. The Christian Democratic Party created proper villages where refugees from the same village or town could stay together, cleverly exploiting their anti-communist rancour at election

[37] Agostino Bistarelli, *La storia del ritorno. I reduci italiani del secondo dopoguerra* (The History of the Return. Italian Ex-combatants in the Second Post-War Era), Turin, Bollati Boringhieri, 2007.

level.[38] Another destination favoured by the government was the Trentino–Alto Adige region, where groups of Istrian and Dalmatian refugees proved useful in strengthening the Italian ethnic and linguistic presence in primarily German-speaking areas.[39]

Many decided to leave again and choose distant destinations for emigration, mainly Australia and North America. This was because they desired for both economic and psychological reasons to be far away as possible from their lost homeland, and also because there was a widespread feeling of helplessness and distrust.

For a long time, the memory of the dramatic events at the Eastern border in the immediate post-war years was kept private among the families and the enlarged families represented by the refugee associations. A political dimension was achieved only in rare moments, and mainly at the local level, in particular when influencing the political debate in Trieste and its surroundings.[40] By contrast, two distinct opposing collective memories were created: of those who had been exiled, and of the minority of Italians who for the most diverse reasons had decided to stay, or at any rate had stayed, in Communist Yugoslavia. Officially, fewer than 35,000 native Italian speakers are numbered in Croatia today, and fewer than 4,000 in Slovenia. These two distinct parties mutually ignored each other, acting as if the other did not even exist and as if there were no reason to take their lives and fate into consideration.

The political exploitation of the exodus was regionally concentrated for at least four decades along the Eastern border, where many of the exiles had settled, playing an important role in local political life. It was a memory forcibly exploited both by the Christian Democratic Party and by the Italian extreme right. Two mutually reinforcing elements merged here: anti-Slavism and anti-Communism. They were both still present in that border territory before the dramatic events of 1943–5.[41] There

---

38 Pamela Ballinger, "National Refugees, Displaced Persons, and the Reconstruction of Italy: the Case of Trieste", in Jessica Reinisch, Elizabeth Withe (eds), *The Disentanglement of Populations. Migration, Expulsion and Displacement in Postwar Europe, 1944–49*, Houndmills, Basingstoke, Hampshire/New York, Palgrave Macmillan, 2011, pp. 115ff.

39 Elena Tonezzer (ed.), *Volti di un esodo* (Faces of an Exodus), Trento, Museo storico in Trento, 2005, partly founded on oral sources and written memoirs.

40 See the path-breaking study by Pamela Ballinger, *History in Exile. Memory and Identity at the Borders of the Balkans*, Princeton NJ, Princeton University Press, 2003.

41 Marina Cattaruzza, *L'Italia e il confine orientale 1866–2006* (Italy and the Eastern Border), Bologna, Il Mulino, 2007.

were two main undisputable "truths" to such a circumscribed public and private memory: (1) the *foibe* were just the first step in an attempted "genocide" of the Italian population in the region, which intended to eradicate it definitively; (2) consequently there was a close link between the *foibe* and the subsequent expulsion of the 250–300,000 Italians from the coastal regions on the Eastern border.

The situation changed radically after 1990. The collapse of the so-called "First Republic", founded on the constitutional agreement between the anti-fascist parties, owing to its internal weakness (highlighted by the "*mani pulite*" affair), caused profound upheaval, bringing new subjects onto the political stage. The first and most important of these was the media magnate Silvio Berlusconi. He created and hegemonized an alleged "new" right, into which the old, post-fascist *Movimento Sociale Italiano* (MSI – Italian Socialist Movement) party had been profoundly transformed in terms of its ideology and programme. This new political subject appropriated the subject of the *foibe*, which was closely intertwined – as we have seen before – with the ensuing exodus. The intention was on the one hand to legitimize the new right wing as a true national and patriotic party, and on the other (especially) to target political opponents by reiterating the old but generally effective anti-communist cliché. It provoked also a weakening of the leftist historiography, which adhered to the so-called "anti fascist paradigm" which has partly hegemonized historical studies in post-war Italy. By combining the two phenomena of mass killings and resettlements, which by rights were distinct entities, and by inflating the number of victims to the extent of calling this a true "genocide", historians and journalists have elevated the *foibe* to the status of a black page in Italian history, which was deliberately ignored in the past owing to the cultural domination of the left in Italy.[42] The Communists were targeted, in fact, as responsible twice over. First, they were guilty of siding in 1943–5 with the Yugoslav Communists, betraying national interests, thereby rendering themselves accomplices, albeit indirectly, of the attempted genocide. Secondly, by maintaining firm control over Italian historiography after 1945, they were guilty of a prolonged silence that caused those dramatic events to be sidelined in public memory. Above and beyond the fact that both these assumptions are highly questionable,

42 Gustavo Corni, *Fascism, Anti-Fascism and Resistance in the Politics of Memory and Historiography in Post War Italy*, in Q. Edward Wang – Franz L. Fillafer (eds), *The Many Faces of Clio. Cross-Cultural Approaches to Historiography*, Oxford, Berghahn, 2007, p. 430f.

it needs to be emphasized how a renewed interest in the topic, favoured by media such as TV, in reaction paved the way for studies to make significant progress.[43] These became increasingly more divergent in comparison with the public account, which presented the Italians from Istria and Dalmatia as "martyrs", taking the events out of context and providing a highly simplified, black and white account.[44] The ordeal for the Italians who had suffered the harsh trials of being displaced and dispossessed has thus been extrapolated from its natural historical context and ascribed to a communist conspiracy perpetrated by the Yugoslav Communists and their Italian accomplices.

The impact of the *foibe* in terms of politics and public opinion was far more significant than just historiographic. It is true that the repeated attempts by *Alleanza Nazionale* (National Alliance), a governing party along with Berlusconi for most of the 1990s and 2000s, to oblige historians to devote more space in their history books and manuals to a preconceived interpretation of those historic events, forcing at the same time teachers to adapt, fell on deaf ears. But political pressure from centre-right governments led to the introduction of a National Memorial Day, in the official denomination *Giorno del Ricordo*, by a law dated 30 March 2004. It must, incidentally, be remembered that a large majority (the centre-right governmental parties as well as the leftist opposition) in both branches of the parliament voted through the law. The law is intended to "preserve and update the tragic memory of the Italians and of all the victims of the *foibe*, the exodus of the people of Istria, Fiume and Dalmatia from their homelands after World War II and the more complex issue of the Eastern border". The date set for the commemoration is 10 February, to coincide with the signing of the Paris Peace Treaty in 1947. This date is historiographically questionable, because there are no links of cause and effect between the signing of the peace treaty and the expulsion of Italians, which had begun already before it. But the significance is clear in the eyes of the legislator: to reiterate the injustice of the peace treaty. In February 2005, to mark its first celebration, a fictional programme,

---

43 Among others, see Guido Crainz, *Il dolore e l'esilio. L'Istria e le memorie divise d'Europa* (The Sorrow and the Exile. Istria and European Divided Memory), Rome, Donzelli, 2005 and Joze Pirjevec, *Foibe. Una storia d'Italia* (Foibe. An Italian History), Turin, Einaudi, 2009.

44 An example of this educational literature is the (pseudo-scientific) book by Marco Pirina, *Dalle foibe all'esodo 1943–1956: il perché del silenzio dei vivi* (From Foibe to the Exodus. The Reasons for the Silence of the Living), Pordenone, Silentes Loquimur, which in 2008 was already in its eighth edition.

Il cuore nel pozzo, was broadcast by state television. It was criticized by historians because of its many inaccuracies, but it won over a broad sector of the public.

The *Giorno del Ricordo* was in those years opposed by many to the International Holocaust Remembrance Day, which the Italian parliament, like many others, had set by law (back in July 2000) on 27 January in remembrance of the extermination of European Jews, following the recommendations of the United Nations. The contrast between the two festivities, which could and should be complementary, is the result of political exploitation, and does not correspond at all to the criteria of historiographic accuracy. It is certain, however, that the new public holiday has from time to time ignited some sort of nationalistic friction. Just think of the diplomatic incident sparked in February 2007 between Italy and Croatia, when the President of the Republic, former Communist Giorgio Napolitano, during an official speech commemorating the *foibe* of Basovizza (near Trieste), spoke of "ethnic cleansing", triggering a resentful response from the Croatian President Stjepan Mesic.

Conclusion

In light of over a decade of celebrating this festivity, it does not seem to have contributed either to disseminating a more widespread awareness of the facets of our country's recent history among larger portions of the Italian population (especially the younger generations) or to surmounting the wall closing off the outside that characterizes the individual or group memory of those involved and their relatives, who have joined together to form specific associations. Once again, it seems rather that, all recent efforts notwithstanding, the silent memory of the victims has – as has happened in the past – remained largely impervious to political exploitation.

The Politics of History of the Lost Land: Shifting European, National and Regional Approaches to the History of Karelia

Kimmo Katajala

Professor of History, Department of Geographical and Historical Studies, University of Eastern Finland

Ilkka Liikanen

Professor of Border and Russian Studies, Karelian Institute, University of Eastern Finland

The war between Finland and the Soviet Union ended with the Moscow Armistice of 1944, whose stipulations, confirmed by the Paris Peace Treaty of 1947, accorded most of the Karelian territory to the Soviet Union. At the time, some 420,000 Finns and Karelians fled from the annexed territories to Finland. The resulting experience created a shared sentiment of loss that has played an essential part in Finnish post-war historiographical approaches to Karelia. Wartime visions of Karelia as an outpost in the civilizational battle between East and West lost ground, and even earlier narratives of exotic originality, minority culture and the transnational history of a borderland gave way to a history of the Lost Land with powerful references to national unity. The Karelian issue came to be associated with the land *we* lost, the land taken away from *us*, the Finns. Even if the majority of people probably shared this sense of loss, the notion of a common belonging did not always reflect earlier attitudes which the population of the border regions had encountered, or the way displaced Karelians were being treated in their new homeland. In many instances, these minority experiences on the margins of the national narrative have come to the fore only gradually, decades after the end of the war.

Figure 5: *Karelian territories attributed to the Soviet Union by the Paris Peace Treaty (1947)*

Even in current discussions, references to Karelia tend to allude to some form of buried wisdom shared by all Finns, suggesting the existence of a suppressed, tacitly approved true history of Karelia. In terms of current politics of history, this practice subscribes – rather innocently –

to the idea of a single authentic historical narrative of Karelia that has to be safeguarded against external pressures and false reinterpretations. This represents an obvious paradox as historical narratives of border regions tend to be complex and subject to multiple interpretations.

In Finnish post-war politics of history, the notion of a concealed true history of the Lost Land was not primarily about the destiny of the population of border regions, but directly linked to the legitimation of national policies during the war. It offered a way to avoid critically addressing inter-war and wartime historical narratives of Karelia – and their connection to wartime politics. At the same time, it pushed aside the manifold older interpretations and obscured the tradition of earlier historical approaches that had been constantly changing since the days of the founding fathers of Finnish national historiography.[1] Today, when new European perspectives are on the rise in the study of border regions, there is an obvious need to examine in detail this variety of competing paradigms of Karelian history and to understand the political rationale behind them.

Before and during World War II, the history of Karelia and the Finnish Eastern border had typically been written up as part of grand narratives of Finnish national and European history, often in terms of a battle between East and West. When Finland tried to recover its international status after the lost war, the major political parties had to suppress references to the lost Karelian lands in their official statements. In high politics, allusions to the loss of Finnish "national" territory – let alone an eternal battle line between East and West – could be interpreted as questioning the Paris Peace Treaty. Finnish political wisdom of the day deemed it utterly ill-advised to feed any suspicions of a revanchist stance as long as Finland struggled to regain full international stature. This was especially important during the period when the Allied Control Committee stayed in the country (1944–7), and it continued to be a serious concern during

1 See Kimmo Katajala, "From Conflict to Cooperation: Paradigm Changes in Finnish Research into the History of Karelia and the Eastern Border", in Kimmo Katajala, Maria Lähteenmäki (eds), *Imagined, Negotiated, Remembered. Constructing European Borders and Borderlands*, Münster, Lit, 2012, pp. 87–118; Ilkka Liikanen, "Origins of the Eastern Border as the Grand Controversy of Finnish National History Writing", in Tibor Frank, Frank Hadler (eds), *Disputed Territories and Shared Pasts: Overlapping National Histories in Modern Europe*, London, Palgrave, 2011, pp. 177–199. These review articles form the main basis of the historiographical analysis presented in this study.

the whole Cold War period, with membership of the United Nations (1955) as a major turning point.[2]

Considerations of what it was politically sensible to voice aloud by Cold War standards did not mean that historical texts about Karelia ceased being published altogether. On the contrary: there was a post-war boom of publications on Karelian history, although with a clear change of focus compared to the inter-war period. At first, the most common forms of writing the History of the Lost Land were regional and local histories, memoirs and studies of everyday life. From the 1960s onwards, political themes and perspectives of European and national history made a reappearance, but they were now presented from new angles and often gave rise to disputes in terms of politics of history.

The historical debates of the 1960s and 1970s can be largely understood as a result of new revisionist approaches that were then spreading across Western Europe. Beyond, there was, however, a long-standing refusal by the academic community, as well as the media, to critically discuss the way in which national and wider European history had been approached in the 1920s and 1930s.[3] Finnish historians and intellectual circles in general felt no need to participate in the broader re-evaluation of nationalist politics and national history that took place elsewhere, for example in Germany.[4] Finland's participation in Hitler's operation Barbarossa (1941) was conceived as a separate front aimed at reconquering Karelia, a consequence of Stalin's 1939 attack rather than a wilful alliance with the Nazis. Over the last decades, authors adopting new comparative European perspectives have distanced themselves from interpretations of national history writing, and this has applied to studies of Karelia's history as well. In terms of history politics, this turn has often

---

2 Ilkka Liikanen, "Finland–Russia: Karelia", in Emmanuel Brunet-Jailly (ed.), *Border Disputes. A Global Encyclopedia*, Vol. 1, Santa Barbara CAL, ABC-CLIO, 2015, pp. 206–216.

3 Pekka Ahtiainen, Jukka Tervonen (eds), *Menneisyyden tutkijat ja metodien vartijat. Matka suomalaiseen historiankirjoitukseen* (Scholars of the Past and Guardians of Methods. A Journey Through Finnish History Writing), Helsinki, Suomen Historiallinen Seura, 1996, p. 151; Ilkka Liikanen, "Raoul Palmgren and the East and West of the Finnish Left", in Heidi Haggrén, Johanna Rainio-Niemi, Jussi Vauhkonen (eds), *Multi-layered Historicity of the Present: Approaches to Social Science History*, Helsinki, Unigrafia, 2013, pp. 61–74.

4 See Edgar Wolfrum, *Geschichtspolitik in der Bundesrepublik Deutschland. Der Weg zur Bundesrepublikanischen Erinnerung 1948–1990*, Darmstadt, Wissenschaftliche Buchgesellschaft, 1999.

been interpreted as bringing closure to the traumas caused by the war and the loss of Karelia. It is being assumed that a broader European perspective would in itself represent a more peaceful approach and a postponed reckoning with "chauvinist" approaches. However, as the earlier grand visions of a battle between East and West testify, shifting the focus to "higher" European perspectives hardly offers any guarantee of a less destructive or less self-righteous approach.[5] There is therefore all the more reason today to study in detail the political uses of European, national and regional narratives of Karelia's history.

In the following, we will sketch how the regional, national and European history of Karelia has been narrated over time and what kind of paradigm shifts can be recognized. We will first outline the main trends in early interpretations of Karelia's history during the period of nation-building and the inter-war period, with special emphasis on the key role of Karelian history in Finnish wartime propaganda. Secondly, we will attempt to analyse which layers of earlier historical interpretations were accepted as part of the narratives that became important for addressing the loss of Karelia after the war – and which were rejected. Finally, we will discuss the renewal of Finnish historical writing since the 1960s and the impact of new perspectives in the politics of history on narratives of Karelia's history.

Karelia in Finnish national master narratives

Conceptual shifts and changing paradigms were a characteristic of historical narratives about Karelia from the very beginning. Clearly, the break with Sweden in 1809, when Finland became part of the Russian empire, meant a major change as historians began to turn away from the political history of a multicultural Swedish empire towards Finnish national perspectives. However, there existed clear differences in the way in which the founding fathers of Finnish national history writing conceptualized the constitution of the Finnish state and the position of Karelia in this process. This can be illustrated by analysing the writings of two leading Finnish nineteenth-century historians and politicians, Yrjö

5 For an earlier critical analysis of narratives of Karelia in the context of the history of World War II, see Outi Fingerroos, "Karelia Issue: The Politics and Memory of Karelia in Finland", in Tiina Kinnunen, Ville Kivimäki (eds), *Finland in World War II: History, Memory, Interpretations*, Leiden, Brill, 2012, pp. 483–517.

Koskinen (Georg Zakarias Forsman, 1830–1903) and Johan Richard Danielson-Kalmari (1853–1933).[6]

Yrjö Koskinen was a well-known public figure and professor of history at the Imperial Alexander University of Helsinki, who started his career during the years of the so-called "national awakening" and the breakthrough of political mass organization in the mid-nineteenth century. The central concept in his interpretation of Finnish history was that of "the people".

Obviously, writing the history of the Finnish people implied an ethnically defined starting point. For Koskinen, however, "the people" does not refer to an organic entity that had existed forever, but rather is conceived as a product of history.[7] When he evokes the medieval Finnish tribes of Tavastia, Savo and Karelia he does not consider the Finnish people as the simple sum of these groups.[8] For him, it was state formation that ultimately distinguished those Finno-Ugric tribes that were to form the Finnish people from those that were not affected by this process. Koskinen explicitly excluded from the Finnish people the Karelians who lived further East.[9]

The maturation of the Finnish people to statehood described by Koskinen was a process connected to Swedish and Russian state formation, which provided its external frame. In this sense, Karelia's division by a border, with a Finno-Ugric population living on both sides of it, was not a major historical injustice for Koskinen as it was precisely within the framework of this (shifting) border that the constitution of the Finnish people as a historical actor had taken place.

Towards the end of the nineteenth century, a shift in emphasis occurred in Finnish politics and historiography that is best illustrated by the work of J. R. Danielson, a pupil of Koskinen and his successor at the helm of the so-called Finnish Party. Danielson openly combined scholarly activities with political activism in defence of the "Finnish state" against Russian

6 See in more detail Ilkka LIIKANEN, "Origins of the Eastern Border as the Grand Controversy of Finnish National History Writing", *op. cit.*, pp. 182–187.

7 Ilkka LIIKANEN, "Kansa. Fennomanian kansa-käsite ja modernin politiikan kieli" (The People. The Fennomanian Concept of the People and the Language of Modern Politics), in Matti HYVÄRINEN et al. (eds), *Käsitteet liikkeessä. Suomen poliittisen kulttuurin käsitehistoria* (Concepts on the Move. The Conceptual History of Finnish Political Culture), Tampere, Vastapaino, 2003, pp. 276–82.

8 Yrjö KOSKINEN, *Oppikirja Suomen kansan historiassa* (Lectures on the History of the Finnish People), Helsinki, Suomalaisen Kirjallisuuden Seura, 1869, pp. 510–11.

9 ibid., pp. 42–43.

attempts to codify and redefine the legal status of the Grand Duchy of Finland within the Russian empire. His interpretation of Karelia's history introduced at least two distinctive features.

First, Danielson strongly emphasized the role of Western political and cultural traditions.[10] For him, Western state traditions formed the basis for the rule of law upon which Finnish autonomy rested. Constitutional acts and international law were paramount to the social, political and cultural ties that bound together the Finnish people.[11] In this view, Karelia's status was primarily defined by international agreements and treaties that legitimized the existing border – and thus the division of the Karelian people.

Second, Danielson early on seems to have adopted a clearly more organic vision of the Finnish people than Koskinen, susceptible to paving the way for notions of a historical injustice. Even in the medieval context he rather straightforwardly employs concepts such as "we" and "our land", and depicts the Finns as a "people" from which the Karelians were "separated" or "torn apart". In Danielson's vision – which perhaps can also be read as a political programme – the Finnish people had been ready for statehood and were only prevented from implementing it by the landing of the Swedes: "Before the different tribes found time to constitute a common state, they were captured by an alien conquest."[12]

Turn-of-the-century cultural Karelianism

From early on, an essential part of Finnish identity building was based on a search for the pastoral past of Finns from Karelia. In his widely read textbook *Maamme kirja* (Book of Our Land) (1876), the professor of history Zacharias Topelius, for example, counted the Karelians as one of the tribes that formed the Finnish people. Karelia was thus culturally part of Finland, although its Eastern part had been attributed to Russia by

10 Johan R. Danielson, "Viipurin läänin palauttaminen muun Suomen yhteyteen" (The Returning of the County of Wiborg to Connection with the Rest of Finland), Helsinki, Weilin & Göös, 1894, pp. 1–2.

11 Jukka Tervonen, *J. R. Danielson-Kalmari. Historiantutkija ja-opettaja* (J. R. Danielson-Kalmari. Historian and Teacher), Suomen Historiallinen Seura, Helsinki, 1991, p. 45.

12 Johan R. Danielson, "Valtiollinen taistelu Norjassa" (The Battle over the State of Norway), *Valvoja*, 1883, pp. 78–79.

the Nöteborg Treaty of 1323.[13] The late nineteenth and early twentieth centuries were the heyday of cultural and political Karelianism, a vital component of Finnish national romanticism. Artists, painters, poets and men of letters became inspired by the region and its culture. A large proportion of the poems included in the Finnish national epic, the Kalevala, were collected in Karelia. The academic elite began to look at the region as either the original home of Finnish culture or some kind of refuge where it had survived almost untouched. Among the earliest manifestations of these ideas was Yrjö Blomstedt and Victor Suckdorff's book on Karelian architecture and ornaments published in 1901.[14]

The 1910s saw the publication of more works that popularized knowledge about Karelia in the spirit of ethnographic Karelianism. It should be noted that although Karelian culture was perceived as exotic, it was at the same time seen as an integral part of trans-boundary Finnish culture and identity. The most influential representative of this notion was a collective volume called *Karjalan kirja* (The Book of Karelia) (1910, second edition 1932).[15] It became a classic in the field of Karelian studies and had many successors that presented Karelian culture in a similarly romantic light through texts and photographs.[16] Perhaps the most influential scientific study of the early twentieth century was Väinö Voionmaa's *Suomen karjalaisen heimon historia* (History of the Finnish-Karelian Tribe) (1915).[17] Drawing on the geopolitical approach of the German geographer and ethnographer Friedrich Ratzel and the Swedish political scientist Rudolf Kjellén, it brought Karelia and the Karelian people back into the fold of the Finnish people and Finnish territory.[18]

---

13 Zacharias Topelius, *Maamme kirja* (The Book of Our Country), Helsinki, Edlund, 58th edition, no date (first edn 1876), pp. 32, 124, 154, 237; Hannes Sihvo, *Karjalan kuva. Karelianismin taustaa ja vaiheista autonomian aikana* (Karelia's Image), Helsinki, Suomalaisen Kirjallisuuden Seura, 2003 (first edn 1973), esp. pp. 334–396.

14 Yrjö Blomstedt, Victor Sucksdorff, *Karjalaisia rakennuksia ja koristemuotoja keskisestä Venäjän Karjalasta I–II* (Karelian Buildings and Ornamental Forms from Central Russian Karelia), Helsinki, Suomen muinaismuistoyhdistys, 1901.

15 Iivo Härkönen (ed.), *Karjalan kirja I–II* (The Book of Karelia), Porvoo, WSOY, 1910.

16 See e.g. I. K. Inha, *Kalevalan laulumailta* (From the Runic Lands of Karelia), Helsinki, Kansanvalistusseura, 1911.

17 Väinö Voionmaa, *Suomen karjalaisen heimon historia* (The History of Finland's Karelian Tribe), Helsinki, Kansanvalistusseura, 1915.

18 Maria Lähteenmäki, *Väinö Voionmaa. Puolue- ja geopoliitikko* (Väinö Voionmaa. Party Politician and Geopolitician), Vantaa, Suomalaisen Kirjallisuuden Seura, 2014, pp. 74–75; Thomas Lundén, "Geopolitik och politisk geografi: Kjellén och Ratzel

The Karelian region that historians showed most interest in was the Vyborg area and, more generally, the Karelian Isthmus, which early on had belonged to Sweden. Significantly, the White Sea area of Karelia and the Olonets region in Russian Karelia, together often referred to as Eastern Karelia in the Finnish literature, did not attract any special attention among Finnish historians during the early years of the twentieth century. Articles written before Finland's independence virtually never expressed a desire to reconsider the border with Russia and focused on topics such as the history of agriculture, forestry and religion. In academic journals, clear anti-Russian undertones appear only in a single paper on changes in land ownership.[19] This was to change abruptly after 1917. After having been mainly the pre-eminent domain of linguists and collectors of folklore, exotic Karelia became the centre-piece of a political programme seeking to unite the Finns with their nearest kinsmen within the boundaries of a "Greater Finland". This ideology was widespread among Finnish intellectuals and civil servants during the inter-war period and deeply influenced contemporary historical and geopolitical interpretations.[20]

Ethnic geopolitics of the inter-war period

After Finland's independence, borders became a popular research topic among Finnish historians. Finding justifications and roots for the national borders was a major task for them, and especially for Jalmari Jaakkola, who in the 1920s published two major studies on ancient Finnish borders. In Jaakkola's studies, Finland was presented as "our country" and thus "we", the Finns was held to have existed well ahead of the first peace treaty between Russia and Sweden, the so-called Nöteborg Treaty of year 1323. In addition, Jaakola's use of the concept of *valtaraja* (boundary of authority) suggests strong state-like features attached to this ancient Finnish community. Jaakkola went to great lengths to identify historical evidence in favour of the existence of territorially fixed

ur kulturgeografisk synvinkel" (Geopolitics and Political Geography: Kjellén and Ratzel from the Perspective of Cultural Geography), in Bet Edström et al. (eds), *Rudolf Kjellén. Geopolitiken och konservatismen* (Rudolf Kjellén. Geopolitics and Conservatism), Stockholm, Hjalmarson & Högberg Bokförlag, 2014, pp. 82–99.

19 Kimmo Katajala, "From Conflict to Cooperation", *op. cit.*, p. 93.

20 See Matti Klinge, *Vihan veljistä valtiososialismiin. Yhteiskunnallisia ja valtiollisia näkemyksiä 1910- ja 1920-luvuilla* (From Brothers in Hate to State Socialism) Porvoo, WSOY, 1983.

provinces that the Finnish tribes were held to have formed. His central argument was that state-like internal region-building had started before the so-called "period of conquest" and that ancient Finland on its own figured as a defender of Western civilization.[21]

During subsequent decades, professional historians examined in detail all peace treaties between Sweden and Russia with the aim of identifying the historical roots of Finland's Eastern border.[22] In many ways, Arvi Korhonen, with his *Suomen itärajan synty* (The Birth of the Finnish Eastern Border) (1938), occupies a special place among them.[23] Published just before the outbreak of the Winter War in 1939, the book made a careful analysis of the process of border demarcation that took place after the Treaty of Stolbovo in 1617. The resulting border had remained stable for a century and, more importantly, coincided with that confirmed by the Treaty of Tartu (1920) between the newly independent states of Finland and Soviet Russia.[24]

Another prominent new topic during the early years of independence was the history of Old Finland, that is, the territories of the Karelian Isthmus and the Lake Ladoga region which Sweden had lost to Russia during the eighteenth century and which had been incorporated to the

21 Jalmari Jaakkola, "Maamme vanhoista valtarajoista" (On the Ancient Finnish Boundaries of Authority), *Historiallinen Aikakauskirja*, Vol. 24, 1926, pp. 192–194, 199. For more detail on the historical debates on Jaakkola's interpretations see Ilkka Liikanen, "Origins of the Eastern Border as the Grand Controversy of Finnish National History Writing", *op. cit.*, pp. 187–189.

22 Werner Tawastjerna, *Pohjoismainen viisikolmattavuotinen sota. Vuosien 1570–1590 välinen aika* (The 25-Year Russian–Swedish War, 1570–1590), Helsinki, Suomen Historiallinen Seura, 1918–1920; Werner Tawastjerna, *Pohjoismainen viisikolmattavuotinen sota. Sotavuodet 1590–1595 ja Täyssinän rauha* (The 25-Year Russian–Swedish War, 1590–1595, and the Treaty of Teusina), Helsinki, Suomen Historiallinen Seura, 1929, see Ilkka Liikanen, "Territoriality, State, and Nationality in the Making of Borders of Finland", *Russian Sociological Review*, Vol. 13, No. 4, 2014, pp. 105–115; Erkki K. Osmonsalo, "Valtion ja valtakunnan rajankäynnit Suomessa Venäjänvallan ja itsenäisyyden aikana" (Border Demarcations of the State and Realm in Finland during the Russian Period and Independence), in *Suomen maanmittauksen historia III:4*, Porvoo, WSOY, 1933; Erkki K. Osmonsalo, *Suomen rajapolitiikka Venäjän vallan aikana. I. Ruotsin vastaista rajaa koskevat kysymykset 1809–1824* (Finnish Border Policy during the Russian Period. I. The Issues of the Swedish Border), Helsinki, Suomen Historiallinen Seura, 1933.

23 Arvi Korhonen, *Suomen itärajan syntyhistoriaa* (On the History of the Birth of the Finnish Eastern Border), Porvoo, WSOY, 1938.

24 Kimmo Katajala, "Zwischen West und Ost. 800 Jahre an der Ostgrenze Finnlands", *Kirchliche Zeitgeschichte*, 23 Jahrgang, Heft 1, 2010, pp. 82–108.

autonomous Grand Duchy of Finland in 1812. During the eighteenth century, distinct traditions and practices of land ownership had caused numerous conflicts between Finnish peasants and their new Russian landlords. Relations between the two remained uneasy until the time when serfdom was abolished in Russia in the 1860s, whereupon the Senate of Finland bought out the Russian fief holders of Old Finland in the 1870s. Old Finland thus became a highly suitable historical model with which to illustrate the Finnish struggle for freedom and the cruelty of the Russian nobility and landlords, as well as to stress the exemplary role of the Finnish state in solving problems of land ownership characteristic of an Eastern form of feudalism.[25]

Eastern Karelia, as the Finns call the regions of Olonets and White Sea Karelia on the Russian side of the border, and the living conditions of the Karelian population there, similarly attracted the attention of Finnish historians and ethnographers. When a group of professional and amateur historians published *Karjalan historiaa* (On the History of Karelia) in 1938, all but one of the eleven contributions dealt with the history of Russian Karelia. Several journals published in the 1920s and 1930s were exclusively devoted to Karelian life and Karelia's history; their contributors were amateur historians or Karelians who had moved to Finland before or after Finnish independence. Some of these publications appeared in German or English to draw international attention to Finnish and Karelian efforts in favour of unification.[26]

Karelia in wartime historical narratives

During World War II, Finland twice entered into armed conflict with the Soviet Union, first in the Winter War (1939–40) after the Soviet attack and later, on Germany's side, in the Continuation War (1941–4). One might expect that under wartime conditions the printing of historical writings and essays would practically have come to a halt. However, this was not at all the case, especially where the history of Karelia was

25 Kimmo Katajala, "From Conflict to Cooperation", *op. cit.*, pp. 95–96; Kimmo Katajala, "Konstruoitu Karjala. Suomalaisen historiantutkimuksen Karjala-paradigmat 1900-luvulla" (Constructed Karelia: The Karelia Paradigms of Finnish History Writing), in Pekka Suutari (ed.), *Karjalan kuvaa rakentamassa* (Constructing the Image of Karelia), Vantaa, Suomalaisen Kirjallisuuden Seura, 2013, pp. 39–40.

26 Kimmo Katajala, "From Conflict to Cooperation", *op. cit.*, p. 94; Kimmo Katajala, "Konstruoitu Karjala", *op. cit.*, pp. 37–38.

concerned. Naturally, many wartime publications served government propaganda and were written by non-professional historians. But, in addition, an almost continuous flow of publications was produced by professional scholars exploring the Karelian region from different angles.

Immediately after the start of the Continuation War and the Karelian offensive of the Finnish army in June 1941, the best brains among Finland's professional historians – established professors of history or leading researchers who were to gain tenure soon after the war – were recruited to explain the Karelian issue. The fourth issue of Finland's main historical quarterly, *Historiallinen Aikakauskirja*, published in 1941 was devoted almost entirely to Karelian history, the general tenor of the contributions being that Karelia was originally part of the West and that Karelians were closely related to the Finns.[27]

Already immediately after the Winter War, Professor Jalmari Jaakkola wrote a short essay, *Suomen historian ääriviivat* (Outlines of Finland's History), in which he repeated his interpretation of Finland as an outpost of Western civilization.[28] This idea now became the main doctrine for Finnish historical research. President Risto Ryti charged Jaakkola with writing a book on the Finnish Eastern question, a task that the historian accomplished just before the outbreak of the Continuation War with his *Suomen idänkysymys* (The Finnish Eastern Question). Both publications, translated into several European languages, were intended to inform the Germans of the Finnish territorial goals in Karelia and to explain the Finnish intervention in Russia to the Western Allies.[29] In a similar vein, Professor Einar W. Juva's *Suomen taistelu itää vastaan* (The Fight of Finland against the East) presented Finland as an outpost of Western

---

27 The articles in *Historiallinen Aikakauskirja 4-1941* are: Jalmari Jaakkola, "Muinaisen "Karialan" – Karjalan alku" (The Birth of the Ancient "Kariala" – Karjala); Kaarlo Blomstedt, "Karjalan ja muun Suomen myöhäiskeskiaikaisista laamanneista" (About the Late Medieval Jurors in Karelia and Other Parts of Finland); Martti Ruutu, "Karjalan nousu Suomen sivistyneistön näköpiiriin" (The Rise of Karelia to the Horizon of the Educated Finns). All book reviews have appeared in the special issue on the Karelian question in terms of war history.

28 Päiviö Tommila, *Suomen historiankirjoitus. Tutkimuksen kuva* (History Writing in Finland. A Research Overview), WSOY, Porvoo 1988, p. 188; Ilkka Herlin, "Linjoilla ja linjojen takana. Historioitsijat sodassa" (On the Front and Behind the Lines), in Pekka Ahtiainen, Jukka Tervonen (eds), *Menneisyyden tutkijat ja metodien vartijat, op. cit.*, p. 88; Kimmo Katajala, "Konstruoitu Karjala", *op. cit.*, p. 43.

29 Kimmo Katajala, "From Conflict to Cooperation", *op. cit.*, p. 97; Kimmo Katajala, "Konstruoitu Karjala", *op. cit.*, p. 43.

culture, and *Finnlands Bollwerk gegen den Osten*, a booklet published by the anthropologist Yrjö von Grönhagen in Dresden, portrayed Karelia as a Finnish bulwark against the East.[30]

The generally best-remembered wartime publication – perhaps because of its title – is a book quickly compiled on the orders of the Finnish government by the historian Eino Jutikkala, the geographer Väinö Auer and the ethnologist Kustaa Vilkuna during the first months of the Continuation War. Its purpose was to prove that Karelia was historically, geographically and culturally an organic and natural part of Finland. Its title was changed to *Finnlands Lebensraum* after the text had been partly revised by Yrjö von Grönhagen, then serving as the representative of the Finnish Army Information Office in Berlin, to better suit the tastes of the Nazi government. The book's main author, Eino Jutikkala, was not happy with the changes made and successfully petitioned the Finnish censorship authorities to forbid its publication in Finland.[31]

In the course of the Continuation War, the Finns occupied most of Russian Karelia, areas that had never belonged to Sweden or Finland. This gave archaeologists, linguists, ethnologists and specialists in architecture the opportunity to collect new material for their studies. Karelian toponyms and family names, for example, were a common research topic for linguists, even after the war. The obvious aim of these studies during the war period was to demonstrate the old historical ties between two kindred peoples, the Karelians and the Finns.

---

30 Einar W. Juva, *Suomen taistelu itää vastaan* (Finland's Battle against the East) Helsinki, Otava 1942; Päiviö Tommila, *Suomen historiankirjoitus*, *op. cit.*, p. 199; Antti Laine, "Tiedemiesten Suur-Suomi – Itä-Karjalan tutkimus jatkosodan vuosina" (The Greater Finland of Scholars – Research on East Karelia during the Years of the Continuation War), *Historiallinen Arkisto 102*, Helsinki, Suomen Historiallinen Seura, 1993, p. 97; Mervi Kaarninen, "Yliopisto sodassa – Opiskelua ja tutkimusta rintamalla ja kotimailla" (The University at War), in Marjatta Hietala (ed.), *Tutkijat ja sota* (Scholars and the War), Helsinki, Suomalaisen Kirjallisuuden Seura, 2006, p. 198; Pekka Ahtiainen, Jukka Tervonen (eds), *Menneisyyden tutkijat ja metodien vartijat*, *op. cit.*, p. 83; Ilkka Herlin, "Linjoilla ja linjojen takana", *op. cit.*, pp. 92–99. Yrjö von Grönhagen, *Karelien, Finnlands Bollwerk gegen den Osten*, Dresden, Franz Müller Verlag, 1942; for narratives of Finland as an outpost against the East, see Kimmo Katajala, "Finland, the Last Outpost of Western Civilization?", *op. cit.*, especially p. 300.

31 Ilkka Herlin, "Linjoilla ja linjojen takana", *op. cit.*, pp. 96–97; Keijo Kulha, *Jutikkala – tinkimätön akateemikko* (Jutikkala – the Uncompromising Academician), Helsinki, Edita, 2006, pp. 169–171; Kimmo Katajala, "From Conflict to Cooperation", *op. cit.*, p. 98; Kimmo Katajala, "Konstruoitu Karjala", *op. cit.*, p. 44.

Enthusiasm for publishing research and propaganda works on Karelian history reached its apogee early during the Continuation War. At first, the main goal was to convince the Finnish public of the necessity of conquering Eastern Karelia and not just the Karelian territories lost in the Winter War. A second objective was to explain to the Germans Finland's "natural rights" to the Karelian territory. Later on, after the Battle of Stalingrad, older and new writings were published in English and French to justify the Finnish occupation in the East in the eyes of the Allies.[32]

The history of the Lost Land

Even if Finland avoided occupation, the war ended in a catastrophe for the Finns. Once more, Finland lost most of its Karelian territories, and the Soviet government resettled the area with people from all over the Soviet Union. On the Karelian Isthmus in the South, people fled in panic ahead of disastrous battles, whereas in the more Northern regions emigration was better organized. Around 420,000 Karelians and Finns from the ceded territories, along with demobilized soldiers, were resettled in what remained of Finland. Those who had owned farms in Karelia (around 55%) were given land in compensation.[33]

Only Finland's northernmost and Swedish-speaking regions were exempt from the compensatory land reform. Often, land was taken from local private owners, causing long-lasting bitter feelings in rural communities. Where land had been state property, it was mostly forest and the new settlers had to start life from scratch. The shock and grief experienced by Karelians over the loss of their homeland, the anguish caused by the land reform and its consequences, the often miserable life of the settlers on their new farms and the sometimes acrimonious conflicts in local societies have later been studied thoroughly by researchers and exhaustively portrayed in works of fiction. The social scientist Heikki Waris and his research team carried out their classic study on the adaptation of Karelian immigrants to Finnish society already in

32 Kimmo Katajala, "From Conflict to Cooperation", *op. cit.*, p. 98; Kimmo Katajala, "Konstruoitu Karjala", *op. cit.*, pp. 44–45.

33 Erkki Laitinen, "Vuoden 1945 maanhankintalain synty, sisältö ja toteutus" (The Land Reform Law of 1945: Origin, Content and Implementation), in Erkki Laitinen (ed.), *Rintamalta raiviolle. Sodanjälkeinen asutustoiminta 50 vuotta* (From Frontlines to Clearing New Fields. 50 Years of Post-War Re-settlement policies), Jyväskylä, Atena, 1995, pp. 85–89, 95–138.

1952. Since then, over two hundred Ph.D. and MA theses and countless other academic writings and studies have been published on the subject. Waris's report concluded that adaptation had generally been successful.[34] In this respect, the second and third post-war generations of researchers have been more critical as their informants voiced more unfavourable views on the reception of their parents and grandparents in Finland.[35]

As for the ceded areas of Karelia, the post-war years saw a stream of essays, articles and books about the refugees' former home regions, local societies, parishes, churches, schools and everyday lives. It seems that people were somehow trying to preserve memories of their forfeited homes, lands and former ways of life. This "conservation work" was mostly expressed in writings published in several small magazines during the 1950s and 1960s. The authors were from highly heterogeneous backgrounds. Some of them were professors, or later became professors, such as Onni Okkonen, Kustaa Vilkuna and Viljo Nissilä; others were government ministers, politicians, diplomats or teachers; and still others were ordinary people, among them many Karelian refugees.[36]

A major feature in the process of "preserving the lost Karelia" were local histories of Karelian parishes and municipalities, most of them published in the 1950s. There has always been a strong tradition of local histories in Finland, but post-war research on the ceded territories of Karelia reached a unique all-time peak. These local histories can be roughly divided into two groups: memoirs and other historical writings by amateur historians and local histories by university-trained researchers. Although rather different in content and outlook, they both answered the same need to preserve the memory of life in people's lost homes in Karelia. In fact, many parish organizations from the lost Karelian

---

34 See Heikki Waris et. al., *Siirtoväen sopeutuminen. Tutkimus Suomen karjalaisen siirtoväen sopeutumisesta* (Integration of the Evacuees. A Study on the Adaptation of Karelian Evacuees in Finland), Helsinki, 1952.

35 See e.g. Hannes Sihvo, "Lunastettava maa – Kaanaanmaat ja Egyptinkorvet" (Lands Under Reform), in *Rintamalta raiviolle. Sodanjälkeinen asutustoiminta 50 vuotta, op. cit.*, pp. 13–26; Tarja Raninen-Siiskonen, "Karjalaisen siirtoväen sopeutuminen tutkimuksen kohteena" (The Adaptation of Karelian Evacuees as a Research Object), in *Karjala-kuvaa rakentamassa, op. cit.*, pp. 122–123; Heli Kananen, "The Adaptation of an Ethnic Minority in Finland in the 1940s and 1950s: Orthodox Displaced Persons and the Lutheran Indigenous Population", *Scandinavian Journal of History*, Vol. 38, 2013, pp. 111–132.

36 Kimmo Katajala, "From Conflict to Cooperation", *op. cit.*, p. 98; Kimmo Katajala, "Konstruoitu Karjala", *op. cit.*, pp. 45–46.

territories continued their life in Finland several years after the war; their funds were often transferred to foundations or associations cherishing the memory of the older home parish, for example by ordering, paying for and publishing the above-mentioned publications.[37] Compared to turn-of-the-century Karelianism, these publications rarely concentrated on the exotic features of Karelian culture and the transnational history of the borderlands, but rather emphasized the significance of a common Finnish cultural heritage and links to general trends of economic and social modernization in Finnish society.

In the academic world, ethnologists and linguists were busy publishing research based on material collected during the war (see above). A number of articles about Karelian place names, Karelian poems and traditional religion appeared in the *Kalevalaseuran Vuosikirja* (Yearbook of the Kalevala Society). These apolitical subjects were unlikely to contradict Finland's new foreign policy orientation and challenge the changed domestic political set-up.[38]

In historical studies, the situation was different, and academic research legitimizing dreams of a Greater Finland ceased altogether. The small number of articles on Karelia published in historical journals now strictly focused on politically neutral topics.[39] Professional historians who had once denounced Russia and the Soviet Union as Finland's arch enemy adjusted to the new political constraints. In the words of Pekka Ahtiainen and Jukka Tervonen, they now tried to secure a *Lebensraum* for historical research by avoiding politically loaded interpretations and topics.[40]

However, one heated historical debate broke this silence and took up key themes of inter-war and wartime research with a barely concealed political angle. In 1960, Kustaa Vilkuna published new ethnographic evidence on the location of the border defined in the Nöteborg

37 Kimmo Katajala, "From Conflict to Cooperation", *op. cit.*, p. 100; Kimmo Katajala, "Konstruoitu Karjala", *op. cit.*, pp. 47–48.

38 About the effects of the new foreign policy on historical research in Finland in the 1940s and 1950s, see Pekka Ahtiainen, Jukka Tervonen, *Menneisyyden tutkijat ja metodien vartijat, op. cit.*, pp. 25–28.

39 Kimmo Katajala, "From Conflict to Cooperation", p. 100; Kimmo Katajala, "Konstruoitu Karjala", *op. cit.*, p. 47.

40 Pekka Ahtiainen, Jukka Tervonen, *Menneisyyden tutkijat ja metodien vartijat, op. cit.*, p. 25; see also Päiviö Tommila, *Suomen historiankirjoitus, op. cit.*, p. 201.

Treaty of 1323.[41] He pleaded that besides recognizing certain areas of domination it was vital to show how the border was linked to the region's everyday economy and the rhythm of life of its inhabitants. Instead of institutionalized state structures, Vilkuna was interested in the kind of agreements that were necessary to organize hunting and taxation in these remote areas. In particular, he deployed great efforts to locate a boat route linking Karelia to the Gulf of Bothnia and expected to prove that the Nöteborg Treaty delineated the border in such a way that it provided the Karelians with access to areas under their control in the North. Vilkuna envisioned a large wilderness and hunting ground North of the border where tax collectors from both sides were operating.[42] By questioning the existence of a clear-cut borderline separating territories belonging to different states, he challenged Jalmari Jaakkola's older thesis of an ethnic-based state-like border – and thus the very premises of how the history of Karelia was written during the inter-war period. In response, the already retired Jalmari Jaakkola accused Vilkuna of "engaging in guerrilla warfare" against the representatives of post-1948 "modern historiography".[43]

By the 1960s, Jaakkola had, however, noticeably "nationalized" his interpretation by dropping the earlier rhetoric of a great clash of civilizations in the European North. For Jaakkola, the question was no longer how the borders of a "Westernized Finland" had become a front line between East and West, but his underlying assumption of borders as fixed territorial lines of authority and power remained unchanged.

Many saw political underpinnings in this debate, since Vilkuna had become a close associate of President Urho Kekkonen, who personified the post-war turn in Finnish politics by advocating peaceful neighbourly relations with the Soviet Union. The setting was paradoxical in a way that was typical of Finnish conditions at the time. Whereas in the 1920s research on Karelian history tended to take place within the framework of grand narratives of national and European history, scholars in the 1960s seemed to favour detailed examinations of the

41 Kustaa Vilkuna, "Pähkinäsaaren rauhan raja kansatieteellisessä katsannossa" (The Border of Nöteborg from an Ethnographic Perspective), *Historiallinen Aikakauskirja*, Vol. 58, 1960. For more on this debate see Ilkka Liikanen, "Origins of the Eastern Border as the Grand Controversy of Finnish National History Writing", *op. cit.*, pp. 190–192.

42 Kustaa Vilkuna, "Pähkinäsaaren rauhan raja kansatieteellisessä katsannossa", *op. cit.*, pp. 407–414.

43 Jalmari Jaakkola, "Pattijoen rajahistoriallinen asema" (The Position of Pattijoki in Border History), *Historiallinen Aikakauskirja*, Vol. 58, No. 2, 1960, p. 227.

local mapping of the borderline. The theme of "civilizational divisions" was no longer openly present. However, this episode of breaking the silence surrounding earlier interpretations of the Finnish Eastern border easily brings to mind parallels with contemporary political frontlines among Finnish intellectuals, between those who supported President Kekkonen and his policies of peaceful coexistence and those who emphasized the historical continuity of this border as a battle line and the significance of military and ideological preparedness. A similar division can be recognized within the organizations of Karelian immigrants, although among them, unlike in the academic community, supporters of Kekkonen's policies often occupied dominant positions. This paradox can probably be read as a further indication of how the politics of writing the history of the Lost Land were rather shaped by national politics and the national political elite than by the situation and aims of the emigrants from Karelia.

Détente in writing the history of Karelia

From the 1960s on, professional historians increasingly returned to the subject of Karelia and the Eastern border region. Among the monographs and articles published during the next two decades, seventeen studies appeared in *Historiallinen Aikakauskirja* alone, most of them on the medieval and early modern periods but some also on the nineteenth and twentieth centuries. The new studies examined Finnish nineteenth-century Karelianism in its artistic and political forms, the so-called Kinship Wars of 1918–22 (the interventions of Finnish volunteer troups to Russian/Soviet Karelia), Karelian emigration to Finland after 1917, the migration of American Finns to Soviet Karelia in the 1930s, and the post-war resettlement of Karelian refugees in Finland. Nothing was yet written about the Finnish occupation of Karelia during the Continuation War, nor was the history of Soviet Karelia in the 1920s and 1930s considered a suitable topic for research, although this may have been due to a lack of access to the necessary sources.[44]

Moreover, historians now broke the silence surrounding politically loaded interpretations of the inter-war period. A much-debated example is Jarl Gallén's new theory about the nature of Finland's Eastern border

44 Kimmo Katajala, "From Conflict to Cooperation", *op. cit.*, pp. 100–101; Kimmo Katajala, "Konstruoitu Karjala", *op. cit.*, pp. 48–49.

in medieval times. Gallén suggested that the border was linear only in its Southernmost parts, whereas the sparsely settled North formed a shared frontier zone located between two vaguely defined boundaries.[45] His interpretation challenged older views prevalent in the 1920s and 1930s of a clear separation of state or proto-state territories and was consequently rejected by the most authoritative "old-school" historians.

Heikki Kirkinen's writings led to a similar paradigm shift.[46] After having traced the contacts of Karelian culture with Byzantium and Russia in his first monograph on Karelian history (1963), he straightforwardly stated in his second book (1970) that Karelia had never been an outpost of Finland or Western civilization. According to Kirkinen, it formed a unique territory with a characteristic identity and culture of its own that was tributary neither to the West nor to the East.[47] This magnum opus of his was followed by a second volume bearing the subtitle *Karjala taistelukenttänä* (Karelia as a Battlefield) (1976).[48] For the first time since Arvi Korhonen, Kirkinen used both Russian and Swedish sources for his study of early modern Karelian history.

In later years, Kirkinen emphasized on many occasions how much he had to struggle throughout most of the 1960s for recognition of his new paradigm. By then, the political climate was, however, gradually changing, and first steps were taken towards cooperation between Finnish and Soviet scientists. For historians, what topic could have served these purposes better than the historical reinterpretation of Karelia as a mediator between East and West?[49] The new attitude was strikingly announced in 1973, when the Yearbook of the Kalevala Society bore the title *Karjala idän ja lännen silta* (Karelia, Bridge between East and

---

45 Jarl Gallén, *Nöteborgsfreden och Finlands medeltida östgräns* (The Treaty of Nöteborg and the Medieval Eastern Border of Finland), Helsingfors, Svenska litteratursällskapet i Finland, 1968; Ilkka Liikanen, "Origins of the Eastern Border as the Grand Controversy of Finnish National History Writing", *op. cit.*, p. 193.

46 Heikki Kirkinen, "Kiistakenttä ja silta. Karjalan historiallinen funktio" (Battlefield and Bridge. The Historical Function of Karelia), *Suomalainen Suomi*, Vol. 33, 1965, pp. 327–334.

47 Heikki Kirkinen, *Karjala idän ja lännen välissä I. Venäjän Karjala renessanssiajalla (1478–1617)* (Karelia Between East and West: I. Russian Karelia During the Renaissance Period, (1478–1617), Helsinki, Kirjayhtymä, 1970.

48 Heikki Kirkinen, *Karjala idän ja lännen välissä II. Karjala taistelukenttänä* (Karelia Between East and West: II. Karelia as a Battlefield), Helsinki, Kirjayhtymä, 1976.

49 Kimmo Katajala, "From Conflict to Cooperation", *op. cit.*, pp. 101–102; Kimmo Katajala, "Konstruoitu Karjala", *op. cit.*, pp. 50–51.

West).[50] In a similar spirit, the first volume of a major series of five about Karelia, published in 1982–3, was entitled *Karjala 1. Portti itään ja länteen* (Karelia. Gateway to the East and to the West).[51]

Hannes Sihvo, editor of the aforementioned yearbook and a specialist in early Karelianism, was another major figure of the new Karelian studies of the early 1970s. His *Karjalan löytäjät* (Founders of Karelia) (1969) and *Karjalan kuva* (Karelia's Image) (1973) are still references for research on these topics.[52] Finally, the political Karelianism of the 1920s and 1930s, too, came under the radar of academic research with Risto Alapuro's Ph.D. thesis, published in the early 1970s, on the radical student movement known as the Academic Karelia Society.[53]

Changes in political conjunctures do not alone explain the growing interest in Karelian affairs. The post-war border between Finland and the Soviet Union had split up former administrative and culturally distinctive regions, resulting in the creation of new administrative territorial units in Eastern Finland: the counties of South and North Karelia.

In 1969, new universities were established in the main towns of these counties, Lappeenranta and Joensuu. Especially in Joensuu, intense research activities were launched in the human and social sciences on Karelian and regional history, with the obvious aim of promoting the cultural and social cohesion of the region.[54] Though efforts in this direction can be traced back to the nineteenth century, the 1960s saw the emergence of a more determined "project" to raise territorial self-awareness in North Karelia and to promote identity building among its inhabitants.[55] Thus a third element was added to the politics of history of Karelia that was not connected in the same way to the

---

50 Hannes Sihvo (ed.), *Karjala – idän ja lännen silta* (Karelia, Bridge between East and West), Helsinki, WSOY, 1973.

51 Markku Haapio et al. (ed.), *Karjala 1. Portti itään ja länteen* (Karelia, Gateway to the East and to the West), Hämeenlinna, Karisto, 1982.

52 Hannes Sihvo, *Karjalan löytäjät* (Discoverers of Karelia), Tampere, Kirjayhtymä 1969; Hannes Sihvo, *Karjalan kuva. Karelianismin taustaa ja vaiheita autonomian aikana* (Karelia's Image: The Background and Development of Karelianism during the Period of Autonomy), Helsinki, Suomalaisen Kirjallisuuden Seura, 1973.

53 Risto Alapuro, *Akateeminen karjala-seura. Ylioppilasliike 1920–1930-luvuilla* (The Academic Karelia Society. A Student Movement of the 1920s and 1930s), Helsinki, WSOY, 1973.

54 Anssi Paasi, *Territories, Boundaries and Consciousness. The Changing Geographies of the Finnish–Russian Border*, Chichester, Wiley, 1996, pp. 31–38.

55 Kimmo Katajala, "Konstruoitu Karjala", *op. cit.*, p. 52.

war's causes and consequences as were the silenced legacy of inter-war history writing and the experiences and aims of Karelian immigrants.

At the same time, the early 1970s saw the tail-end of the movement devoted to publishing local histories of former parishes of the ceded territories. The histories of the town of Sortavala (1970) and the parish of Virolahti (1970) were the last to be written by university-trained historians. The tide of memoirs published by amateur historians had already ebbed away in the mid-1960s.[56]

Beyond national imaginaries of Karelia

The opening up of the hitherto largely closed Soviet scientific community to cooperation with Western and Finnish scientists during the 1980s had a visible impact on the volume of research on Karelia. New opportunities to consult Russian archives enabled professional historians to take up new topics and an increasingly open border after 1991 made it possible for people in general, and amateur historians interested in Karelia in particular, to cross freely into Russian Karelia.

Already in the mid-1980s, Raimo Ranta published in quick succession several academic studies about Old Finland and the process of border demarcation between the Kingdom of Sweden and the Russian empire in the eighteenth century.[57] These works were strictly based on archival sources and notably lacked the propagandist or anti-Russian undertones characteristic of writings on this topic from the 1920s and 1930s.[58]

---

56 Kimmo KATAJALA, "From Conflict to Cooperation", *op. cit.*, pp. 102–103; Kimmo KATAJALA, "Konstruoitu Karjala", *op. cit.*, pp. 52–53.

57 Raimo RANTA, "Kaakkois-Suomi kiistana rauhanneuvotteluissa 1718–21 ja 1743" (South-Eastern Finland as a Controversy in the Peace Negotiations of 1718–21 and 1743), *Viipurin suomalaisen kirjallisuusseuran toimitteita 7* (Publications of the Finnish Literary Society of Wiborg 7), Helsinki, Viipurin suomalainen kirjallisuusseura, 1985, pp. 15–98; Raimo RANTA, *Vanhan Suomen talouselämä vuosina 1721–1743 I–II* (The Economic Life of Old Finland), Helsinki, Suomen Historiallinen Seura 1985, 1986; Raimo RANTA, *Viipurin komendanttikunta 1710–1721: valtaus, hallinto ja oikeudenhoito* (The Commandant County of Wiborg, 1710–1721), Helsinki, Suomen Historiallinen Seura, 1987.

58 About the character of research on Old Finland, see Jyrki PAASKOSKI, "Gamla Finland och paradigmskiftet i historieforskningen" (Old Finland and the Paradigm Change in History Writing), *Historisk Tidskrift för Finland 2016*, p. 446; Jyrki PAASKOSKI, *Vanhan Suomen lahjoitusmaat 1710–1826* (Donated Lands of Old Finland 1710–1826), Helsinki, Suomen Historiallinen Seura, 1997, p. 2.

During the 1980s, several Soviet historians in turn published articles on Old Finland in Finnish journals. Although perhaps not true cooperation, the situation can be described with a term borrowed from the vocabulary of Finnish–Soviet foreign policy as "peaceful co-existence".[59]

A rising number of historical studies on border issues finally led to an open revival and critical processing of earlier debates on Finland's Eastern border. Professor Kyösti Julku, who took pains to locate the places through which the medieval border ran in 1323, still seemed to be attached to the concept of a linear border.[60] By contrast, the Danish historian John Lind became interested in Jarl Gallén's idea of a zonal border in the largely uninhabited forest areas of the North and, jointly with Gallén, published new evidence that challenged the older still predominant concept typical of inter-war national history writing.[61] Lind's interpretation drew inspiration from recent debates on medieval and early modern state-building processes in Europe and compared the treaty of 1323 with others concluded by the Principality of Novgorod. Today, his views have largely been accepted in academic circles, though the older notion of a linear border still survives in textbooks for elementary schools and colleges.[62] Lind's explication failed, however, to convince Heikki Kirkinen, who in his earlier work had built great visions of the ancient past of Karelia developing in the neighbourhood of the Novgorodian state.[63]

---

59 Päiviö. TOMMILA, *Suomen historiankirjoitus*, *op. cit.*, pp. 295–306; Kimmo KATAJALA, "From Conflict to Cooperation", *op. cit.*, p. 194; Kimmo KATAJALA, "Konstruoitu Karjala", *op. cit.*, p. 54.

60 Kyösti JULKU, *Suomen itärajan synty* (The Birth of the Finnish Eastern Border), Rovaniemi, Pohjois-Suomen historiallinen yhdistys, 1987.

61 New arguments in support of the Gallén's theory presented in different articles during the 1980s were gathered in the volume Jarl GALLÉN, Johan LIND, *Nöteborgfreden och Finlands medeltida östgräns 2* (The Nöteborg Treaty and the Medieval Eastern Border of Finland 2), Helsingfors, Svenska litteratursällskapet i Finland, 1991.

62 Kimmo KATAJALA, "From Conflict to Cooperation", *op. cit.*, pp. 104–105; Kimmo KATAJALA, "Konstruoitu Karjala", *op. cit.*, p. 55.

63 On Kirkinen's argumentation, see Heikki KIRKINEN, "Mikä oli Pähkinäsaaren rauhan raja?" (What Was the Border of the Treaty of Nöteborg?), *Historiallinen Aikakauskirja*, Vol. 90, 1992, pp. 304–317; Heikki KIRKINEN, "Salainen lisäpöytäkirjako Pähkinäsaaren rauhansopimuksessa?" (A Secret Supplementary Protocol to the Treaty of Nöteborg?), *Historiallinen Aikakauskirja*, Vol. 102, 2004, pp. 393–406; Ilkka LIIKANEN, "Origins of the Eastern Border as the Grand Controversy of Finnish National History Writing", *op. cit.*, pp. 193–195.

In spite of partly overlapping interpretations, the debaters of the 1990s understood themselves as revisionists or reformers with regard to earlier Finnish national historiography by disentangling the concept of border from that of the Finnish proto-nation and traditional understandings of ethnicity. Heikki Kirkinen abandoned the canon of national history writing to produce the history of a trans-boundary region, albeit in a manner reminiscent of national historiography. John Lind – and Jarl Gallén before him – even more openly rejected the old concept of an ethnically defined border in favour of a broader view on European processes of state formation.

The opening up of Finland's Eastern border in the late 1980s and early 1990s enabled Finnish researchers to reach places in Karelia which had been closed to foreigners since the war. Finnish archaeologists were now able to visit Karelia and take part in excavations there in cooperation with their Soviet colleagues. Similarly, works by Finnish and Soviet researchers "co-existed" in the 1980s in the field of Karelia's Iron Age and medieval history.[64] Soviet – and later Russian – archives became accessible to Finnish historians, who were able to prepare numerous studies on new subjects such as the role of the Red Finns in Soviet Karelia during the 1920s and 1930s, which laid the groundwork for later research. By the 1980s, Finnish historians widely studied the Kinship Wars, the idea of Greater Finland and the period of Finnish occupation during the Continuation War, topics deliberately avoided in the 1950s and 1960s.[65]

---

64 For examples from the reports on the Finnish–Soviet meetings of historians, see Rauno Enden, Vesa Laulumaa (eds), *Suomalais-neuvostoliittolainen historiantutkijoiden symposium 7.12.1985* (Finnish–Soviet Symposium of Historians, 7.12.1985), Helsinki, Suomen Historiallinen Seura, 1986; Eero Kuparinen (ed.), *VIII suomalais-neuvostoliittolainen yhteiskuntahistorian symposiumi Turussa 2–6.9.1984* (The Seventh Finnish–Soviet Social History Symposium in Turku 2–6.9.1984), Turku, Turun historiallinen yhdistys, 1986; for more, see Kimmo Katajala, "From Conflict to Cooperation", *op. cit.*, p. 105; Kimmo Katajala, "Konstruoitu Karjala", *op. cit.*, pp. 56–57.

65 See e.g. Reino Kero, *Neuvostokarjalaa rakentamassa. Pohjois–Amerikan suomalaiset tekniikan tuojina 1930-luvun Neuvostokarjalassa* (Building Soviet Karelia. North American Finns as Importers of New Technologies into 1930s Soviet Karelia), Helsinki, Suomen Historiallinen Seura, 1983; Reino Kero, "The Role of Finnish Settlers from North America in the Nationality Question in Soviet Karelia in the 1930s", *Scandinavian Journal of History*, Vol. 6, 1986, pp. 229–241; Auvo Kostiainen, "Dominating Finnish Minority? On the Background of the Nationality Problem in Soviet Karelia in the 1930s", *Faravid*, 8, 1984, pp. 341–366; Auvo Kostiainen, *Loikkarit. Suuren lamakauden laiton siirtolaisuus Neuvostoliittoon* (Defectors. The Illegal Migration to the USSR during the Period of the Great Depression), Helsinki, Otava, 1988.

During the post-Soviet period, effective cooperation between Finnish and Russian historians on the study of Karelia's history, and especially the history of the Russian–Finnish border and borderlands, took off. Neither exclusively dividing line nor bridge, the border was now being approached as one element among others in the life of a borderland that had a long tradition of mutual economic cooperation and cultural interaction.[66] This development owed much, of course, to the opening up of the Finnish–Russian border, but can also be explained by the boom in a new kind of border studies inspired by the great historical changes of the time, European integration, the end of the Cold War and globalization. Formerly enclosing and dividing borders were becoming more diffuse and more porous, a situation that also seemed to apply to Karelia in the 1990s, resulting in similar research interests across most of Europe.[67]

It is hardly surprising that the rapidly changing geopolitical environment of the early 1990s saw the re-emergence of public calls for the restitution of Finland's lost Karelian lands. In the 1950s and 1960s, President Kekkonen had secretly and repeatedly discussed the return of the ceded areas with Soviet leaders – without success. When the Baltic States became independent and the Soviet Union collapsed, the issue was once more put on the agenda by the Finnish political leadership. For the Soviet Union and its successor state, the Russian Federation, the case has, however, remained closed. In their view, the 1947 Treaty of Paris had been about a broader European settlement; questioning the course of the Finnish–Russian border was likely to have repercussions for numerous other similar borders and was therefore strongly discouraged. Throughout the post-war period, the main organizations of Karelian immigrants have been taking a moderate stance on this issue, most often backing the country's official foreign policies. Calls for the restitution of the ceded territories were confined to smaller

66 One example of this is the history of the Karelian people in Heikki Kirkinen, Hannes Sihvo, Pekka Nevalainen, *Karjalan kansan historia* (History of the Karelian People), Porvoo, WSOY, 1994. See also Tapio Hämynen, Aleksandr Paškov (eds), *Nation Split by the Border: Changes in the Ethnic Identity, Religion and Language of the Karelians from 1809 to 2009*, Joensuu, University Press of Eastern Finland, 2012.

67 See e.g. Anssi Paasi, *Territories, Boundaries and Consciousness, op. cit.*; Heikki Eskelinen, Ilkka Liikanen, Jukka Oksa (eds), *Curtains of Iron and Gold. Reconstructing Borders and Scales of Interaction*, Aldershot, Ashgate, 1999; Kimmo Katajala, Maria Lähteenmäki (eds), *Imagined, Negotiated, Remembered, op. cit.*; Heikki Eskelinen, Ilkka Liikanen, James Scott (eds), *The EU–Russia Borderland: New Contexts for Regional Co-operation*, London, Routledge, 2013; Ilkka Liikanen, James W. Scott, Tiina Sotkasiira (eds), *The EU's Eastern Neighbourhood. Migration, Borders and Regional Stability*, London, Routledge, 2016.

radical groups.[68] In the recent past, such activist demands have been mainly voiced in times of major geopolitical change, such as during the dissolution of the Soviet Union, Finland's accession to the European Union and the EU's Eastern enlargement. In spite of notable peaks in public discussions of the Karelian issue, claims on the ceded territories generally have been steadily declining in number and force.[69]

Conclusion

Before World War II, the history of Karelia and the Finnish Eastern border was predominantly written as part of the grand narratives of Finnish national and European history, often in terms of an eternal battle between East and West. After the lost war when Finland attempted to recover its international status, the Karelian issue was actively silenced in the domestic political debate. Questioning the Paris peace treaty was out of the question as long as the Allied Control Committee remained in the country (from 1944 to 1947). Even later during the Cold War years, the Karelian Issue remained a problem for policies of promoting Finland's international status, particularly before the country became a member of the United Nations in 1955.

The Cold War standards of what was politically sensible did not mean that publishing historical texts concerning Karelia was altogether censored during the post-war years. They did, however, take quite a different approach than during the inter-war period. The most common form of publication was regional and local histories, memoirs and studies of everyday life. In the 1960s, political themes of and perspectives on European and national history returned to the interpretations of Karelia, but they were now influenced by new theoretical perspectives and often followed by historical political disputes.

In Finland, the history of Karelia has been a vital element not only in addressing the loss of the region ceded to the USSR after World War II

---

68 Pekka Nevalainen, "Luovutetun Karjalan palautuskeskustelun vaiheet" (Phases of Discussion on Returning the Ceded Areas of Karelia), in Pekka Nevalainen, Hannes Sihvo (eds), *Karjala. Historia, kansa, kulttuuri* (Karelia. History, People, Culture), Helsinki, Suomalaisen Kirjallisuuden Seura, 1998, pp. 250–254.

69 Jussi Laine, Miika Tervonen, "Remaking the Border: Post-Soviet Borderscapes in the Finnish Media", in Chiara Brambilla, Jussi Laine, James Scott, Gianluca Bocchi (eds), *Borderscaping: Imaginations and Practices of Border Making*, Farnham, Ashgate, 2015, pp. 65–76.

but also in addressing the national trauma of lost war and legitimizing Finnish choices in regard to wartime European frontlines. The heated Finnish historical debates of the 1960s and 1970s clearly resulted from new, fast-spreading revisionist approaches but, even more so, from the refusal of the Finnish academic community to discuss pre-war and wartime historical interpretations during the first post-war decades. After the war, Finnish historians and intellectual circles in general did not feel the need to re-evaluate nationalist politics and national history as was being done in Germany and in many other European countries. In Finland, participation in Hitler's Operation Barbarossa was perceived as a separate front for the reconquering of Karelia and thus a consequence of Stalin's attack in 1939, rather than as the wilful cooperation with the Nazis in the World War. Among Finnish academics and media it was deemed that this specific situation did not give cause to critically consider how the national history or broader European history had been depicted in the 1920s and 1930s. Although this tradition was not openly referred to after the war, it is plausible to ask to what degree Karelian history published in the form of local or regional histories still echoed – in the sense of a hidden transcript – earlier national and civilizational paradigms.

Since the end of the Cold War, academic researchers working on Karelia and the Finnish–Russian border have sought to distance themselves from the "nationalist" history writing of the inter-war period. In terms of the politics of history, the rise of new European and transnational perspectives in the study of borders and borderlands can be considered the latest trend in addressing the experience of loss in the aftermath of the war. An analysis of the historical debates on Karelia shows, however, the difficulty of distinguishing national and European conceptualizations of the border as two separate discourses producing interpretations that clearly differ in the policies they subscribe to.

In the light of the scholarly debate about the nature of the post-war turn in Finnish historiography that took place in the 1990s, this issue can be placed within a broader context. Professor Päiviö Tommila, who became a member of the Finnish Academy, spoke of this change of direction in rather positive terms. He described it as a shift from romantic nationalism to realistic craftsmanship, fashioned by modern trends in

Nordic history writing.[70] At the time, his argument about the progressive modernization of Finnish history writing was, however, criticized by younger scholars who saw the post-war shift more in terms of a tactical adaptation to new political circumstances: a turn from grand visions to flat empiricism in a climate of self-censorship.[71]

These alternative interpretations reflect conflicting visions of the nature of both the earlier and later periods. Were the inter-war years characterized by a particular self-centred Finnish romantic nationalism or rather by grand supranational narratives of a battle between East and West typical of most European nationalist history writing at the time? And accordingly, should the revisionist tendencies since the 1960s be understood as a mere side-attack against Finnish history writing's natural evolution towards modern European approaches, or did the 1960s, after a period of flat empiricism and opportunist political silence, inaugurate a true revival of a grand theory in the Finnish academic community, as Pekka Ahtiainen and Jukka Tervonen have concluded?[72]

In light of our analysis, it is easy to recognize these general trends in the study of Karelian history as well. During the inter-war period, European perspectives of a civilizational divide were emphasized in the historical "bordering" of Finland. After the war, grand narratives of European history were abandoned – or no longer referred to – but the practice of projecting a deep civilizational dividing line persisted in approaches to Karelian history. In the 1970s and 1980s, historical studies of the borderlands became open to new regional perspectives, research on the experiences of Karelian immigrants adopted a more critical tone and, lastly, since the 1990s, studies addressing the problematic areas of

---

70 Päiviö Tommila, "Historiantutkija kansakunnan opettajana – yleisesitysten maailma" (The Historian as the Teacher of the Nation), in Päiviö Tommila (ed.), *Historiantutkijan muotokuva* (Portrait of the Historian), Helsinki, Suomen Historiallinen Seura, 1998, pp. 164–165; Päiviö Tommila, *Suomen historiankirjoitus*, *op. cit.*, pp. 202–204.

71 Pekka Ahtiainen, "Suomalaiskansallinen historiankirjoitus. Jatkumo vai varjo menneisyydestä" (Finnish National History Writing. A Continuing Line or a Shadow of the Past), in Pekka Ahtiainen et al. (eds), *Historia, sosiologia ja Suomi* (History, Sociology and Finland), Helsinki, Hanki ja jää, 1994, pp. 20–22 and pp. 25–31; Pekka Ahtiainen, Jukka Tervonen, "Menneisyyden tutkijat ja metodien vartijat", *op. cit.*, pp. 24–33.

72 Pekka Ahtiainen, Jukka Tervonen, "A Journey Through Finnish Historiography from the End of the 19th Century to the Present Day", in Frank Meyer, Jan Eivind Myhre (eds) *Nordic Historiography in the 20th Century*, University of Oslo, Oslo, 2000, pp. 50–80.

Karelian history have openly challenged the fundamentals of inter-war research. Today, when new European perspectives have been again on the rise in historical discussions on Karelia, the question that remains is the degree to which they represent less pronounced intentions to establish fixed dividing lines in the past.

The core of the politics of history addressing the loss of Karelia can no longer be credibly posed simply as a question of a silenced or self-censored national narrative of Karelian history. Such an approach, which is typical to early post-war decades, tends to conceal rather than address the link between Finnish wartime policies and the particular combination of national and European historical narratives dominant before the war. The critical point of inter-war historiography on Karelia was not simply the nationalistic undercurrent of its arguments but the way in which the idea of a supranational, civilizational divide was tied to conceptions of territoriality and borders. Since the early 1990s, we have witnessed the rise of new supra- and transnational perceptions of territoriality and borders in the context of deepening European integration. For current politics of history, the crucial question is whether the supranational perspectives of borders will once more be associated with theories of a clash between civilizations or whether – even in the case of Karelia – new approaches can contribute to a better understanding of shared European experiences.

The *Kresy* in Polish Memory: Between a Lost Arcadia and the Bloodlands of East-Central Europe

Beata HALICKA
Professor of Cultural History of East Central Europe,
Adam Mickiewicz University, Poznań

In the history of Poland, which is more than one thousand years old, the borders have been changed many times. Poland's territory grew regularly until it reached its peak of over one million square kilometres at the beginning of the seventeenth century. After the third partition of the state in 1795, Poland disappeared from the map of Europe until it regained independence in 1918. At the end of World War II, Poland was fighting on the side of the winners, but it nevertheless lost around 20% of its land as a consequence of the country shifting Westwards in 1945. Around 1.5 million Poles then fled or were expelled from their homeland. Today, Poland's territory covers 312,600 km^2 and most of the lands it lost were in the East.

Figure 6 – *Poland (1918-1945)*

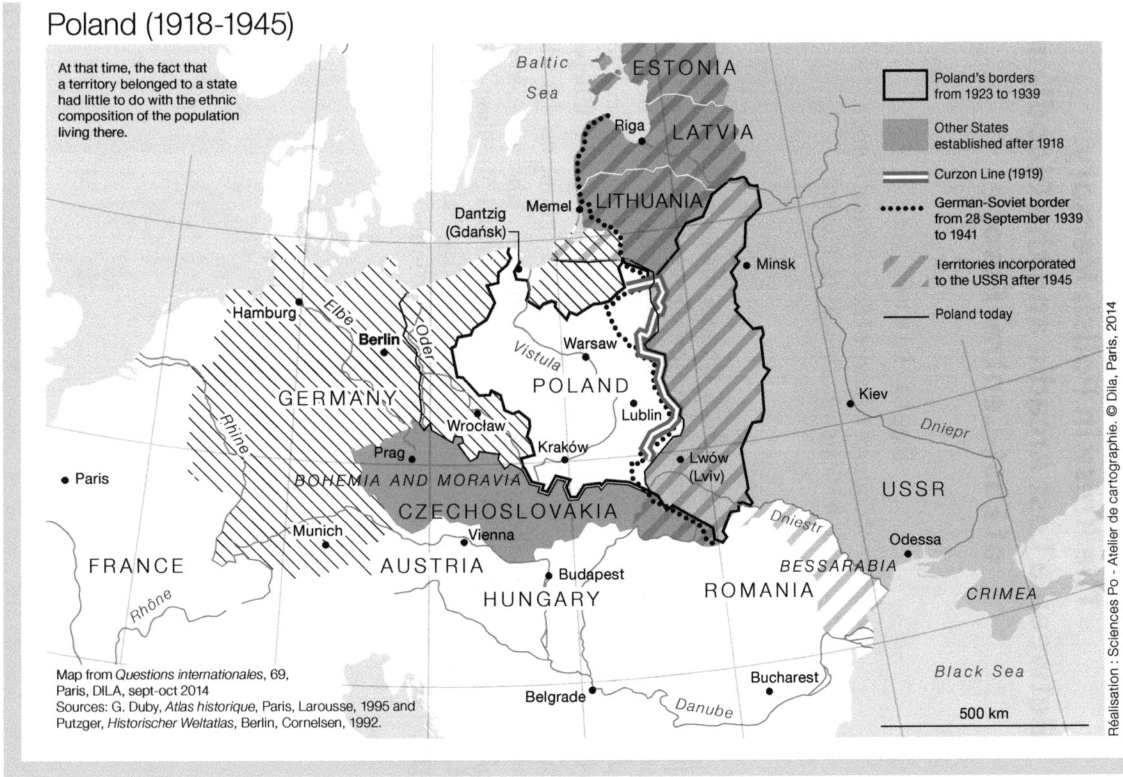

Considering these multiple changes in the lands making up the country, it is not surprising that there is a special word in Polish for the borderlands in the East: *kresy*. This concept has a long tradition and it holds an important place in the Poles' collective memory. When defining *kresy*, historians usually have to specify the period they are referring to; *kresy* during the Polish-Lithuanian Commonwealth was not the same as *kresy* in the inter-war period or after 1945. This chapter discusses the contemporary Polish memory of the most recent loss of territory in 1945, when the *kresy* regions were forcibly emptied of Poles and the long tradition of Polish culture among the other ethnic groups in that area almost completely disappeared. In these terms, the loss of territory was combined with a significant loss of culture.

To understand the impact of this loss, it is necessary to explain the historical context of the Eastern Polish borderlands, especially at the beginning of the twentieth century. Over the last seventy years, there have been a variety of interpretations of the historical facts in Poland and different actors have tried to impose their point of view. Under the Communist regime, the government and members of the Communist party were one group, and the refugees as well as expellees resettled in (mostly Western) Polish territories and those who went into exile made up another group. The latter group was divided into conservatives fighting for a revision of Poland's borders and a group of intellectuals looking for reconciliation with Ukrainian, Belarussian and Lithuanian neighbours. In the 1970s and 1980s, this group found many supporters in the Polish opposition movement. After the political changes of 1989–90, the interests of acting groups converged, but there were still different views and goals. In the last twenty-five years, the most important actors have been government representatives, with their vision of politics of history, and different organizations of refugees and expellees that were founded after 1990 to represent their particular interests.

The origins of *kresy*

A map of the territory, at its greatest extent in 1619, of the Polish-Lithuanian Commonwealth superimposed over present-day borders of East-Central Europe shows that all of Belarus, Lithuania and Latvia, a large part of today's Ukraine, central and Eastern Poland, half of Estonia and the Western territories of Russia around the city of Smolensk made up this early Polish state. As Timothy Snyder argued: "the nation of this Commonwealth was its nobility, Catholic, Orthodox, and Protestant. United by common political and civil rights, nobles of Polish, Lithuanian, and East Slavic origin alike described themselves, in Latin or Polish, as 'of the Polish nation'. They took for granted that, in the natural order of things, the languages of state, speech, literature, and liturgy would vary."[1] During the religious wars in Western Europe, this Commonwealth offered near-unprecedented religious tolerance guaranteed by the Warsaw Confederation Act of 1573. As a country on the frontier between the Catholic and Orthodox Churches, this Commonwealth gave birth to the hybrid United Church, which recognized the Catholic pope but used Orthodox rituals. It is also known as the Pale of Jewish Settlement, and the Hasidic movement originated in these lands. As the Commonwealth fell apart in the late eighteenth century, the tsarist empire claimed the Eastern part as its frontier for two decades until the Russian empire moved Westward, swallowing up large portions of Poland in 1795.[2] In the nineteenth century, modern nationalism arrived in this part of Europe. Patriots started to recast the nation as the people and nationality as the language they spoke. The most advanced in this field were the Poles. In the second part of the nineteenth century, competition emerged between Poles and other ethnic groups, especially with Lithuanian and Ukrainian patriots who also fought for a state independent from the Russian Empire.

Polish borderlands in the East at the turn of the nineteenth and twentieth centuries

After Napoleon's defeat, a new European order was established at the Congress of Vienna in 1815. A small area under Russian occupation took the name of the Kingdom of Poland. It was joined to the Russian Empire under the Tsar and was granted very limited autonomy. East of this Kingdom, large areas of the former Polish–Lithuanian Commonwealth were directly incorporated into the Russian Empire. Those lost lands were for first time called *kresy*, with the meaning of lost borderlands.[3]

---

1 Timothy Snyder, *The Reconstruction of Nations. Poland, Ukraine, Lithuania, Belarus, 1569–1999*, London, Yale University Press, 2003, p. 1.

2 Kate Brown, *The Biography of No Place. From Ethnic Borderland to Soviet Heartland*, Cambridge MA/London, Harvard University Press, 2003, p. 3.

3 Andrzej Szwarc, "Narodziny mitu" (The Birth of Myth), in *Kresy Rzeczpospolitej. Wielki mit Polaków* (Kresy of Respublica. The Great Myth of the Poles), Warszawa, Seria Biblioteka Polityki (Series Library of „Polityka"), 2016, p. 39.

In order to unify the newly acquired territory with the rest of the state, the Russians introduced a strong policy of russification, which the Poles fought to oppose. While the efforts of Polish nationalists had some success in the Kingdom of Poland, sustaining Polish culture and language in the lands joined to Russia was much more difficult. Many myths were invented or developed at that time. In the spirit of Romanticism, many looked for inspiration in the Middle Ages and wrote the history of Poland as beginning in 966. Polish Eastern borderlands were described as *antemurale christianitatis* – a bulwark of Christianity.[4] Some Polish writers supported the doctrine of Poland as the "Christ of nations", which identified Poles collectively with the messianic suffering of the Crucifixion and saw Poland as destined, like Christ, to return in glory.[5]

Literature played an important role in creating the collective identity of a nation without a state. Adam Mickiewicz, a major figure in Polish Romanticism, was one of the most influential writers at that time. In 1834, in exile in Paris, he published one of his masterpieces, the epic poem *Pan Tadeusz*, and depicted the historical Grand Duchy of Lithuania on the eve of Napoleon's 1812 invasion of Russia.[6] Mickiewicz's homeland Lithuania, as part of the Polish-Lithuanian Commonwealth, appeared in this poem as "an idyllic chronotope of childhood and early youth, locus amoenus colored by nostalgia".[7]

Another author, Henryk Sienkiewicz, played a similarly important role in the creation of the Polish myth of *kresy*, especially its Southern part in today's Ukraine. He received the 1905 Nobel Prize for Literature. His *Trilogy* of historical novels[8] recounts dramatized versions of famous events in the seventeenth-century Polish-Lithuanian Commonwealth, weaving together fact and fiction. Sienkiewicz's goal was to strengthen national resolve by invoking Poland's glorious past. The work became an

---

4 Janusz Tazbir, *Polskie przedmurze chrześcijańskiej Europy. Mity a rzeczywistość historyczna* (Polish Bulwark of Christian Europe. Myths and Historical Reality), Warszawa, Wydawnictwo Interpress, 1987.

5 Maria Janion, "Romanticism and the Beginning of the Modern World", *Dialogue and Universalism*, No. 10, 2000, pp. 45–67.

6 Czesław Miłosz, *The History of Polish Literature*, University of California Press, Berkeley/Los Angeles/London, 1983, p. 208.

7 Tomas Venclova, "Native Realm Revisited: Mickiewicz's Lithuania and Mickiewicz in Lithuania", *Lituanus: Lithuanian Quarterly Journal of Arts and Sciences*, Vol. 53, No.3, 2007. http://www.lituanus.org/2007/07_3_03%20Venclova.html

8 Henryk Sienkiewicz's Trylogy: *Ogniem i mieczem* (With Fire and Sword, 1884), *Potop* (The Deluge, 1886) and *Pan Wołodyjowski* (Sir Michael, 1888).

instant classic and was enthusiastically received by Polish readers. It also influenced the imagination of most Poles at the time, as well as today, about *kresy* and the role of the Polish state in this part of Europe. A mix of chivalric heroes, a wild landscape and dynamic action makes this *Trilogy* a sort of Wild West story of East-Central Europe.[9] Sienkiewicz used protagonists from Ukrainian history, such as Bohdan Chmielnzykyi and other Cossack leaders, as well as figures from Ukrainian folk legends. They were all part of the Slavic community of the Polish-Lithuanian Commonwealth and revealed Sienkiewicz's fascination with Ukrainian folklore. However, the central protagonists of his novels are Polish nobles, who represent sarmatism.[10] It was unique for its cultural mix of Eastern, Western and native traditions. In Sienkiewicz's novels, the image of the nobles corresponds to the stereotyped picture of a Pole as a Polish-speaking Catholic, fighting for "God, Fatherland and Freedom".[11] The Polish nobles seem to live in a world free of internal social, religious and ethnic conflicts and all members of the state fight together against external enemies. It is interesting to note that Sienkiewicz wrote his *Trilogy* at the end of the nineteenth century – at a time of rising of national movements, especially among people of Lithuanian and Ukrainian (called at this time Ruthenian) descent and at a time when tsarist repression of the borderlands served to marginalize the region economically and socially and led to its backwardness.[12] Most of these contemporary problems are not contextualized by Sienkiewicz in his historical novels, as his main goal was to strengthen Polish national identity with a narrative about its glorious history and dominant position at the time of the Polish-Lithuanian Commonwealth.[13]

---

9 Jacek Kobuszewski, *Kresy*, Wrocław, Wydawnictwo Dolnośląskie, 1996, p. 84.

10 Sarmatism was the dominant Baroque culture and ideology of the Polish nobility from the sixteenth to the eighteenth centuries.

11 Christoph Klessmann and Robert Traba, "Kresy und Deutscher Osten. Vom Glauben an die historische Mission – oder Wo liegt Arkadien?" in: Hans Henning Hahn and Robert Traba (eds), *Deutsch–Polnische Erinnerungsorte, Parallelen* (Vol. 3), Paderborn, Ferdinand Schöningh, 2012, p. 45.

12 Kate Brown, *The Biography of No Place*, *op. cit.*, p. 5.

13 Ahmet Ersoy, Maciej Górny, Vangelis Kechriotis, *Modernism: Representations of National Culture: Discourses of Collective Identity in Central and Southeast Europe 1770–1945: Texts and Commentaries*, Budapest/New York, Central European University Press, Volume III/2, 2010, p. 164.

The Great War in *kresy*

The first two decades of the twentieth century brought considerable changes to the territory of *kresy*, understood as the part of Polish-Lithuanian Commonwealth incorporated into Russia, as well as in the meaning of the word *kresy*. The Great War and the Bolshevik Revolution also left their mark on towns and cities. At the end, many lands in the territories of the former Russian and Austro-Hungarian Empires became independent states, according to the doctrine of national self-determination.[14] Poland and Lithuania did so, but the border between them was complicated by the Polish Army's occupation of the city of Wilno. The Lithuanians, who considered Wilno the historical capital of the Grand Duchy of Lithuania, had to move their capital to Kaunas.

Ukrainian nationalists were also fighting for an independent state. They wanted Lwów as their capital, but the city was dominated by the Poles. At the beginning of World War I, it seemed that the Ukrainians had greater hope for success than the Lithuanians with the Russian Empire. The Ukrainian "ethnic group" numbered in the tens of millions.[15] They lived both in the territory of the Russian Empire and in Austrian Galicia. The new government of the independent Polish state decided to fight for Galicia militarily. This ethnically mixed borderland became the scene of the Polish–Ukrainian and then of the Polish–Soviet war. The Treaty of Riga signed on 18 March 1921 set the border between these two states. The Ukrainians did not gain international recognition of their independence and remained divided between Poland and Soviet Russia. Poland became a multi-ethnic country and had to guarantee minority rights for all ethnic and national groups living in its territory. Yet Polish officials conducted a policy of strengthening Polishness in the mixed borderlands and repeatedly violated the rights of minorities.[16] In this situation, it is not surprising that morale among the Ukrainian minority was very poor and a feeling of injustice prevailed. Poland was thus in a devil's circle, as were all the newly founded states of Eastern Central

---

14 Edward McWhinney, *Self-Determination of Peoples and Plural-Ethnic States in Contemporary International Law: Failed States, Nation-Building and the Alternative, Federal Option*, Leiden/Boston, Martinus Nijhoff, 2007.

15 Timothy Snyder, *The Reconstruction of Nations, op. cit.*, p. 133.

16 Ryszard Torzecki, *Polacy i Ukraińcy. Sprawa ukraińska w czasie II wojny światowej na terenie II Rzeczypospolitej* (Poles and Ukrainians. The Ukrainian Affair during the Second World War on the Territory of Respublica), Warszawa, Wydawnictwo Naukowe PWN, 1993, p. 12f.

Europe at this time. To grant national rights to an extent that would satisfy minorities was considered too dangerous for the cohesion of the young republic.

The new Polish Eastern border was a kind of compromise based on the borders of the second partition of the Polish-Lithuanian Commonwealth in 1793. The part of the Commonwealth taken by Russia in the first partition of 1772 remained part of the Russian-Soviet state. With the Treaty of Riga, the meaning of the word *kresy* changed. It was no longer used to refer to the land lost in 1772, and a new myth of *kresy* as a part of the new Polish state emerged.

Kresy in the inter-war period and during World War II

The many military conflicts over the Eastern border of the Polish state in the years 1919–21 led to the creation of a new national narrative. In particular, the disputed areas, which were claimed by Lithuanians, Belarussians, Ukrainians and the Soviet Union, had added value because their belonging to Poland had been won by a fierce battle. The otherness of the new *kresy* was also manifested in the cultural, religious and ethnic diversity of the Eastern borderlands of the new Polish Republic. Both independent Lithuania and the Soviet Union contested the 1921 border and hoped to change it to their advantage. Compared to the other lands of Poland, which were much more nationally homogeneous with only the Jews as the only large minority of less than 10% of the population, the ethnic structure of the new *kresy* created a mosaic of four large (Ukrainians, Poles, Belarussians and Jews) and several smaller groups.[17] The *kresy* made up around 45% of the Polish state (180,000 km^2) and was inhabited by 30% of Polish citizens.[18]

---

17 According to the census of 1931, the largest group were the Ukrainians with 41.3% of population; the Poles numbered slightly less than 30%, the Belarussians 16.9% and the Jewish people 9.3%. When dealing with the results of national census, it should be taken into account that the national identity of the inhabitants of this part of Europe in the first half of the twentieth century was often unstable; many people considered themselves locals or, first, members of a religious group. Witold Sienkiewicz/Grzegorz Hryciuk, *Wysiedlenia, wypędzenia i ucieczki. 1939–1959. Atlas ziem Polski*, Warszawa, Demart, 2008, p. 14. German edition: *Zwangsumsiedlung, Flucht und Vertreibung 1939 bis 1959. Atlas zur Geschichte Ostmitteleuropas*, Bonn, Bundeszentrale für politische Bildung, 2009, p. 16.

18 Włodzimierz Medrzecki, "Panorama Kresów" (Panorama of Kresy), in *Kresy Rzeczpospolitej. Wielki mit Polaków*, *op. cit.*, p. 57.

During the fight for independence, as well as in the inter-war period, two different visions of Poland were used by Polish politicians. The first, describing Poles as descendants of the culture and traditions of the Polish-Lithuanian Commonwealth, was led by Józef Piłsudski, the Chief of State in 1918–22 and 1926–35. He believed in a multicultural Poland, *a home of nations*, recognizing numerous ethnic and religious nationalities and existing as a federation with the neighbour states of Lithuania and Ukraine. His main opponent was Roman Dmowski, who called for a national state of Poland founded mainly on an ethnically Polish people and on Roman Catholic identity. As he saw the ethnic minorities in Poland as a direct threat to the cultural identity, integrity and ethnic cohesion of Poland, they should either be "polonized" or forced to emigrate.[19] Polish governments had a mixture of both positions in their policy.

Especially in the politics of history, Polish governments made great efforts to strengthen the Polishness of the *kresy* areas. This kind of activity only increased the antagonism of other national groups living in this territory. One good example of this is the Tomb of the Unknown Soldier created in Warsaw in 1925, dedicated to the unknown soldiers who gave their lives for Poland. As a symbolic cornerstone of this tomb, an unidentified body of a young soldier who fell during the Defence of Lwów was chosen. His ashes were transferred from Lwów, where the city's historic Lychakiv Cemetery has a monument and a burial place for Poles and their allies who died in Lwów during the Polish–Ukrainian War and the Polish–Soviet War. Out of almost 3,000 tombs, 300 were for the Eaglets, as the young Polish defenders of the city from 1918 are known. The fact that most of the people buried there fought on the Polish side against the Ukrainians generated a great deal of controversy among Ukrainians.[20]

The Polishness of *kresy* was an important component of education in schools and universities. The border region was presented as a place of heroic struggles for Polish independence. The cultural diversity and the interests of other ethnic and national groups were not discussed. Nobel Prize winner Czesław Miłosz, who spent his youth in Wilno in

[19] Mikolaj Stanislaw Kunicki, *Between the Brown and the Red: Nationalism, Catholicism, and Communism in Twentieth-Century Poland. The Politics of Boleslaw Piasecki*, Athens, Ohio University Press, 2012, pp. 10–12.

[20] After World War II, as the city became part of Soviet Ukraine, the Polish historical monuments located at the cemetery were destroyed or neglected. It first reopened in 2005 and the reconstruction and official opening were seen as a major improvement in Polish–Ukrainian relations.

the inter-war period, in his book *Rodzinna Europa* (The Native Realm, 1959) regrets that the Polish education system eliminated any signs of Lithuanian culture and folklore from schoolbooks. Children and young people living in Wilno had no way of knowing about the culture and tradition of the Lithuanians living among them, who made up the majority in the countryside near the city. The same must be said about the relation with the Jews. Czesław Miłosz remembers: "Such a school, by replacing a many-cultured heritage with national attitudes cut according to the latest fashion, must also have laid the foundation for anti-Semitism among its pupils. The Jewish religious literature that sprang from this part of Europe was translated into many languages and won recognition all over the world … But we, in the very city where those books were printed, knew literally nothing about them."[21]

An important part of constructing national identity was the memory of the battle of Warsaw as a decisive Polish victory in 1920 during the Polish–Soviet War. It was celebrated as one of the most important battles in European history and it was stressed that the Polish victory over the Soviets stopped the spread of communism towards Europe. At the same time, Soviet leadership was looking for ways to change the border drawn in the Treaty of Riga in 1921. Stalin and Hitler were interested in revising the post-war Versailles order in Europe. These plans culminated in late summer 1939 as Germany and the Soviet Union signed a Non-aggression Pact complete with a Secret Protocol on the "territorial-political reconfiguration" of Eastern Europe. Stalin demanded that his influence on the Polish *kresy* reach the so-called Curzon Line. With the outbreak of World War II, the two dictators in Berlin and Moscow destroyed the Polish Republic and divided it among themselves.

Soon after the Soviet army and security organizations moved into the *kresy*, they began mass arrests and deportations of Polish citizens, sending them to prison camps and hard labour in Siberia, Soviet Central Asia and the Soviet Arctic region. The Soviets forcibly removed as many as 330,000 Polish citizens. Many of those deported died. Around 150,000 Poles were forcibly recruited into the Red Army.[22] "Stalin's primary goal was not ethnic, but 'social' cleansing. He wanted to remove the 'ruling classes' in Eastern Poland in order to prepare the annexed territories for

---

21 Czesław Miłosz, *The Native Realm. A Search for Self-definition*, New York, Doubleday, 1968, pp. 97.

22 Philipp Ther, Ana Siljak (eds), *Redrawing Nations. Ethnic Cleansing in East-Central Europe, 1944–1948*, Lanham (u.a.), Rowman & Littlefield, 2001, p. 3.

rapid sovietisation."[23] The most brutal part of this plan was a series of mass executions of around 22,000 Polish prisoners of war carried out by the Soviet secret police NKVD in April and May 1940. Most of the victims were officers and high-ranking soldiers in the Polish Army; there were also many thousand police officers and Polish intelligentsia whom the Soviets deemed to be "intelligence agents, gendarmes, landowners, saboteurs, factory owners, lawyers, officials, and priests".[24] The murder of these prisoners of war took place in camps in Ostashkov, Starobelsk and Kozelsk, and the murder of the civilians held in prisons occurred in the territory of today's Western Ukraine and Belorussia. The massacre is named after the Katyń Forest where some of the mass graves were first discovered by the Nazi soldiers in 1943.[25] The Soviet Union claimed that the victims had been murdered by the Nazis in 1941 and continued to deny responsibility for the massacres until 1990. In Polish collective memory, especially according to the loss of *kresy*, the memory of the Katyń massacre has a very important place and was highly significant in the context of post-war communist political history. Even today, Russia and Poland are divided on the legal description of the Katyń crime. The Poles consider it a case of genocide and demand further investigations. Despite the commitment expressed by Russian President Dmitry Medvedev in December 2010 and the Russian State Duma calling for the massacre to be investigated further to confirm the list of victims, many pro-Soviet and national Russian politicians continue to deny all Soviet guilt.

With the military aggression of September 1939 and the German occupation, the Polish government left the country and went into exile. Staying in Paris and then in London, it started to organize an underground state and resistance forces in Poland. Despite this, the conditions for liberating Poland were dictated by the USSR from the beginning. Polish communists staying in the Soviet Union came to Poland with the Red Army and formed the Polish Committee of National Liberation (*Polski Komitet Wyzwolenia Narodowego*) with Stalin's support. This Provisional Government started to work on 22 July 1944 in Lublin without legitimization from Polish society.

---

23 Philipp Ther, "A Century of Forced Migration: The Orgins and Consequences of 'Ethnic Cleansing'", in Philipp Ther, Ana Siljak (eds), *Redrawing Nations*, *op. cit.*, p. 51.

24 Małgorzata Kuźniar-Plota, "Decision to Commence Investigation into Katyn Massacre". Departmental Commission for the Prosecution of Crimes against the Polish Nation. 2004. http://www.ipn.gov.pl/en/news/77,dok.html.

25 "Katyń – zapowiedź śmierci Kresów" (Katyń – Sign of Death of Kresy), in *Kresy Rzeczpospolitej. Wielki mit Polaków*, *op. cit.*, pp. 9–13.

Despite this, it could act freely because anyone who openly opposed it had to reckon with arrest by the NKVD, deportation and even death. In this way, within a few months the mostly anti-communist Polish society found itself deprived of any way to fight against the communist takeover. In exchange for recognition of the (slightly modified) Curzon Line as the border between Poland and the Soviet Union, in a secret agreement concluded on 27 July 1944 between the Polish Provisional and the Soviet governments, the Soviets supported the idea of a Polish–German border on the Oder and Neisse Rivers, which later became the basis for the decisions at conferences in Yalta and Potsdam.[26]

The Polish government in exile had a different position. In the hope of support from Western Allies, on 17 December 1944 Minister Tomasz Arciszewski gave an interview to the *Sunday Times* in which he not only emphasized claims to the cities Lwów and Wilno in *kresy*, but also refused to take over the German cities Breslau and Stettin, as he argued they had a numerically strong German minority.[27] With the Soviet victory over Nazi Germany, as the Polish government in exile weakened and the Western Allies supported Stalin's territorial demands, Poland was shifted approximately 200 km to the West and lost the *kresy*.

An important part of Polish collective memory about this *kresy* is the Polish–Ukrainian civil war and the flight and expulsion of Poles from Volhynia and Galicia in 1943–4. Both Nazi Germany and the Soviet Union aggravated ethnic tensions in the occupied territories. The Soviets encouraged Ukrainians to shake off the economic and cultural dominance of the Poles and literally to "beat up" their former lords.[28] When the Nazis conquered Eastern Poland in the summer of 1941, they supported radical Ukrainian nationalist forces, used them as helpers in the Holocaust and pitted them against the Poles. The Ukrainians wanted to seize the opportunity offered by the war to create their own nation-state. The Organization of Ukrainian Nationalists (*Orhabizacja*

---

26 First published in Tadeusz Cieślak, *Stosunki polsko-radzieckie w latach 1917–1945. Dokumenty i materiały* (Polish–Soviet Relations between 1917 and 1945. Documents and Materials), Warszawa, Książka i Wiedza, 1967, pp. 339.

27 The interview with Tomasz Arciszewski in *The Sunday Times*, 17 Dec. 1944, quoted in Tadeusz Cieślak et al. (eds), *Sprawa polska w czasie drugiej wojny światowej na arenie międzynarodowej. Zbiór dokumentów* (The Polish Affair during the Second World War in the International Arena. Documents), Warszawa, Państwowy Instytut Naukowe, 1965, p. 655–657.

28 Philipp Ther, *A Century of Forced Migration*, *op. cit.*, p. 51.

Ukarinskych Naionalistiv) started to expel Poles in 1942. They were not only fighting with Polish military units, but also massacring entire villages. Up to 350,000 Poles fled West over the San River. The Polish underground retaliated by attempting to drive Ukrainians from areas they controlled in today's South-Eastern Poland. The ruthless nature of these encounters between both nationalities was a difficult obstacle to coexistence after the war.[29] Because of this, and under Soviet pressure, in September 1944 the communist Polish Committee for National Liberation signed treaties with the Ukrainian, Lithuanian and Belarussian Soviet Socialist Republics regarding the "exchange" of the population from these territories. Between 1944 and 1948, more than 480,000 Ukrainians were expelled from Poland to the Soviet Union. From the whole *kresy*, over 1.1 million Poles were forced to leave their homes and were brought by train to the West.[30] In official communist propaganda, these people have been called the repatriates (*repatrianci*). Repatriation means coming back home, but most of them were expelled from their homes. The way in which the Poles had to leave their homeland differed depending on the region. In the Belarussian area, most of them could choose between staying and becoming a Soviet citizen or leaving. In the Lithuanian part, the inhabitants of Wilno had to leave because the city was to become a homogeneous Lithuanian capital. The Poles in the countryside were allowed to stay, as long as they were ready to assimilate with the Lithuanians. In the territory of the new Ukrainian Soviet Republic, the Poles had no choice. They knew the Ukrainians would not accept any Poles. Despite their differences, all these people were treated as one group by the new Polish communist authorities. In their eyes, they were not victims, but just migrants who came to be settled in the Western and Northern territories joined to Poland. They were not allowed to use any term for themselves other than "repatriates".

The population losses in the *kresy* were immense. Almost all Jews living there (c. 1 million people) were murdered in the Holocaust. As mentioned, around 330,000 Polish citizens were deported to Siberia and around 400,000 were taken to Nazi Germany for forced labour. As a consequence of the Polish–Ukrainian civil war and the shifting of borders, c. 1.1 million Poles were transferred to the new Polish territories in the West and North. Around 250,000 Poles who first chose to remain in

---

29 ibid., p. 52.

30 Witold Sienkiewicz, Grzegorz Hryciuk, *Wysiedlenia, wypędzenia i ucieczki. 1939–1959*, *op. cit.*, p. 238.

their homeland in the *kresy* moved to Poland after the death of Stalin in the 1950s.[31] All these people can be considered lucky in the end because they survived. Timothy Snyder counted 14 million people of different ethnic groups murdered in the territory he named *bloodlands*, which at its largest extent covers the lands of the historical Polish-Lithuanian Commonwealth.[32] Unfortunately, the memory of these dramatic events is not shared by the nations now in this territory and the Holocaust survivors. The dominant tendency is that each group remembers its own sufferings and not the sufferings of the neighbouring group. In general, the East-Central Europeans see themselves mostly as victims and only to a very small extent see the victimhood of "others".

Polish communists and dealing with the loss of *kresy*

The political change, the communist takeover and the social revolution in the late 1940s divided Polish society depending on the position a person took in relation to the new regime. Not only did the communists seize power over the country by violence, but they also seized power over the official narrative about World War II and its consequences. Anyone who espoused a different opinion was treated as an enemy of the state and persecuted. One of the founding myths of the new communist Poland was that of the "Recovered Territories". The Communists described the annexing of Eastern German lands to Poland as their huge success and the solution for the demographic problems of the inter-war period in Poland, as the peasants suffered because of land hunger. With the shifting of Poland, every peasant could receive around 10 ha of land in the new territories. In addition, the development of industry and better living conditions were promised to those who settled in the "Recovered Territories". This name refers to the fact that those lands had been part of Poland in the tenth and eleventh centuries under the medieval Piast dynasty, the first kings of Poland. Over the centuries, however, they had become Germanized through German Eastward settlement and political expansion.[33] This kind of propaganda attempted to secure legitimacy domestically and internationally for the new borders. At the same time,

31 ibid., p. 238.

32 Timothy Snyder, *Bloodlands. Europe between Hitler and Stalin*, London, Bodley Head, 2010, p. viii.

33 See the political text by Zygmunt Wojciechowski, *Polska – Niemcy. Dziesięć wieków zmagania* (Poland – Germany. Ten Centuries of Struggle), Poznań, INNE, 1945.

it minimized the importance of the loss of *kresy* and the depriving of millions of Polish citizens of their homeland.

Public discussions about the fate of the refugees and expellees from the Eastern borderlands of Poland were not allowed, and their memories could only be cultivated in family circles.[34] Journalistic and literary works, as well as remembrance literature, came under censorship, with the result that most authors practised self-censorship, wrote for the proverbial drawer, or later tried to publish their work abroad. Thus, the people who had endured a journey of several weeks in freight trains, often having already suffered the trauma of the Soviet and German occupations, as well as the Polish–Ukrainian civil war, were not allowed to speak or to write freely. On their arrival, most of them found themselves in a state of culture shock. Depending on their physical and emotional state, they made a place for themselves in their new environment and began to engage with it, albeit at different tempos. Most of them shut themselves away in their private lives and isolated themselves, thereby losing the possibility of satisfying their needs for recognition, social contact or self-development. Frequently, this had a negative impact on their health, with some sitting on their unpacked suitcases for years afterwards or reliving the trauma of the war.

The situation changed with the political thaw of 1956, and many started to believe that they would be able to speak and write freely about their experiences. At that time, various institutions (research institutes, cultural centres and newspapers) announced competitions for the best memoirs, looking for stories from before and during the war, reasons for resettlement in the newly gained territories, the process of resettlement, and the first years in the new homeland.[35] In studying the memoirs sent for a competition initiated by the Institue for Western Affairs (*Instytut Zachodni*) in Poznań in 1957, I chose texts written by Poles expelled from the *kresy* and settled in Western Poland.[36] Most of these people did

34 See the interesting study showing the parallels between the fate of the German and the Polish refugees and expellees: Philipp Ther, *Deutsche und polnische Vertriebene. Gesellschaft und Vertriebenenpolitik in der SBZ/DDR und in Polen 1945–1956*, Göttingen- Zürich, Vandenhoeck and Ruprecht, 1998.

35 Paul Andrew Vickers, *Peasants, Professors, Publishers and Censorship: Memoirs of Rural Inhabitants of Poland's Recovered Territories (1945–c.1970)*, Ph.D. thesis, University of Glasgow, 2014, available at: http://theses.gla.ac.uk/4821/ (accessed 5 February 2016).

36 Beata Halicka (ed.), *Mój dom nad Odrą. Pamiętniki osadników Ziem Zachodnich po 1945 roku* (My Home on the River Odra. Written Memories by Settlers in Polish Western Territories), Kraków, Universitas, 2016; German edition: Beata Halicka

not suit the ethos of the settler who was meant to be actively involved in the resettlement and economic growth of the Western and Northern territories. This was the main narrative expected by the organizers. Because of the political thaw, some authors decided to express their criticism of shortages, deficiencies, mistakes and failed projects. I also found some accounts concerning human tragedies they witnessed during the flight and expulsion as well as on the journey to the West. All this, however, was written under self-censorship, which prevented discussion of certain topics such as the Soviet occupation, the loss of the homeland in *kresy*, or bemoaning lost property. The authors avoided presenting their fate from the point of view of a victim and did not write (or wrote only indirectly) about their own suffering, apathy, or longing for the life they had lost. Their position as victims appears significantly more often in memoirs written in the 1990s and later.

Since the late 1960s, the collective imagination about the fate of the Poles from the *kresy* has been influenced by a comedy film *Sami swoi* (literally "Only Ours" by Sylwester Chęciński, 1967), which became a hit for many decades. The film tells the story of two warring families from *kresy* who arrived in the same transport in a Lower Silesian village, where they settled next to each other. The old homeland is presented in the spirit of state propaganda as poor and backward areas, with the new Western territories as modern and progressive. Older generations insist on tradition and idealize their previous lives, which in the eyes of the young arouses ridicule and does not fit the new situation. Unfortunately, the film offers a distorted, far too naive and optimistic picture of the historical facts and ignores a number of problems. Its popularity and the lack of other good films on the subject meant that the Poles who did not come from the East had a greatly simplified and even trivial image of forced migration and the loss of the Polish Eastern borderlands.[37] This simplified picture may have satisfied a mass audience, but not intellectuals

(ed.): *Mein Haus an der Oder. Erinnerungen polnischer Siedler nach 1945*, Paderborn, Ferdinand Schöningh, 2014. See also Beata Halicka, "Polish Wild West: Forced Migration and Cultural Appropriation of the Oder Region after 1945", in Midwest Slavic Conference. Ohio State University. Center for Slavic and East European Studies 2015, URI: http://hdl.handle.net/1811/71166.

37 Beata Halicka, *"Polski Dziki Zachód". Przymusowe migracje i kulturowe oswajanie Nadodrza 1945–48* ("Polish Wild West". Forced Migration and Cultural Appropriation of the Oder Region 1945–48), Kraków, Universitas, 2015, p. 382; German Edition: Beata Halicka, *Polens Wilder Westen. Erzwungene Migration und die kulturelle Aneignung des Oderraumes 1945–48*, Paderborn, Ferdinand Schönigh, 2013, p. 300.

and writers trying to find an alternative to the state narrative that would be closer to the facts and accepted by the communist censors.

Contesting the phantomization of *kresy*

While some general topics about the history of Polish Eastern lands since the political thaw of 1956 were allowed in public discussion, the word *kresy* remained taboo until 1989. Its phantomization can clearly be seen in the *Dictionary of Myths and Cultural Traditions* by the famous Polish lexicographer Władysław Kopaliński.[38] In this 1985 opus, there are many terms very closely connected with the cultural tradition of the Polish Eastern borderlands, but the term *kresy* is not to be found.[39] This phantomization is especially strange considering that the *kresy* made up 46% of Polish territory in 1939 and two-thirds of it in the seventeenth century. How to educate children and young people at the universities while avoiding the term *kresy?* The communist leader proceeded pragmatically: all facts calling the Polish–Soviet brotherhood into question were deleted from schoolbooks and publications. At the same time, the most important persons born in the *kresy*, especially writers such as Adam Mickiewicz, Juliusz Słowacki and Henryk Sienkiewicz and composers like Stefan Moniuszko, Karol Szymanowski and many others, were allowed to be mentioned, even though they had a hostile relationship with Russia.

Contemporary writers living in communist Poland and looking for a solution for their writing often moved the action of their works into the deep past. The other possibility was an escape to the world of imagination. Jarosław Iwaszkiewicz, for example, set the action of his novel *Sława i Chwała* (Glory and Vainglory, 1966) in this part of *kresy*, which in 1945 became the Western Ukrainian SSR, but the landscape he portrayed was a nostalgic one in which the line between real and unreal worlds is strongly blurred. His saga depicts a panorama of the life of Polish intelligentsia in the years 1914–47, but the characters do not "make history" or live in a concrete social and geographical context. They are at first busy considering their role in the world, discussing such philosophical problems as life, death,

38 Władysław Kopaliński, *Słownik mitów i tradycji kultury* (Dictionary of Myths and Cultural Tradition), Warszawa, Wydanictwo PIW, 1985.

39 Christph Klessmann and Robert Traba, *Kresy und Deutscher Osten, op. cit.*, p. 51.

action, betrayal, love and hate.[40] The end of the Polish *kresy* is presented not a personal defeat, but as the necessary twilight of a decadent society in the capitalistic Poland of the inter-war period.

This kind of political argument was not satisfying for most Poles who were transferred from the East to the West. Deprived of writing public memoirs about their lost homeland, they had nothing left but historical novels about the *kresy*. The strength of this need is shown in the unprecedented success of the filming of two parts of the already mentioned *Trilogy* by Henryk Sienkiewicz in 1969 and 1974. To satisfy specific Polish nostalgia, sentimental longing and wistful affection for the lost Eastern territories, the communist leaders then in 1976 allowed the director Jerzy Hofmann to film the screen version of the novel *Trędowata* (The Leper) by Helena Mniszkówna, a bestseller in 1909. In this way, the historical film acted as a safety valve, giving vent to the need to keep the memory of *kresy* alive; since the 1970s there has been a feeling that this subject is no longer completely taboo.

The *kresy* as a political programme of Polish émigrés in Western Europe

The government-in-exile, formally called the Government of the Republic of Poland in Exile, remained in London after the Potsdam conference in July/August 1945, despite the fact that most European states recognized the new Polish, mostly communist government supported by the Soviet Union. The government-in-exile found itself in a very difficult position: without the recognition of Western Allies and without effective power, it became largely symbolic of continued resistance to the foreign occupation of post-war Poland. It insisted on making a stand in defence of Poland's pre-1939 Eastern border and demanded the returning of *kresy* to the Polish state. It took the official position that "Poland should renegotiate its Eastern borders. This was grounded in the idealist conviction that since Poles had been wronged by the Molotov–Ribbentrop pact, decimated by the Second World War, sold out by the Allies at Yalta, and oppressed by Communism for decades, Poland deserved justice in a future European settlement."[41] This political programme was shared by many Polish émigrés in Western Europe and

---

40 Andrzej Zawada, Jarosław Iwaszkiewicz, "Profile" (Profiles), Warszawa, 1994.

41 Timothy Snyder, *The Reconstruction of Nations*, *op. cit.*, p. 226.

both Americas; anyone who adopted a different position was treated as a traitor to Polish interests.

But this was not the only political programme of the Polish émigrés. An alternative political and cultural programme around the *kresy* was developed by two Polish intellectuals in exile in Paris: Jerzy Giedroyć and Juliusz Mieroszewski. The former was the founder, chief editor and publisher of the literary-political journal *Kultura*, initially in Rome, then in Paris in the years 1947–2000. Mieroszewski was the chief editor of the English section of the journal between 1950 and 1972 and closely collaborated with Jerzy Giedroyć. They managed to make *Kultura* the leading Polish émigré journal, and with time won over many Polish intellectuals to their cause. Their guiding assumption was that certain wartime changes should not be reversed. They saw *kresy* not as Polish lands lost to the Soviet Union, but as contested territories that could now serve nations comparable to the Polish nation. In the early 1970s, Mieroszewski provided the theoretical justification for the Eastern grand strategy of a future sovereign Poland. He proposed strengthening the Lithuanian, Belarusian and Ukrainian nations within the respective Soviet Socialist Republics, including in territories taken from Poland in 1945. Even if during the Cold War this seemed rather romantic, Giedroyć and Mieroszewski contended that a future sovereign Poland should support the independence of Lithuanian, Belarussian and Ukrainian nation-states. Their great political achievement was to communicate the programme in such a way that, before the revolution of 1989, this position was taken for granted by the Poles who would matter thereafter.[42] This crucial, and at the time unique, consideration of the *Kultura* programme found an increasing number of supporters and helped lay the groundwork for Poland's successful Eastern policy after the fall of Communism. Poland was the first state to recognize independent Ukraine in 1991.

The journal *Kultura* was published by the Literary Institute (*Instytut Literacki*) and presented not only political and historical articles but, primarily, the best of Polish twentieth-century writing, including Czesław Miłosz, Witold Gombrowicz, Czesław Straszewicz, Józef Czapski, Gustaw Herling-Grudziński and others. It offered them also the printing of their books. The home of the Literary Institute in Paris became something of a mecca not only for Polish émigrés but also for Poles from communist Poland. With the support of the latter, thousands

42 ibid., p. 220.

of books were smuggled into communist-dominated Poland. When a world of underground independent letters came into being in Poland and the democratic opposition of the 1970s began to consolidate, the Literary Institute in Paris had already become a strong reference point for many members of the Polish opposition movement.[43] A similarly important role in printing and smuggling books to Poland was played by Jerzy Kulczycki, who founded Odnowa Press in London in 1964 and ran the Orbis Books bookstore in the years 1972–2008. Both the Literary Institute in Paris and Jerzy Kulczycki in London cooperated with the National Committee for a Free Europe, which in the years 1954–91 financed the sending of around 4 million books to Poland.[44]

Polish writing in exile

Polish writing published in exile usually comprised issues not allowed in communist Poland, and a large part of this work dealt with *kresy*. Bolesław Hadaczek divided this body of literature into works dealing with the experience of war, those about deportation and exile, and those called *kresy*-nostalgia.[45] Consistent with its Greek root meaning "homecoming" and "pain", nostalgia in Polish exile literature was often considered a feeling of extreme homesickness. Many authors were living in the past, idealizing their lost homeland and unable to take root in their new place of residence. Loyalty to the homeland required them to embellish and give an idyllic nature to the "good old days". It was also very strongly connected with patriotic feelings and often with nationalism, alien to all those who participated in taking the homeland away. Some authors discussed the danger posed by strong nostalgia. Józef Wittlin, author of a nostalgic book *Mój Lwów* (My Lwów, 1946), wrote in his essays about losing the ability of rationally selecting events and assessing the situation.[46]

---

43 See the webside of the Instytut Literacki, which today is called the Fundation Paryska Kultura: http://kulturaparyska.com/en/ludzie/pokaz/g/jerzy-giedroyc.

44 Since 1971 the smuggling of books to East Central Europe has been organized by the International Advisory Council and also the International Literary Centre and funded by the US Central Intelligence Agency. See, for more, Jerzy Kulczycki, *Atakować książką* (To Attack with a Book), Warszawa, IPN, 2016, pp. 154, 205.

45 Bolesław Hadaczek, *Historia literatury kresowej* (The History of the Literature of Kresy), Kraków, Universitas, 2011, pp. 306–390.

46 Józef Wittlin, *Orfeusz w piekle XX wieku* (Orpheus in the Hell of the Twentieth Century), Paryż 1963, quoted from: Bolesław Hadaczek, *Historia literatury kresowej*, *op. cit.*, p. 324.

One of the writers who managed to overcome nostalgia and to create literature of the highest level was Czesław Miłosz, winner of the 1980 Nobel Prize and from 1961 to 1998 Professor of Slavic Languages and Literatures at the University of California, Berkeley. He was born in 1911 in the village of Szetejnie (today Lithuania) as *kresy* was a part of the Russian Empire. In the novel *Dolina Issy* (The Issa Valley, 1955) and in the memoir *Rodzinna Europa* (Native Realm, 1959), he described his childhood and emphasized his identity with the multi-ethnic Grand Duchy of Lithuania.[47] Dealing with his life in the multi-ethnic Wilno of the inter-war period, he distanced himself from every form of nationalism and criticized the way in which some Polish leaders treated ethnic and religious minorities living in his homeland. Miłosz became famous with his book *Zniewolony umysł* (The Captive Mind, 1953), a study about Polish intellectuals under Communism and their behaviour under a repressive regime.[48]

Czesław Miłosz and other writers with a similar way of thinking developed a critical political and cultural programme, which showed a way of dealing with the loss of *kresy* that offered an alternative to the nationalistic one. This programme was open to dialogue and partnership contacts with the Jewish diaspora and the Eastern neighbours of Poland. It was based on cultivating the *kresy*'s own cultural traditions, but at the same time understanding the differences of other national groups and their attempts to be acknowledged as independent nations. Many books by these authors were smuggled into Poland in the late 1970s and 1980s. They were distributed in the underground and enjoyed great popularity. They also inspired many writers living in the country to work at their own books, and a real boom in works on the subject began after 1989.

Kresy in independent Poland

With the political changes of 1989–90, a process began during which the pent-up longing for the lost Eastern territories was enthusiastically released for the first time in forty-five years. The way of describing the lost, "forbidden" homeland had to be redefined. There was not only the transformation of the political system and the abolition of censorship,

47 Aušra Paulauskienė, *Lost and Found: The Discovery of Lithuania in American Fiction*, Amsterdam, New York, Rodopi, 2007, p. 24.

48 Andrzej Franaszek, *Miłosz. Biografia* (Miłosz. Biography), Kraków, ZNAK, 2011, see also: http://www.milosz.pl.

but also intensive contacts with Poles living in exile who started to visit their country and even moved back home – all of which opened up new possibilities for dealing with the loss of the *kresy*. This development was seen in the context of similar narratives in other European countries, especially in Germany, first divided into East and West and then, after 1989, looking for a new way of presenting its own history stressing the perspective of victimhood. All these components influenced an intense and often emotional public discussion, which started in Poland after 1989 and continues today. A presentation of the different actors taking part in this discussion would go beyond the scope of this chapter. Generally, there are two groups: a Polish-centred, national narrative and a group of activists interested in more transnational and multi-perspective approaches. In the first, some similarities can be found with groups representing German expellees, for example organizing "nostalgic" journeys to the places of origin or stressing the dominant role of Polish culture in the *kresy*. Unlike the German expellees, however, the Poles did not make revisionist demands as they were aware of the right of Lithuanians, Belarussians and Ukrainians to have independent states. Looking for an alternative to the propaganda term "repatriates", some of them started to use the word "expellees" (*wypędzeni*).[49] This has not found widespread acceptance. The term "expellees" was very strongly connected with the fate of Germans and interpreted as a German propaganda term, because of German revisionisms about current Polish Western and Northern territories. As a better solution, some prefer the word *wygnańcy*, which also means expellees, but is an old-fashioned term used in the Bible and in Polish Romantic literature.[50]

As mentioned above, after the first free elections in 1990, the new Polish government was open to friendly cooperation with independent Lithuania, Belarus and Ukraine in its foreign policy developed by Jerzy Giedroyc and Julian Mieroszewski in Paris. A large number of NGOs had been established not only to preserve and cultivate Eastern Polish

---

49 See e.g. an anthology of Polish and German memoirs in which victims of forced migration are called expellees from the East: Hans-Jürgen Bömelburg, Renate Stössinger und Robert Traba (eds), *Vertreibung aus dem Osten. Deutsche und Polen erinnern sich*, Osnabrück, fibre Verlag, 2001; Polish edition: *Wypędzeni ze wschodu. Wspomnienia Polaków i Niemców*, Olsztyn, Stowarzyszenie Wspólnota Kulturowa Borussia, 2000.

50 The idea comes from: Jan M. Piskorski, *Wygnańcy. Przesiedlenia i uchodźcy w dwudziestowiecznej Europie* (The Expelles. Resettlement and Refugees in 20th Century Europe), Warszawa, Państwowy Instytut Wydawniczy, 2010; German edition: *Die Verjagten. Flucht und Vertreibung im Europa des 20.* Jahrhundert, München, Siedler, 2013.

traditions, but also to look for possibilities of working together with people still living in territories that had belonged to Poland until World War II. Most organizations had a regional or local character such as the Association of Friends of Lwów, or the Association of Friends of Wilno. They collected information about history and culture and organized cultural events and sentimental journeys, in which the remnants of Polish culture were the main points of interest.

Two other organizations located in the Eastern Polish periphery, close to the Polish–Lithuanian and Polish–Russian border, were founded with very different ideas: the Association of the "Borussia" Cultural Community (*Stowarzyszenie Wspólnota Kulturowa "Borussia"*) in Olsztyn and the centre "Borderland of Arts, Cultures and Nations" ("*Ośrodek Pogranicze – sztuk, kultur, narodów*") in Sejny. The leaders of these organizations came to the small cities in Polish North-Eastern periphery[51] from Warsaw, having had experiences in the anti-communist opposition. They offered an alternative to presenting Poland as a homogeneous state of one ethnic group. They viewed the landscape on both sides of Poland's current Eastern border as a space of overlapping cultures, religions and languages, very heavily affected by the historical cataclysms and totalitarian ideologies of the twentieth century. Krzysztof Czyżewski described the region as a ruined "Atlantis" in which everything had been destroyed.[52] In his opinion, the area was filled with traces of the end of the world, the end of the "old civilization". The physical evidence is still present and the goal of this activist is to discover different shifts of the past and deal with them in order to work on cultural bridge building.[53] The second organization, *Borussia*, based its action programme on similar ideas and developed a method of activism with the name "open regionalism". It works on building and deepening the culture of dialogue and tolerance

[51] Olsztyn (Allenstein) is a city in a formerly Eastern Prussian territory. Sejny has a large Lithuanian minority and a rich Jewish heritage and is very close to the birthplace of Czesław Miłosz.

[52] Krzysztof Czyżewski is a Polish author from Poznań with a degree in Polish literature. He was closely related to avant-garde theatre movements and some underground periodicals, e.g. *Czas Kultury* (Time of Culture) in the 1970s and 1980s. In 1990, he was one of the initiators of the 'Borderland' Foundation and became its president.

[53] This idea can probably be traced back to Karl Schlögel, *Die Mitte liegt ostwärts. Die Deutschen, Mitteleuropa und der verlorene Osten*, Berlin, Siedler, 1986. The webside of the Centre Borderland: http://pogranicze.sejny.pl/?lang=en. See also: Matthew Carr, *Fortress Europe: Dispatches from a Gated Continent*, New York, New Press, 2012, p. 226.

among people of different nationalities, religions and traditions, and on supporting the development of civil society.[54] Both organizations have been awarded international prizes and are still organizing many artistic, editorial, historical and other projects.

A similar point of view can be found in the writings of Andrzej Stasiuk, one of the most successful and internationally acclaimed contemporary Polish writers and journalists. His travel literature and essays deal with the reality of East-Central Europe and its relationship with the West. In his books *Opowieści galicyjskie* (Tales of Galicia 1995), *Przez rzekę* (Across the River 1996) and *Dukla* (Dukla, 1997), he makes a point of presenting the diversity of this part of Europe and, drawing on postcolonial ideas, criticizes "Polishness as a sort of feeling of superiority".[55] With this statement, Stasiuk stresses an important point that has been often overlooked. Many authors, researchers and organizations dealing with the past of *kresy* mention the multicultural character of this region and describe the more or less peaceful coexistence of different ethnic and religious groups. Yet they do so from the perspective of Polish leaders holding power, or landowners or intellectuals bringing culture and civilization to "less developed" minorities. Jacek Kolbuszewski already noted some aspects of this problem in his book about *kresy* published in 1995.[56] Other works by two historians, Timothy Snyder and Daniel Beauvois, also opened up new perspectives. The first looked for circumstances in which the modern nations of Poles, Lithuanians, Belarussians and Ukrainians were born.[57] The second was more interested in the relationship between different social strata in the *kresy* of the late eighteenth and nineteenth centuries.[58] This study shows some similarities with colonialism in other

---

54 http://borussia.pl/. See also Robert Traba, *Kraina tysiąca granic. Szkice o historii i pamięci* (Land of a Thousand Borders. Drafts about History and Memory), Olsztyn, Stowarzyszenie WK Borussia, 2003, p. 155–276.

55 Tomasz Machała, "Andrzej Stasiuk's European lesson", *Wprost*, 26 December 2011. See also http://www.voxeurop.eu/en/content/article/1319171-andrzej-stasiuk-s-european-lesson

56 Jacek Kolbuszewski, *Kresy*, *op. cit.*

57 Timothy Snyder, *The Reconstruction of Nations*, *op. cit.*

58 Daniel Beauvois (ed.), *Les confins de l'ancienne Pologne: Ukraine, Lituanie, Biélorussie XVIe–XXe siècles*, foreword by Czesław Miłosz, Villeneuve d'Ascq, Presses Universitaires de Lille, 1988; Daniel Beauvois, *Histoire de la Pologne*, Paris, Hatier, 1995; Daniel Beauvois, *Polacy na Ukrainie 1831–1863. Szlachta polska na Wołyniu, Podolu i Kijowszczyźnie* (The Polish Nobility in Wolyn, Podole and the Region of Kiev), Paris, Instytut Literacky, 1987; Daniel Beauvois, *Trójkąt ukraiński. Szlachta, carat i lud na Wołyniu, Podolu i Kijowszczyźnie 1793–1914* (Ukrainian triangle. The

parts of the world at that time and raises many new questions that helped deconstruct the myth of *kresy* that embellishes the Polish role and its civilizing power. Many of these issues were dealt with in a 2015 special edition of the popular Polish journal *Polityka* with the title "Kresy – The Huge Myth of the Poles".[59]

In light of the changing nature of official memory and public discourse, two important viewpoints can be observed in Poland in the last few years. On 10 April 2010 a Polish government aircraft crashed near Katyń, on Smolensk Military Air Base. A delegation of 96 key political figures led by the Polish President Lech Kaczyński was on board, travelling to commemorate the Massacre of Katyń in 1940. This tragedy brought all Poles together in deep mourning, but over time it became an increasing cause of division in Polish society. The conservative party, *Prawo i Sprawiedliwość* (PiS), led by Jarosław Kaczyński, the brother of the President Lech Kaczyński, challenged the results of the investigation declaring that the crash was an accident and instead suggested it had been caused by Russia. As the party won the Polish parliamentary elections in 2015 and created a majority government, a second viewpoint appeared. The government not only started a new investigation into the plane crash, it also introduced a new history policy with the goal of glorifying and secularizing Poland's past. To assess the impact of these changes, historians will need some distance over time to gain perspective. But we may expect that under the influence of these new policies, collective memory about the lost *kresy* will also change.

Hopefully, communicative memory will not be dominated by one political option and its contents that will be deposited in cultural memory[60] in a few decades, and instead a kind of melting pot of different ideas will emerge. The loss of the Eastern Polish lands remains an important part of national remembrance. The challenge is to work on this issue with critical analysis and open dialogue to find a middle way between the imaginings of a lost Arcadia and the bloodlands of East-Central Europe.

Nobility, Tsarism and Folk in Wolyn, Podole and the Region of Kiev 1793–1914), Lublin, UMCS, 2005; Daniel Beauvois, *Wilno – polska stolica kulturalna zaboru rosyjskiego 1803–1832* (Wilnus – Polish Culture Centre of Russian Annexation 1803–1832), Wrocław, Wydawnictwo Uniwersytetu Wrocławskiego, 2010.

59 *Kresy Rzeczpospolitej. Wielki mit Polaków, op. cit.*

60 Aleida Assman, *Cultural Memory and Western Civilization: Functions, Media, Archives*, Cambridge, Cambridge University Press, 2012.

The Ties of Greek and Turkish Refugees and "Exchangees" to their Lost Homelands: An Asymmetry of Memory

Michel Bruneau
CNRS-Bordeaux

From the Balkan Wars (1912–13) to the population exchanges under the Treaty of Lausanne (1923), the disappearance of the Ottoman Empire reordered the territories and populations of the Greek and Turkish states. Muslim refugees from the Balkans and Greece, and Greek Orthodox Christians from Asia Minor and Eastern Thrace, were torn from their places of birth, their "homelands", and reimplanted in their new homelands.[1] This violent uprooting and reinsertion caused pain on both sides. However, the memory of the "lost homelands", long ignored or concealed in both countries, subsequently fared quite differently in Greece and Turkey. In Greece, beginning in the 1970s there have emerged many voluntary associations of refugees from Asia Minor in the broadest interpretation, shrines and commemorative monuments have been erected, and pilgrimages have been held. Demands that a "genocide" should be recognized became central from the late 1980s. In Turkey, the expression of this memory occurred later, in the 1990s, among descendants of the "exchanges",[2] and has been less widespread and publicized. Are these differences to be explained by sharply differing historical, social and political contexts in the two countries? How involved,

1 Greece is known as the 'motherland'. Turkey was a new state, the republic of Kemal Atatürk, which was from the outset revered in nationalist terms so as to fill the vacuum caused by the disappearance of the Ottoman Empire.

2 The word 'exchangees' (tr: *mübadilleri*) is used only by Turkish associations, whereas in Greece the more general term 'refugees' (el: *prosfuges*) is used, which includes the exchangees. This may be because the Turkish government organized the exchange and it lasted around a year, whereas the Greeks left hastily, often in panic, as a result of war and ethnic cleansing.

if at all, were the two governments? What relations do the refugees and their descendants in these two nation-states maintain with the memory of their lands and cultures of origin? What commemorative frameworks have official Greek and Turkish historical discourses provided for this memory? Have they enabled this memory to express itself or have they rather marginalized it?

Achieving ethnic homogeneity in the Greek and Turkish nation-states

The consequences of Greece's military defeat ("Asia Minor Catastrophe", 1922) and the massive arrival of refugees before and after the Treaty of Lausanne (1923) changed the nature of the Greek nation-state and brought about the birth of a Turkish one. By abandoning the "Great Idea" (*Megali Idea*), with its echoes of the Byzantine Empire, the Greek nation-state became more ethnically homogeneous as it lost many of its Muslim and other minorities and began to look more like the Turkish nation-state of the Kemalist republic that had emerged after the Armenian genocide and the ethnic cleansing of the Christian minorities.

While the Young Turks of the CUP (Committee for Union and Progress) were relinquishing multi-ethnic Ottomanism to push for a Turkish nation-state on the Western model, finally achieved by Kemal Atatürk, the Greeks, who on Independence had first followed the same model with reference to Ancient Greece, then reintroduced an imperial concept inspired by Byzantium, the ideology of the *Megali Idea*. This grand dream was irrevocably destroyed by the Great Catastrophe (*Megali Katastrofi*), which brought Greece back to the more modest size of a nation-state that had become ethnically homogeneous with the settlement of over a million refugees, most from Asia Minor and Eastern Thrace, taking the place of half a million Muslim exchangees, mainly from Northern Greece and the Aegean islands. The Greek nation-state became the mirror image of the Turkish Kemalist republic across the Aegean.[3]

---

[3] Michel Bruneau, *De l'Asie Mineure à la Turquie: Minorités, homogénéisation ethno-nationale, diasporas*, Paris, CNRS-Editions, 2015, 412 p; Bruce Clark, *Twice a Stranger: How Mass Expulsion Forged Modern Greece and Turkey*, London, Granta Books, 2006, 274 p.

Figure 7: *Expulsions and displacement of minorities in Turkey and surrounding lands (1830–1924)*

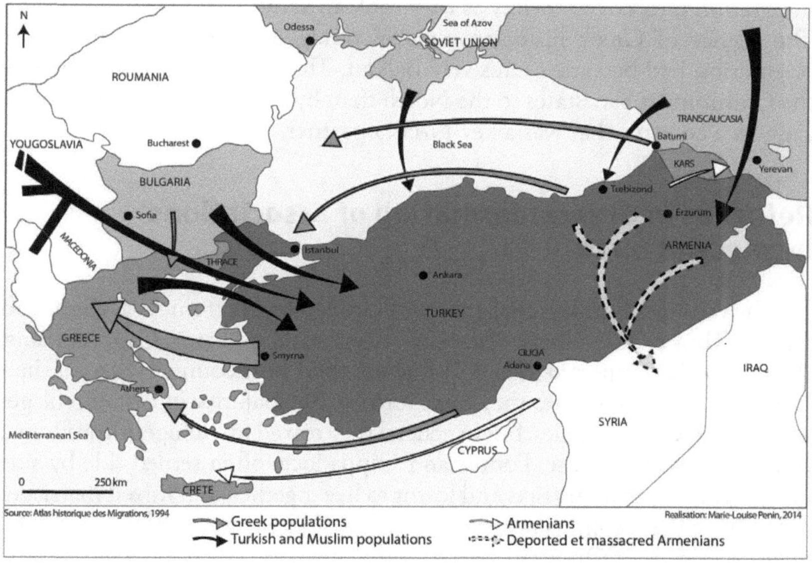

The Greek authorities long ignored this period of their country's history, largely so as to maintain good relations with their Turkish neighbours (Inönü–Venizelos Greek–Turkish Friendship Treaty, 1930). This enabled them to avoid revealing the real responsibilities of the various political and military leaders for the catastrophe, and not embarrass the Western powers who needed Turkey's support against the Eastern Bloc during the Cold War. Until the 1980s, those who had survived the Great Catastrophe and the massacres were required to erase from their memories what had happened in Turkey from the turn of the twentieth century till 1922.[4]

4 In the first years after the refugees' arrival in Greece they were poorly received by the 'autochthones'. In Athens, for example, they settled in districts of Piraeus and the Athens suburbs outside the older inhabited areas. First the Royalists and then the dictator Metaxas encouraged hostility against them and even racism from the Greek population against refugees called *Tourkosporoi* (Turk seeds) or *Tourkomerites* (Turk born). Politically, most refugees backed Venizelos, at least until the Greek–Turkish friendship treaty of 1930 whereby the Greek government gave up any claim for damages from the Turkish government for property 'abandoned' by the refugees. Then they turned more to the Left and the Communist Party. See Vlassis Agtzidis, "Mnimi, tavtotita kai ideologia ston pontiako ellinismo" (Memory, Identity and Ideology in Pontic Hellenism), in Giorgos

The refugees' first concern had been survival. World War II and German occupation then froze the situation, and incidentally enabled their better integration into Greek society as they took an active part in the Resistance. The silence of Greek historians was encouraged by governments whose orientation had become exclusively Balkan. They were more concerned by the Communist Slav states to the North than by Turkish nationalism to the East, in a country that was a key NATO partner.

Refugees in Greece: formation of associations by place of birth

The various ethno-regional groups of Greek refugees from Asia Minor and Eastern Thrace (Anatolians, Thracians, Constantinopolitans, Cappadocians, Pontic Greeks) dispersed after 1914 across their host country, Greece, their "motherland". Sometimes they even formed the majority in certain villages and districts of major cities, but in general they mixed in. Refugees from Ionia, Bithynia, Eastern Thrace, Pontus and Cappadocia often settled side by side in villages and urban districts and learnt to live together, and mixed marriages occurred in the second generation. A "refugee" identity emerged, marked by their experience of Ottoman society, more open and cosmopolitan than the closed peasant society of mainland Greece at that time. A key feature of the identity they shared that distinguished them from "autochthonous" Greeks was the strength of their commitment to the Orthodox faith, maintained by the Ottoman *millet* system. This found expression in a strong attachment to their churches and monasteries as places of pilgrimage.[5]

Kokkinos, Elli Lemonidou, Vlassis Agtzidis (ed.), *To travma kai i politikes tis mnimis* (The Trauma and the Politics Of Memory), Athens, Taxidevtis, 2010, pp. 240–246.

5 Renée Hirschon, *Heirs of the Greek Catastrophe: The Social Life of Asia Minor Refugees in Piraeus*, Oxford, Clarendon Press, 1989, 280 p.

Figure 8: *Refugees in Greece (1928)*

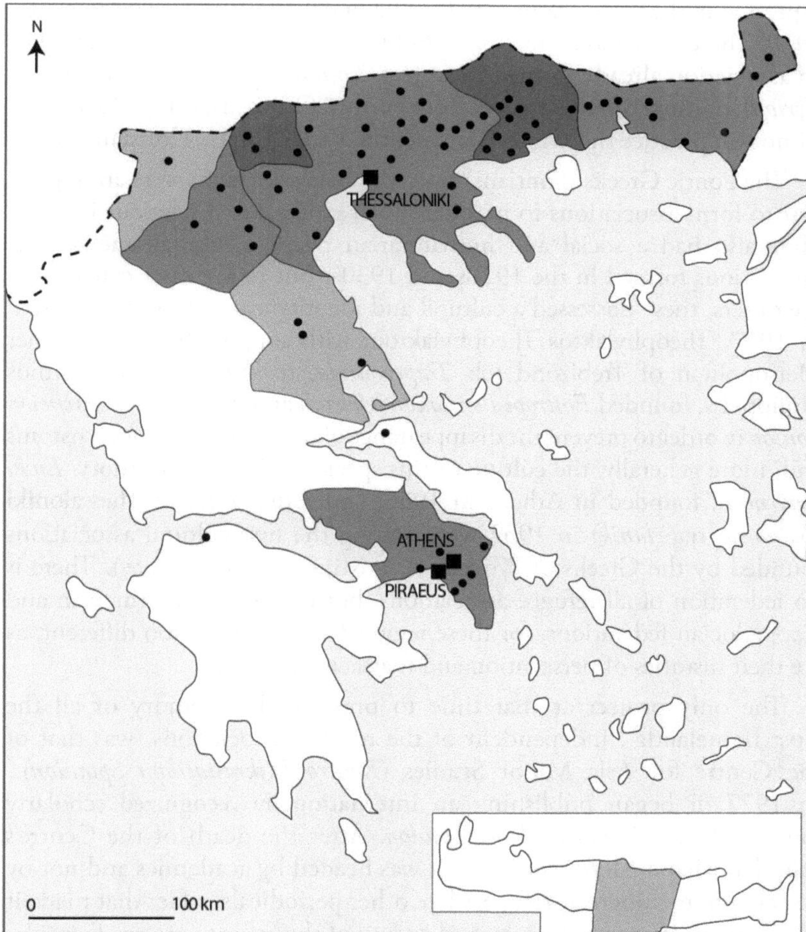

Source: J. Sion, 1937, p.516

Realisation: Marie-Louise Penin, 2014

Percentage of refugees

- 10 - 20% of the population of the departement (nomos)
- 25 - 50% of the population of the departement
- More than 50% of the population of the departement
- ■ Cities with more than 100,000 refugees
- • Main settlement centres: about 1 per 10,000 refugees

Their relationship to the memory of their "lost homelands" was best expressed in the associations they formed in the 1930s and even more after 1970. These were based on a place of birth (e.g. Smyrna, Bafra, Santa) or an association already formed there (e.g. *Efxinos Leschi*, *Merimna Pontion Kyrion*), or more often a larger region: Pontus, Caucasus, Cappadocia, Asia Minor (in practice the Western and central part), Thrace, Constantinople.

The Pontic Greeks (Pontians) from the Black Sea coast were among the first to form associations to maintain their cultural and religious identity. They also had a social and humanitarian purpose, like all the refugee associations formed in the 1920s and 1930s. But to a greater extent than the others, these possessed a cultural and identity aspect from the outset.[6] In 1927, Theophylaktos Theophylaktou, with support from the former Metropolitan of Trebizond (el: *Trapezounda*, tr *Trabzon*), Chrysanthos Philippidis, founded *Epitropi Pontiakon Meleton* and its periodical *Archeion Pontou* in order to prevent the disappearance of the Pontic language, customs and, more generally, the culture of this special society and territory. *Enosi Smyrneon*, founded in Athens in 1936, and *Ioniki Estia* in Thessaloniki (*Salonica*, tr *Selanik*) in 1952 were among the first cultural associations founded by the Greeks of Western Asia Minor (el: *Mikrasiates*). There is no federation of all refugee associations, but rather Pontic, Thracian and Cappadocian federations, for these regional identities are too different, as are their histories of persecution and massacres suffered.

The only project at that time to preserve the memory of all the "lost homelands", independent of the refugee associations, was that of the Centre for Asia Minor Studies (*Kentro Mikrasiatikon Spoudon*).[7] In 1977, it began publishing an internationally recognized scholarly journal, *Deltio Mikrasiatikon Spoudon*. After the death of the Centre's founder, Melpō Merlié, in 1976, it was headed by academics and not by association members or refugees like other periodicals, a fact that made it exceptional. It cannot be attached to any of the refugee groups from the

6 K. St. Hatzikyriakidis, "I syllogiki organosi ton Ellinon tou Pontou prin kai meta tin 'Exodo' tou 22" (The Associations of Pontic Greeks Before and After the Exodus of 1922), *Evxinos Pontos*, 16 (182), March 2012, pp. 14–16.

7 It was due to a private initiative by the ethno-musicologist Melpō Merlié with support from the *Institut Français*, whose director was her husband, Octave Merlier. Its purpose, stated more accurately in 1949, became the recording, collection and conservation of data and testimony on the history and culture of the Greek communities of Asia Minor, some of which were published in the *Exodos* volumes classified by major region of origin.

"lost homelands", but is devoted to all of them without distinction.[8] The *Kentro* is a scholarly research and documentation centre with no other purpose than the scholarly study of the refugees' territories and societies of origin.

It was thus among the refugee associations that the collective memory of the "lost homelands" was cultivated by members and friendly historians, who wanted to make those lands "unforgettable" and not admit they were irrevocably lost. This concern for memory was all the stronger for being attached to a society and territory that were clearly distinct from Greece, which was now their shared "motherland".[9] In the years following the Treaty of Lausanne (1923), and the refugees' settlement and integration in Greece, as the second generation became wealthier, the refugees and their descendants were increasingly faced with a choice: either assimilate almost entirely into Hellene society, maintaining only a minimal or symbolic identity and commemorative link with their "lost homeland", or preserve a strong identity and commemorative attachment to their territory and society of origin, by assembling a rich "iconography", building places of memory in Greece and the Diaspora, and holding large numbers of cultural and commemorative events. The former option was chosen by most of the *Mikrasiates* and Thracians, who were a statistical majority of the refugees (57% in the 1928 census), and the latter by most of the Pontic Greeks and to a lesser extent the Cappadocians. The Pontians and Cappadocians were the least numerous of the refugees (some 17%). There is thus no correlation between the size of a group and its relationship with its memory.[10]

---

8 Paschalis M. Kitromilidis, *Exintapente chronia epistimonikis prosforas* (Sixty-five Years of Scientific Offering), Kentro Mikrasiatikon Spoudon, 1996, 138 p.

9 In the first generation, the 'entrepreneurs of memory' were intellectuals, writers or notables from the 'lost homelands', such as Philon Ktenidis, the playwright and poet behind the project to re-create the Pontic Sumela Monastery in Macedonia, and Chrysanthos Philippidis, the former Metropolitan of Trebizond, who became Archbishop of Athens. In the second generation, they were more often association heads and historians such as Kostas Fotiadis, the historian of the Pontic 'genocide', Vlassis Agtzidis, who runs a research seminar into the history of the refugees supported by the town council of Kifissia (Athens), and the publisher Tassos Kyriakidis in Thessaloniki.

10 According to the latest statistics on refugee associations in Greece (Hellenic Resources Network, *Organisations of the Greek Refugies in Greece*, 2012, http://www.hri.org/forum/diaspora/mikrasia/organ.htlm.), Pontic Greeks have 286 associations in three federations, plus 32 associations of people repatriated from the former USSR (*Palinostountes*) since 1990, making a total of 318, the *Mikrasiates* 120 associations in two federations, and the Eastern Thracians 32. In addition, the *Panellinia Enosi*

Ethno-regional groups of Orthodox Greek refugees and their relationship with memory

The memory work of refugees thus varied according to their places and territories of origin and the local cultures and histories connected to those origins. The great mass of refugees from Western Asia Minor, Ionia, Aeolia, Bithynia and central Anatolia belonged to the Aegean Basin that was the heartland of Hellene culture. They had maintained many uninterrupted relations of all sorts (migration, trade, cultural exchange) with continental Greece and those islands that since 1821 had made up a nation-state on the European model. Eastern Thrace also belonged to this Aegean group, but its closeness to, indeed location within, the Balkans made it a special case, particularly because of the presence of many Bulgarians seeking to extend their own nation-state.

Conversely, two more distant territories, cut off from the Aegean Basin by lands with a Muslim majority, were distinguished by clear geographical and linguistic features, namely mountainous Pontus beside the Black Sea (*Pontus Euxinus*) in North-Eastern Asia Minor and Cappadocia in central Anatolia, a plateau of easily excavated volcanic tuff (troglodyte dwellings, churches and monasteries), where they mostly spoke Turkish or an archaic Greek dialect. Each of these two regions had its own special history going back to the Byzantine period, which was different from the Aegean regions directly linked to Greece. Since the nomadic Seljuk, and later Ottoman, Turks found it harder to settle in densely populated Pontus, the region had done better at preserving its language and religion. Its location by the Black Sea, near the Caucasus, had caused its emigrants to head round along the coastline and towards the Russian Empire, not the Aegean Basin. The Pontic Greeks began their memory work much sooner than the other refugees by assembling an

Kappadokikon Somation, founded in 2008, comprises 52 Cappadocian associations. These figures show the vigorous commitment of the Pontians and Cappadocians, the fewest in number but the most active. Similarly, there is no correlation between the population size of each of these groups and the number of commemorative monuments dedicated to them, since of the sample of 62 monuments we studied in 2004 (see Michel Bruneau and Kyriakos Papoulidis, "La mémoire des patries inoubliables", *Vingtième siècle, Revue d'Histoire*, No. 78, Vol. 2, 2003) more than half are paid for and dedicated to the Pontians (36: 58%), while the refugees from Asia Minor in the most restricted sense (Ionian coast and Bithynia), far more numerous, have only built 12 monuments (19%). The many Thracians have built only 3 monuments (5%) and the Cappadocians 1 (2%).

"iconography" and constructing places of memory first in Greece and then in the Diaspora.[11]

From the Sumela Virgin icon to Pontic Greek "iconography"

In Macedonia, the Pontic Greeks reconstructed the Byzantine monasteries that had been their focal points in Pontus, so that the first generation of refugees, who had known the original monasteries, could pass on to following generations the memory of their homeland and identity via "iconography".[12] These monasteries – Panagia Soumela, Saint John Vazelon, Saint George Peristereota, Panagia Goumera, Saint Theodore Gavras – reconstructed in the Greek region of Macedonia (1950–80) are the objects of annual pilgrimages lasting from one to three days, on their saints' days.[13] These revered reconstructed monasteries contain most of the symbols that make up the Pontic iconography, outside the main shrines and sacred objects. Buildings have been erected by associations with their own resources to house pilgrims (*xenones*). This is particularly striking at Panagia Soumela. Each smaller region (Sanda), city (Tripoli) and town (Kromni, Imera, Livera) in Pontus that had set up its own active association in Greece was eager to have a presence at

---

11 Their unbroken history dating back to the Byzantine period of the Komnenos Empire of Trebizond (1204–1461), when they had their own state, and their remoteness from Greece encouraged the formation of a separate identity. Consequently, at the Peace Conference (1919), the Metropolitan of Trebizond, Chrysanthos Philippidis, had pressed for the creation of an independent Republic of Pontus.

12 The concept of iconography is taken from Jean Gottmann: "An iconography is the sum of beliefs, symbols, images, ideas, etc. that a community has inherited and to which its members are attached. This bond between the people and their 'icons' is the glue that holds the group together, and leads to the definition of a territory from which members of other communities, attached to other iconographies, are excluded"; see Jean Gottmann, *Eléments de géographie politique*, Paris, Cours de droit, 1955, II, 2000. This "set of abstract and concrete symbols that summarise a group's shared beliefs and interests is the glue that provides the group with its cohesion and political personality". Jean Gottmann, *La Politique des Etats et leur géographie*, Paris, Armand Colin, 1995, 228 p.; Michel Bruneau, "De l'icône à l'iconographie, du religieux au politique, réflexions sur l'origine byzantine d'un concept gottmanien", *Annales de Géographie*, 616, 2000, pp. 563–579.

13 Thousands of pilgrims are bused out from cities and countryside, and some fly in from distant countries. There are roughly one hundred thousand at Panagia Soumela every 15 August.

Panagia Soumela in the form of a hostel for its own pilgrims. It became a sort of scale model of the homeland.[14]

Since the Pontic Greeks built a shrine (chapel and later basilica) at Kastania in the Vermio Mountains to house the Virgin Mary icon from Sumela (*Panagia* [all-holy] *Soumela*) and revived the pilgrimages on 15 August, the Feast of the Dormition, they have accumulated an extensive "iconography" to support their memory and assert their identity. These symbols are published in their magazines and feature on their commemorative monuments and websites. In addition to the Virgin of Sumela, the key most emblematic element, there are the resistance fighter *Antartis*, the single-headed eagle of Sinope (fourth century BC), the bottle-shaped bowed lyra (*kemençe*), the last two lines of a folk lament for the loss of *Rhōmania*, *Agia Sofia* and the *Phrontisterion* school in Trabzon (Trebizond), Pontic dances, language and theatre. All of these are emblematic symbols of Pontic Greek culture and identity. They are the firm foundation on which this identity rests and from which it can be transmitted. Attempts since 1988 to have the 'genocide' of the Pontic Greeks internationally recognized have become another driving force in the assertion of the identity of the refugees and their descendants, now spreading to the *Mikrasiates* and Thracians despite their differences.

In the 1980s, a debate arose within the Pontic associations and among Greek politicians about whether there was a "genocide" of the Pontic Greeks, and then of all Ottoman Greeks, between 1916 and 1923, for which responsibility lay with the Young Turk senior Ottoman authorities, particularly Talaat Pasha, Minister of the Interior, and then Mustafa Kemal. The debate began in 1985, the year of the first world Pontian congress when Polychronis Enepekidis, an Austrian historian of Pontic Greek origin, revealed documents found in Vienna and Berlin in the foreign ministry archives of Turkey's two allies during World War I. Other Pontic historians, particularly Kostas Fotiadis and Charalambos Tsirkinidis, brought together

14 The erection in Macedonia of these places recalling the original monasteries in Pontus, with their importance for identity, is echoed in more distant lands of exile, such as America and Australia. The Pontians in America got together to create a site of pilgrimage and shrine devoted to Panagia Soumela at West Milford (NJ). A copy of the Sumela Virgin icon was sent to Australia in 1967, and Flagpole Hill, 80 km North of Melbourne, renamed Mount Mela, is currently being prepared for it. Since 2003, a large gathering has been held every year on the model of the one at the Panagia Soumela shrine in Greece. Michel BRUNEAU, "Des icônes aux églises et aux monastères reconstruits par les Réfugiés grecs d'Asie Mineure sur les lieux de leur exil", *Diasporas, Histoire et Sociétés*, numéro thématique *Dieux-valises*, No.12, 2008, p. 36.

documents from the archives of the UK Foreign Office, Greek foreign ministry and French defence ministry (Château de Vincennes). Most of these documents and various first-hand testimonies were published (2004) by Fotiadis in Thessaloniki (Irodotos, 10 vols). The massacres and deportations (forced marches) caused many deaths from 1916 to 1923: the figure of 350,000 victims is claimed by the associations, for a Pontic Greek population estimated at some 700,000 at the start of the twentieth century. This estimate appears to have been put forward because it corresponds to half the Greek population of Pontus in 1914, one element in the definition of a genocide according to Raphael Lemkin. The figure has not been subject to any careful discussion or debate.

The demand for international recognition of this genocide became from 1988 a central topic at world Pontian meetings, with the aim of obtaining an official apology from the Turkish government like the one the Jews obtained from the German government. So far only the Greek (1994) and Swedish (2011) governments have recognized this genocide. Outside Greece, those who are pressing most actively for recognition, particularly at the United Nations, are members of the Diaspora in the USA, Canada and Australia. A monument in honour of the victims of the Pontic Greek genocide has been erected in Toronto and in Munich (2018), another is planned for Boston. The research for evidence is well advanced but still incomplete. It is easier to establish genocide in the case of Pontus, which was always outside the scope of Greek military intervention, than for Ionia and Eastern Thrace, where the Greek army fought the Turkish army (May 1919–September 1922). The use of the term "genocide" seems more justified for the Pontic Greeks, because their case presents the same patterns and characteristics as the earlier example of the Armenians.

Vlassis Agtzidis makes the point that twenty-one years after the first commemorative law concerning the Pontic Greek "genocide" (1994), on the initiative of parliamentarians of Pontic Greek origin, Greek public opinion and most Greek historians still do not feel concerned by the question of the "genocide" of the Ottoman Greeks and do not wish to recognize it as a genocide.[15] The Greek government still does not want to compromise its good relations with Turkey by supporting the memory of

[15] Vlassis, Agtzidis, "Genoktonia ston Ponto: peri ton pragmatikon megethon kai orion tou istorikou gegonotos" (Genocide in Pontos: About the Real Extent and Limit of the Historical Event), *Evxinos Pontos*, 214, Maios, 2015, p. 260–279.

the refugees of 1923. The academic community, with few exceptions, has never really sought to find evidence and arguments to support recognition of this genocide by the Turkish authorities. Only a handful of historians with a background in the refugee community and Pontic Greek associations continue to research and take part in the annual commemorations (19 May and 24 September). Left-wing Turkish historians (Taner Akçam, Fuat Dündar, Uğur Ümit Üngör),[16] working with fewer restraints, have produced new data from their study of Ottoman and other archives. Pontian Diaspora associations in Australia, Canada, Sweden and the USA have been much more active and effective than those in Greece itself, and have obtained recognition of the genocide by the local, and in the case of Sweden national, authorities in their host countries.

Over the last twenty years, it has been the commemorative monuments dedicated to the victims of the "genocide" of either Pontic Greeks or Asia Minor Greeks that have been the most visible manifestations of the memory work carried out by the associations of refugees and their descendants.

Commemorative monuments, vectors of refugees' narrative of memory/history

Between 1986 and 2001, the Greek government established a legal framework for commemoration. Since the Greek parliament's official recognition in 1994 of the Pontic Greek "genocide" and the commemorative date of 19 May, followed in 1998 by a further law establishing 14 September as a "Day of National Memory of the genocide of the Greeks of Asia Minor by the Turkish authorities", monuments have

16 Taner Akçam, "The Young Turks and the Plans for the Ethnic Homogenization of Anatolia", in Omer Bartov, Eric D. Weitz (ed.), *Shatterzone of Empires: Coexistence and Violence in the German, Habsburg, Russian, and Ottoman Borderlands*, Bloomington, Indiana University Press, 2013, pp. 258–279; Fuat Dündar, *Ittihat ve Terraki'nin Müslümanlari Iskân Politikasi (1913–1918)* (The Code of Contemporary Turkey: The "Union and Progress" Engineering of Ethnicities (1913–1918)), Istanbul, Iletisim, 2008, consulted in a Greek translation published in 2014; Ugur Ümit Üngör, "Seeing Like a Nation-state: Young Turk Social Engineering in Eastern Turkey, 1913–50", in Dominik J. Schaller, Jürgen Zimmerer (eds.), *Late Ottoman Genocides: The Dissolution of the Ottoman Empire and Young Turkish Population and Extermination policies*, London, Routledge, 2009, pp. 9–33.

been built in each town, and even each village, inhabited by descendants of refugees.[17]

These monuments in public spaces are due above all to the action of associations and local authorities, with the decisive financial support of the Greek government, which, seventy years after the exile, recognized the right to and duty of memory. Their presence and the commemorative ceremonies held once or twice a year are a visible manifestation for the Greek people of this right to memory and difference. These monuments have, therefore, the dual function of transmitting both the memory and the identity of the refugee Greeks within the Greek "motherland".[18]

---

17 The Greek parliament and government finally recognized a right to and duty of memory for the former refugees from Asia Minor and their descendants under pressure from associations and some parliamentarians. The motion for parliament to recognize 19 May as the date of commemoration of the Pontic Greek genocide was sponsored by 22 Pasok members of Pontic origins in 1991. The bill prepared within the Pasok parliamentary party was passed in 1994.

In this way, a legislative framework was gradually created between 1986 and 2001. The first act, passed in 1986, declared 14 September to be a "Day of national memory for the victims of the Asia Minor disaster in 1922", and a commemoration in honour of those who were massacred was to be held each year by the prefect of Piraeus in the municipality of Nea Smyrni. The choice of municipality was a symbolic one, because it was considered to comprise a high proportion of refugees and bore a particularly significant name. It was on 14 September 1922 that King Constantine abdicated and fled to Italy, while Kemal's Turkish army had entered Smyrna (tr: *İzmir*) on 9 September and a revolutionary committee was set up in Mytilene on 11–12 September to organize the repatriation of what was left of the Greek army in Asia Minor and prepare the installation of a military government of national salvation. This date also recalls the start of the Great Fire of Smyrna, which lasted three days. It is thus a symbolic date representing the army's final defeat and rout, the fire of Smyrna and the massacres that occurred during the forced deportation of the Greek population of that city and its region.

In March 1994, a new act was passed establishing 19 May as a "Day of memory of the genocide of the Greeks of Pontus", the date of Kemal Atatürk's landing in Samsun, marking the start of a series of massacres, and considered by the associations as the beginning of the Pontic Greek genocide (19 May 1919). In October 1998, another act was passed by the Greek parliament establishing 14 September as a "Day of national memory of the genocide of the Greeks of Asia Minor by the Turkish authorities". Although the two acts were passed unanimously by members of all parties, the presidential decree laying down the organization by prefects of "ceremonies of commemoration including a Te Deum, speeches and the laying of wreaths at the head offices of departments and provinces with the participation of representatives of refugees' and women's associations" was not signed until September 2001. See Vlassis Agtzidis, "Mnimci, tavtotita kai ideologia ston pontiako ellinismo", *op. cit.*, pp. 260–279.

18 Michel Bruneau, Kyriakos Papoulidis, *I Mnimi tou prosfygikou Ellinismou: ta anegerthenta mnimeia stin Ellada (1936–2004)*, Thessalonique, Adelfon Kyriakidis,

Figure 9: *"Pontic Greek genocide", commemorative monument in Kastoria (built in 2001). Bas-relief of the Pontians' mythical history; bust of the nationalist hero Kapetanidis; map of the Pontic Republic territory claimed at the 1919 Peace Conference*

© Michel Bruneau

The emblematic bronze figure found on most of these monuments is the "Pontic hero", also often called *Akritas*, that is, guardian of the frontiers of the Byzantine Empire (*Akrita tou Pontou*), or *Antartis*, resistance fighter.[19]

2004, 133 p; Michel Bruneau, Kyriakos Papoulidis, "Remembering the Genocide and the 'Unforgettable Homelands': The Erection of Commemorative Monuments in Greece by the Refugees of Asia Minor", in Matthias Bjornlund, Tessa Hofmann, Vasileios Meichanetsidis (eds.), *The Genocide of Ottoman Greeks*, Athens and New York, A. D. Caratzas, 2011, pp. 350–369.

19 Carved life-size or larger (2.2 metres in Kozani), wearing traditional Pontic uniform (*zipkas*), he is the symbol of the fierce resistance put up by the Pontic Greeks in the mountains of Pontus from 1916 to 1922, and more broadly, the legendary hero, Digenis Akritas, lord of the Byzantine borders, emphasizing the territorial aspect of this memory.

The Greeks of Western Asia Minor (*Mikrasiates*) have also built memorials, but these are less numerous and varied than the Pontic ones. The emblematic figure of Chrysostomos, the last Metropolitan of Smyrna, martyred in 1922, looms large in Athens and Thessaloniki. It is in the Greater Athens district of Nea Smyrni (New Smyrna) that the largest memorial site to the Hellenism of Asia Minor (Estia) can be found.

Figure 10: *Monuments to the memory of Hellenism of Asia Minor (Ionia, Cappadocia, Eastern Thrace) (1936-2004)*

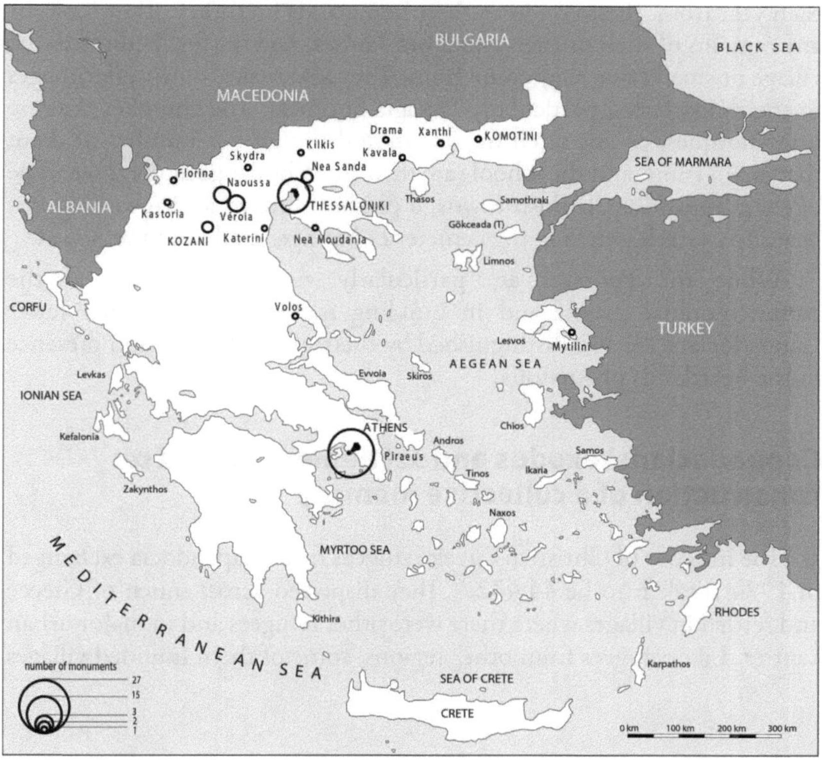

The right to memory demanded by the refugees and not least their descendants has now found other forms of expression. The refugee associations seek the creation of a museum of Anatolian or Oriental Greeks in Athens. *Enosi Smyrneon* initiated the plan for a national museum of Oriental Greeks. And the Pontians were not slow to set up their own museum in the building of *Epitropi Pontiakon Meleton*, in Nea Smyrni. They have designed a travelling exhibition on the history and memory of the Pontic Greeks.[20] The associations of Greek refugees from Asia Minor and Eastern Thrace all over the world also have their own websites containing educational texts and images on the major themes of their culture and demands for the "genocide" to be recognized. Some also publish historical and cultural magazines about their activities and events.

Since the 1980s, the refugees from Asia Minor, especially the Pontians, and their descendants who could afford it have gone on pilgrimages by bus each year from Thessaloniki to their homelands in Turkey. They look for any remains of their or their ancestors' houses, and see for themselves the village or small town they come from. They also make tourist pilgrimages to the monasteries, particularly Panagia Soumela. The churches that are now mosques, or less often museums, and the greater number of them that are in ruins, and the schools are their main bearings in the townscape of these expanding Turkish towns, a physical link to an irrevocably lost past. Any Greek graves in the cemeteries have generally been removed.

While the Pontians are particularly visible in Greece at the commemorative events and in building memorials, the much fewer Cappadocians are also distinguished by their special history and presence in the heartlands of Anatolia.

Cappadocians' exodus and settlement in Greece: construction of a collective memory

The number of Christian Greek refugees from Cappadocia exchanged in 1924 is taken to be 44,432.[21] They dispersed across much of Greece and settled in villages where there were other refugees and in major urban centres. Like refugees from other regions, some of them founded villages

20 The museums and travelling exhibitions highlight traditional life in Pontus (ethnography) and the persecutions, deportations and massacres that are arguments for the case of a 'Pontic Greek genocide', and their position in Russia and the USSR before and after the Bolshevik Revolution. For other, non-Pontic, refugees, there are only plans for museums or exhibitions.

21 Vasso Stelaku, "Space, Place and Identity: Memory and Religion in two Cappadocian Greek Settlements", in Renée Hirschon (ed.), *Crossing the Aegean*, Oxford, Berghahn Books, 2003, p. 180.

where they formed the majority and some kept their homeland place-name, particularly in some areas in Northern Greece and Thessaly.[22]

We focus here on two places that evoke for Cappadocians their memory of and continuity with their homeland. They are national pilgrimage sites: Nea Karvali in the Greek region of Macedonia and Nea Prokopi on the island of Euboea. The former even claims to be the centre of the worldwide Cappadocian Diaspora. The two villages were created in 1925–6 following the population exchange (1923), on land available because it was marshy and deserted by Muslim inhabitants who had also been exchanged. Nea Karvali, in a swampy coastland plain 10 km East of Kavala near the village of Lefki, was first an estate of 300 houses built by the refugee settlement commission (EAP) for those who mainly came from Karvali (Gelveri, tr: *Güzelyurt*) in Cappadocia. In 1996, the population of Nea Karvali was still largely Cappadocian (1,894). The refugees had brought with them into exile the relics of Saint Gregory of Nazianzus and various sacred items, and began in 1929 to build a church for them that was not completed until 1950. This became the centre of the village's religious and social life. Since these refugees called Saint Gregory "our saint" (*o agios mas*), they became rooted in an identity closely bound up with their homeland through the man who was one of the four main Church Fathers from Cappadocia. The saint's feast day on 25 January is the most important annual event in Nea Karvali, attracting pilgrims from far away who believe in his power to work miracles.[23]

The Turkish-speaking refugees of the first generation had great difficulty in integrating locally in Greece because of their Karamanli cultural features, particularly the Turkish language. Their descendants tended to forget their painful past, which was an obstacle to their integration but at the same time was mythologized by their parents. Younger members of the third generation, on the initiative of Kaplanis Iosifidis, set up a cultural association aimed at (re)discovering, transmitting and celebrating the memory of the Greek Orthodox community from Cappadocia, particularly Gelveri. They

---

22 Near Giannitsa (Axos, Nea Aravissos, Neo Milotopo), Chalkidiki (Flogita, Simandra, Nea Silata), Kavala (Nea Karvali), Larissa-Karditsa (Neo Ikonio, Vounaina, Kappadokiko), Ioannina (Neokaisaria, Bafra), Euboea (Nea Prokopi, Nea Sinasos), Kozani (Vathilako), Thessaloniki (districts of Nea Moutalaski, Nea Malakopi-Toumba, Xirochori, Sykies) and in Greater Athens (Eleusis, etc.).

23 Beside the shrine a cultural centre (*Stegi Politismou Neas Karvalis*) was built in 1975 and completed in 1995, following on from the *Nazianzos* association created in Constantinople in 1884 by traders from Karvali. It houses a historical and ethnographical museum, a library and archives used for Cappadocian studies.

ran their first pilgrimage trip to Gelveri (tr: *Güzelyurt*) in 1981, interviewed first-generation refugees, collected archives and miscellaneous items brought along during the 1923 population exchange, and assembled all this in the centre for the study of Cappadocian civilization they set up in 1987. They reversed the identity of a group whose cultural characteristics were no longer a shameful stigma to be hidden but a rich heritage and source of assertion of identity.[24]

The refugees in Nea Karvali and Nea Prokopi all spoke Turkish and at school had learnt only a little scholarly Greek (*katharevousa*), so that for years they could not communicate easily with or be fully accepted by their neighbours in Greece. But bonds with their memories of their homeland and its history were formed by establishing places of memory, mainly churches housing the relics of the saint who had become the symbol of their attachment to Cappadocia, located where they had been resettled. The village name recalling their homeland was also a way of strengthening their feeling of belonging in this new home. The churches of Nea Karvali and Nea Prokopi and the associated iconography were bearings and reference points for their collective memory. All the more since it was religion rather than language that lay at the heart of their identity.

From "Refugee" to "Pontian", "Cappadocian", "Mikrasiate" and "Thracian": memory in the plural

All the Greek Orthodox refugees, whose assertion of identity contained a strong religious component, began their memory work by building churches dedicated to their homeland saint, housing an icon brought by the refugees themselves: for example, the Cappadocians' churches in Nea Karvali and Nea Prokopi and Panagia Faneromeni in Nea Michaniona. Where the icons were believed to work miracles, the churches became pilgrimage sites attracting people from well beyond their local village. Most of the refugees from Asia Minor, Eastern Thrace and Cappadocia were satisfied with this manifestation of their identity and memory.

24 Lisa Montmayeur, "Migrations et mémoires croisées des réfugiés de l'Echange de population de 1923 entre la Grèce et la Turquie: l'exemple de Güzelyurt et Nea Karvali", in Françoise Rollan (ed.), *Quand la violence déplace: mémoires et migrations forcées depuis et vers la Turquie*, Bordeaux, Maison des Sciences de l'Homme d'Aquitaine, 2013, pp. 97–98.

Some wider commemorative events, not exclusively related to a local community, village or town, were the result of initiatives by distinct regional bodies. The Pontians were the first to advance their commemorative demands and press them in a highly active and militant way, particularly from the 1970s on. Even in the 1950s they started reconstructing their major monasteries. They were the first in the 1980s to raise the question of a "genocide" of Pontic Greeks, on the Armenian model. They obtained recognition of this genocide by the Greek government in 1994 and were behind the commemorative laws that in 1994 established 19 May 1919, and in 1998 14 September 1922, as "Days of national memory of the genocide" first of the Pontic Greeks and then of the Asia Minor Greeks. The Pontians built the largest number of memory sites in Greece and the Diaspora, and produced numerous books, largely owing to an active publisher in Thessaloniki, Tassos Kyriakidis. The strength of their commemorative movement was closely bound up with their remarkable ability from the earliest years to put together an abundant and varied "iconography".

Figure 11: *Annual 19 May commemorative demonstration for the recognition of the "Pontic Greek genocide" in the centre of Thessaloniki (2008)*

The Thracians have in recent years begun to follow the Pontic model of Panagia Soumela, establishing the monastery of Ferres (Evros prefecture, near the Turkish border) and its icon, *Panagia Kosmosoteira*, as the focus and emblem of the Thracians. They have recently unveiled the first monument commemorating the "genocide" of the Thracians by the Bulgarians and Turks (1885–1941).[25] Since the seventh world congress of Thracians in Didymoteicho in 2006 they have begun a commemorative process like that of the Pontians before them. Their "genocide" differs greatly from those of the Pontians and Armenians, because it involves two countries, Turkey and Bulgaria, and is more an ethnic cleansing over fifty-odd years than a genocide like that of the Armenians, which was much more systematic and concentrated in time (1915–16).

It is remarkable to see the Pontians' commemorative model repeated twenty years later by the Thracians. The Cappadocians did not follow that model, since they did not undergo any similar massacres, but have recently organized in their Diaspora to preserve the memory of their history, holy places and pilgrimages (1975–2008). The Greeks from the rest of Asia Minor, on the other hand, have not developed memory activities to the same extent. Apart from *Estia Neas Smyrnis*, there are no major commemorative monuments for the refugees from Western Asia Minor, although they were statistically the largest group of refugees recorded in 1928.[26]

Ninety years after the Great Catastrophe (*Megali Katastrofi*) of Smyrna, the Greek refugees from Asia Minor and Eastern Thrace thus maintain a relationship with the memory of their "lost homelands" that differs in force, intensity and topic according to their original region. All of them, however, even in the fourth and fifth generations, preserve a referential memory of the "lost homelands", which have become "unforgettable".

In Turkey, the "Lausanne exchanges" (*Lozan Mübadilleri*), as they call themselves, have only recently begun to show an interest in the memory of the lands and culture of their origins, with no support from their

---

25 The Greek confederation of Thracian associations requested its own commemorative law, the recognition by the Greek government of a day of memory for the "genocide of Thracian Hellenism", to mark 6 April 1914, the "black Easter" when the Young Turks began to expel and uproot the Greeks of Eastern Thrace.

26 These *Mikrasiate* refugees' linguistic, cultural and socio-economic closeness to Greece and the Greek islands meant that they did not feel the need to form an 'iconography' and identity of their own, distinct from the other Greek communities within the nation-state.

nation-state of the sort the Greeks eventually gained more than sixty years after their settlement in their "motherland".

The Muslim "exchanges" from Salonica vilayet

The Ottoman censuses of 1906–7 show that Muslims made up 45% of the total population of the *vilayet* of Salonica (tr: *Selanik Vilayeti*), 40% of the *sanjak* of Salonica and 26% of the city of Salonica (el: *Thessaloniki*). The Muslim population of this city, the third largest and most cosmopolitan of the Ottoman Empire, were mainly officers, diplomats, civil servants and shopkeepers, whereas the Muslims in the rest of the *vilayet* were mainly engaged in peasant farming (olives, tobacco, vines, fruit trees, etc.).

Some 200,000 to 300,000 Muslims in the former Salonica *vilayet* and districts bordering it to the West, corresponding to the current Greek region of Macedonia, the South of the Former Yugoslav Republic of Macedonia (FYROM) and the South-West of Bulgaria (Pirin Macedonia), had to leave their homes and lands as part of the population exchange laid down by the Treaty of Lausanne (1923). These *Selanikli* (Salonicans) were distributed across Turkey by the Turkish Directorate-General of Exchange and also dispersed of their own accord, mainly to provinces and districts left by the Greek Christians of Asia Minor, who had also been exchanged but were twice or three times as numerous. The region of Marmara (Eastern Thrace, regions of Istanbul and Bursa) took in 58% of them.[27]

Before 1914, 115,000 Muslims from Greece, most from Salonica *vilayet*, had gone into exile, followed by 185,278 just before the population exchange. The Muslims from Greece who sought refuge in Turkey from 1914 to 1925 thus totalled 623,251, of whom roughly half were exchangees. Their destination was often influenced by their professions or trades in Salonica *vilayet*. The Directorate-General of Population Exchange, Development and Settlement (*Mübadele, İmâr ve İskân Vekâleti*) mainly placed the self-employed, shopkeepers and civil servants in towns and city suburbs. The farmers were placed either in villages of "autochthonous"

27 The Aegean region, particularly around Izmir (el: *Smyrna*), took in 13%, and the Black Sea region around Samsun 11%. The Central, Eastern and South-Eastern Anatolia regions received 13% dispersed across them. These exchangees settled in areas where the Greeks had been numerous before 1923. Gökce Bayindir Goularas, "L'exil et la mémoire: étude du cas des Turcs de Thessalonique", *op. cit.* pp. 59–62.

Turks, or in the villages of earlier refugees, or in former Greek villages abandoned after the population exchange.[28]

A distinction must be made between the exchangees and the refugees who arrived before (Balkan wars) or after them, the migrants and the "autochthonous" population who were there before all the others. Among these exchangees and refugees a Salonican identity was formed, defined as superior to and more prestigious than more local identities (Drama, Edessa, Serrès) or more ethnic ones (Pomaks, Valachs, Roma, Patriots), which often combined with the Salonican identity or simply with that of exchangee or refugee. The cosmopolitan city of Salonica was a reference of some prestige because of its past and its importance to the Ottoman Empire. That it was also the birthplace in 1881 of Mustafa Kemal Atatürk conveniently enabled the exchangees to claim an attachment to the Turkish national, and indeed nationalist, identity that formed the nation-state in 1923. The exchangees also sought out any Anatolian origins (Karaman, Konya) and strongly asserted their Sunni Muslim religious identity in order to achieve greater integration locally and within the Turkish nation-state, which was founded on the Turkish language and Sunni Islam.[29]

Traditional costumes, songs, dances and food are the main cultural elements that make up this Salonican identity. They are hard to pass on beyond the third generation, except perhaps for the music, which appears to thrive. The lack of interest in associations (compared with in Greece) is perhaps the crucial reason for the difficulty in transmitting this "Salonican" culture from one generation to the next. Various local and ethnic components of identity connect to the shared dominant Salonican identity. They are complementary but not necessarily present as part of the Salonican "mother-identity". Their importance with respect to the main culture varies by local context and geographical origin.[30]

---

28 In this last case, whole communities of exchangees or earlier refugees were able to preserve the continuity of their community life and previous culture for quite a long time. But where they settled in towns, integration into Turkish society was rapid and much of their original identity and culture was lost. Gökce Bayındır Goularas, "L'exil et la mémoire: étude du cas des Turcs de Thessalonique", *op.cit.*, p. 60.

29 Gökce Bayındır Goularas, "L'exil et la mémoire: étude du cas des Turcs de Thessalonique", *op. cit.*, p. 64.

30 These local identities were often connected to a job or trade, like tobacco farming for the exchangees from Drama. Those from Edessa and the former border districts (*kaza*) of Salonica *vilayet* included Muslims speaking not only Turkish, but also Greek (Patriots or *Vallahades*), Slav languages (Bulgarian, Macedonian) and Romanian (Vlachs).

The first-generation exchangees had difficulty, especially in the early years, in being accepted by local communities, just like the Turkish- and Pontic-speaking Greeks in Greece. Their different language or accent in Turkish and their daily habits sometimes led to rejection from the host society. The women in particular behaved in more open and modern ways than local women. This resulted in mostly community-based marriages in the second generation.[31] The exchangees supported policies of modernizing reforms and voted more to the Left than the average citizen. The places they used for transmitting their identity have been cafés patronised solely by men that reflect the divisions between the various local or ethnic sub-identities and, only since 2000, associations and foundations (26 in all for Salonicans).

The association of Lausanne exchangees (*Lozan Mübadilleri Vakfı*), created in 2001, is the most active. It collects data on the population exchange and the exchangees' traditions, and holds a commemorative ceremony every year on 30 January, the anniversary of the Convention Concerning the Exchange of Greek and Turkish Populations. It also runs pilgrimage trips to the homelands. But it is not specifically Salonican. The strictly Salonican local associations are few in number and very recent. There have recently been some pilgrimage trips to native villages, like those made by the Greeks, who have done this for decades and whom the exchangees have seen visiting their own host villages. Meetings between exchanged Turks and Greeks, whether in Turkey or Greece, are generally perfectly cordial and for some people highly emotional occasions, although they receive no official political encouragement in either country.

Memory hard to transmit among Lausanne Muslim "exchangees"

Memory appears to be easier to transmit widely over the Internet, on websites, discussion forums and blogs. There are more young people there, looking for information either about their home or host towns and villages, or about "exchanges" and "Salonicans" in general. Commemorative ceremonies have barely got going (30 January). There are virtually no place-names reminiscent of the homelands, because the Turkish authorities have insisted on Turkish ones. There are relatively few

---

31 Gökce Bayındır Goularas, "L'exil et la mémoire: étude du cas des Turcs de Thessalonique", *op. cit.*, pp. 63–64.

or no symbols or "iconography". The difference is striking with the Asia Minor Greeks and not least Pontians in Greece, who have an extensive iconography, and many associations, commemorative ceremonies and sites. Gökçe Bayindir attributes this difference mainly to pressure from the Turkish authorities, whose main concern until recently has been to strengthen a homogeneous Turkish national identity, focusing on its Anatolian roots rather than an Ottoman past that is more open to religious and identity differences that were deliberately ignored by the Kemalist republic.[32] One may also mention the proportionately much larger number of Greek refugees, and not least their more traumatic past (massacres), laying upon them the duty to remember their family victims, and perhaps also the longer history of the Greeks in their homelands in Asia Minor. Indeed it is remarkable how resilient the Salonican identity is in Turkey and one wonders what its chances of survival are.

Lisa Montmayeur has studied the relations with memory of the Muslim refugees from Kozani settled in Güzelyurt (el: *Geverli*) in Cappadocia, who, unlike the Greeks in the exchange who left that village and settled in Nea Karvali in Greek Macedonia, appear to suffer from a sort of amnesia both collective and individual.[33] The Muslim refugees were mostly workers and tobacco farmers who failed to transfer their crop to Cappadocia, where the natural conditions rather favoured the vines tended by the Greeks before the exchange. Their young people consequently soon migrated to the major Turkish cities or abroad (Germany and Russia), so that at present the population of Güzelyurt is less than one third of what it was at the time of the exchange. The mainly old residents are relatively poor in economic terms and poorly educated. The village does not contain the equivalent of the third generation in Nea Karvali, with university degrees, who have begun to construct a collective memory.

Furthermore, the Muslims from Kozani moved into a village where part of the population was "autochthonous". These locals rejected them for their socio-cultural[34] and language differences (Greek or Macedonian Slavic). So these Muslims from Kozani "rather sought to erase the differences that

---

32 Gökce Bayindir Goularas, "L'exil et la mémoire: étude du cas des Turcs de Thessalonique", *op. cit.*

33 Lisa Montmayeur, "Migrations et mémoires croisées des réfugiés de l'Echange de population de 1923 entre la Grèce et la Turquie" , *op. cit.*, pp. 89–117.

34 Their less conservative religious practices meant that they were seen as infidels (*gâvur*) replacing other infidels (Orthodox Greeks). They also had first claim to the houses abandoned by Greeks that the less well-housed locals had had their eyes on.

set them apart from the local Muslim population than to keep alive their community's specific memory. Forgetting in this case was a necessity."[35]

The urban Muslim refugees from Greece had largely belonged to the military and bureaucratic elite of the Ottoman Empire. They were westernized and well-educated, and took part in the construction of the Kemalist Turkish Republic. They put their efforts into building a new nationalist model of Turkish citizenship, obliterating the Ottoman period rather than bothering to preserve the memory of a lost past.[36]

Cretan Turks on the fault line between Greek and Turkish nation-states

Crete was not conquered and included in the Ottoman Empire until relatively late, in 1645, after being part of the Venetian sphere of influence since 1204. Many of the island's Greek population, variously estimated at between one third and a half, converted to Islam.[37] By the eighteenth century, these Muslims were a majority in the towns. They gradually lost their predominant position following the repeated uprisings by Christian Greeks throughout the nineteenth century (1821–9, 1858, 1866–9, 1896–7). Most of them left the countryside to seek refuge in the fortified coastal towns or emigrated, so that they declined to become only one quarter of the total population.[38] The Cretan Turks were a majority in three towns only: Heraklion, Rethymnon and Chania.

Between 1881 and 1900, more than 40,000 Cretan Turks left the island, and in 1898 an independent Cretan state under the Sultan's suzerainty was created, after pressure from the Great Powers; it kept this official status until 1912, when Crete was attached to Greece. By then the Cretan Turks were only 11% of the island's population. They finally had to leave in 1923–4 after the Asia Minor Catastrophe and the Lausanne

---

35 Lisa Montmayeur, "Migrations et mémoires croisées des réfugiés de l'Echange de population de 1923 entre la Grèce et la Turquie", *op. cit.*, p. 114.

36 ibid., p. 104.

37 The usual reason for converting was to escape the status of *raya* subject to poll tax and avoid the arbitrary actions of the local authorities, the forced labour imposed by the *aghas* and the depredations of fanatic renegades.

38 Emile Kolodny, "Des musulmans dans une île grecque: les 'Turcocrétois'", *Mediterranean World*, XIV, Tokyo, 1995, p. 1–10.

Convention of 30 January 1923 on compulsory population exchange.[39] The Turkish 1965 census recorded 3,500 of them who claimed to speak Greek (in fact a Cretan Greek dialect), distributed, according to other sources, across 44 villages and towns.[40]

Let us examine the case of the island of Moschonisi, now Cunda, off Ayvalik just East of Mytilene. In 1925, 4,500 Cretan Turks (*Kritiki*) landed in the bay of Edremit and many of them settled on Cunda.[41] Local natural conditions were not too different from in Crete except for noticeably harsher winters. Olive, sheep and goat farming were similar in both places. The exodus of the former Greek Christian middle class on Moschonisi had disrupted trade networks between Ayvalik and Greece. But the practical knowledge and skills of the Cretan Turks who spoke a Greek dialect were used to re-establish the links to their advantage.[42]

Initially these Greek-speaking *Kritiki* were treated as foreigners by the local Turks, who called them *gavur fidani* (infidel saplings) because they did not speak their language, just as the Turkish-speaking refugees in Greece were called Turk seeds (*tourkosporoi*). Like the Turkish-speaking Greeks they made up for this hereditary disability by more strongly affirming their religious identity within Sunni Islam, one of the pillars of Kemal's Turkish nation-state along with the Turkish language, despite the official secularity of its institutions, and some of them even gave up their *bektashi* or *alevi* practices. Furthermore, their knowledge of Greek enabled the Cretan Turks and their descendants to easily find jobs catering to Greeks visiting Turkey, a tourism that developed from the 1980s. They were able to engage in many activities related to the border between the two countries, using their three identities (Turkish, Cretan,

---

39 They settled along the Mediterranean coast: in Ayvalik in the bay of Edremit (on Moschonis), Smyrna (İzmir), Çesme (Krini), Vourlá (Urla), and Phocaea (Foça), in the plain of Pamphylia. They are also to be found on the Southern coast of the Sea of Marmara and in Greater Istanbul.

40 Peter Alford Andrews, *Ethnic Groups in the Republic of Turkey*, Wiesbaden, Dr Ludwig Reichert Verlag, 1989, pp. 145, 370–373.

41 Sophia Kouphopoulou, "Muslim Cretans in Turkey: The Reformulation of Ethnic Identity in an Aegean Community", in Renée Hirschon (ed.), *Crossing the Aegean*, Oxford, Berghahn Books, 2003, pp. 212–217.

42 Those who had produced or traded in olive oil in Crete resumed those professions on Cunda (Moschonisi), while the poorer exchangees took up fishing. Later, this fisher folk smuggled much of their catch into Mytilene and as far away as Thessaloniki, from where it was re-exported to Italy, and still is. Emile Kolodny, "Des musulmans dans une île grecque: les 'Turcocrétois'", *Mediterranean World*, XIV, Tokyo, 1995.

Cundan). Their integration into their host region was not as difficult as it was in Greece for the Turkish-speaking Greek refugees from Asia Minor.

Is there a Pontic Question? Preserving a physical and intangible heritage between Turkey and Greece

In the last twenty years there has been a boom in publications about Pontus, the Pontians and "Pontianness" (*Pontiosyni*), first in Greece and then in Turkey. The Pontic Greeks' attachment to their "lost homeland" and the unsuccessful proposal for a Republic of Pontus (1919–24) lie behind this Pontic question, which could be a stumbling-block for relations between Greece and Turkey. The memory work done by the Pontians causes alarm among some Turks concerning their minority of Pontic Greek-speaking Muslims, who may have doubts about their identity, and the former proposal for a "Greek" state with or without the Armenians, which had embarrassed Kemal's Turkish Republic in its early days.

Since 1924, neither the Pontic Greek associations nor the Greek government have made any territorial claims on Pontus. They ask solely for a right to memory, that is, recognition of the "genocide" of Pontic Greeks perpetrated by the Young Turks and then the Kemal regime from 1916 to 1923, the preservation and maintenance of the monuments their ancestors left behind in their former homeland, and the right to visit their original houses and towns. They also ask for the protection of the language and culture of the Muslim Pontic Greek-speaking minority living in these original towns and countryside.

Nationalist Turks disapprove of these demonstrations of memory and the relations that are developing with the Greek-speaking minority. They see them as a threat to the territorial integrity and ethnic homogeneity of their nation-state. Yet despite possible misunderstandings, relations are improving. In 2010, the Turkish government allowed Ecumenical Patriarch Bartholomew I to celebrate mass in the Panagia Soumela monastery on 15 August for the first time since 1924. Every year Pontians make pilgrimage trips to Pontus. The Pontic Question belongs to the past, but the preservation of this heritage is still a matter of concern.

The Pontic Greeks have a physical heritage currently located in Turkish territory. This architecture and these precious objects with symbolic value (*keimilia*) have partly been destroyed, plundered and dispersed, but the major monuments remain in their original location in Pontus in Turkey.

The Turkish government has taken them over for other uses, especially the churches, which have become places of worship (mosques), or for various other functions, or they have simply been left abandoned, while most of the schools are still educational establishments, such as the famous *Phrontisterion* of Trebizond, which is now the Suleyman the Lawgiver Anatolian High School (*Kanuni Anadolu Lisesi*). Some of the architectural heritage has also disappeared under the coastal towns' infrastructure modernization plans. Some sites have retained considerable symbolic value as part not only of Pontic heritage but also of world cultural heritage, with or without UNESCO recognition. One example is the Saint Sophia church in Trebizond, which the Turkish government turned into a museum from 1964 to 2013, but which the Islamists in the AKP party wanted to take over as a Muslim place of worship. Pontic associations in Greece were slow to react and alert public opinion in Greece and then Europe. The Greek and Turkish governments, like public opinion in both countries, have not as yet shown much concern for this issue.

The language the Greeks call the Pontic dialect, and the Turks Rumca (language of the *Rum*), has so far been treated as a private matter for families. As a result of urbanization, migration and not being taught in either country's schools, its use has declined and it is currently under threat of extinction. The Greek-speaking Muslim minority in Turkey is not recognized as such, nor is its cultural heritage protected, and the same was long true in Greece too. In the last two years, however, Pontic Greek cultural associations, particularly of teachers, have mobilized to defend and transmit the language, and have finally obtained the support of the Greek Ministry of Education and of local authorities (*dímoi*) for it to be taught to adults as part of the continuing education programme. In the near future it should be extended to primary and secondary pupils in those *dímoi* where there is an extensive Pontian presence. A textbook and three-year teaching programme have been produced.

Although the growing awareness of a "right to memory" has taken the form among the Pontians, as among the Armenians, of requiring that the Turkish government recognize the "genocide" of which they were victims, the question of religious and cultural heritage has often come second. Only in the recent past, at the initiative of individuals like Parysatis Papadopoulou-Simeonidou, an architect and art historian, and a few associations, has it been raised and taken on a certain international dimension in the European institutions. The Greek and Turkish governments have as yet shown little concern. And yet this is a major question of identity and memory, because the disappearance of monuments or their non-commemorative use, and the loss of the language, pose a threat to the very existence of this minority as such, a "cultural genocide" that would extend and complete the actual demographic "genocide". The Pontians themselves took action in the latter half of the twentieth century to stave off this danger by building commemorative sites in their places of exile, in Greece and the Diaspora (monasteries, museums, commemorative monuments).

An asymmetry of memory on both side of the Aegean

The differences in this relationship with the memory of the "lost homelands", a term used by the Greeks but not the Turks, can only be understood against the historical background of the events that led to the uprooting of these communities, how their forced exile occurred and the societies in the two nation-states that emerged from the fall of the Ottoman Empire.

The Greek Orthodox refugees arrived in huge numbers in Greece from 1914 to 1924, by which time they were statistically around a quarter of the country's population, which threatened to seriously destabilize Greek society, if major international aid had not enabled a major disaster to be avoided. They were brutally driven from their lands and homes in Asia Minor and Eastern Thrace by massacres and the rout of the Greek army in 1922. Most of them left in a panic and the number of victims (except for the Cappadocians) was very high.

The Turkish Muslim refugees from Greece left in 1923–4 under a negotiated population exchange as part of the Treaty of Lausanne (1923). Their departure was prepared and organized by the newly created Turkish Republic of Mustafa Kemal. The Greek military expedition to Anatolia (1919–22) and the crimes committed by the Greek army against the Turkish Muslim communities had convinced them that no further coexistence in Greece between Christians and Muslims was possible. They consequently had no difficulty in espousing the Turkish nationalist ideology of Kemal, whom they saw as their saviour.[43] This ideology made it easier for them to integrate into Turkish society, where they were proportionately less numerous than the Greek refugees in Greece. It was also easier to move into the lands and homes "abandoned" by the massacred, expelled or exchanged Christians more than twice their number. Official policy to

[43] Bruce CLARK, *Twice a Stranger*, *op. cit.*

forget was therefore more effective and lasting in Turkey than in Greece, and it was not until the 1990s that memory began to show itself, whereas in Greece it had always been present and had grown from the 1970s on, because of the larger number of victims whose descendants felt a duty of memory, while the government only officially recognized their existence in the 1990s. In Turkey the government maintained a policy of denial and forgetfulness with respect to the massacres and the former Christian presence in Anatolia. This can be seen in the way Erdoğan's government began to convert into mosques the Byzantine churches dedicated to Saint Sophia (*Agia Sofia*), particularly the one in Trabzon that had been turned into a museum by Kemal Atatürk's secular republican regime. There is talk of doing the same to the one in Istanbul, which is a popular international tourist site.[44]

The population exchange on the basis of religion, intended and negotiated by Kemal and Venizelos, was a determining factor in the organization of two ethnically homogeneous nation-states living in peace, but at the cost of denying or not recognizing the memory of the refugees and exchangees on both sides. In Greece, the strength of their assertion of identity and right to, or even duty of, memory eventually took shape in townscapes and achieved official recognition by the government, whereas in Turkey, the descendants of the Lausanne exchangees only tardily and shyly began to express their ties of memory. The Muslim exchangees had no religious faith as a basis for a collective memory of their homelands like the Ottoman Greek refugees. On the contrary: most of them abandoned their special religious practices (*bektashi*, *alevi*) so as to melt into the dominant Sunni Islam of the new Turkish nation-state. For the Greeks, religion, their close attachment to Orthodoxy, was crucial to constructing a collective memory so as to maintain links with "lost homelands" never to be forgotten. They used their religious faith to put together an "iconography" supporting their identity and the memory of their origins. The difficult question of the recognition of the "genocide" of the Pontic Greeks, and of the Ottoman Greeks in general, which has become a central theme in the refugees' memory, developed after and parallel with the demands of the Armenians. But whereas the Armenian genocide occurred over a limited period of just over a year (1915–16), and was committed in a coordinated, radical way by the Young Turk

---

44 Michel Bruneau, "Le patrimoine menacé des Grecs pontiques, entre Turquie et Grèce", *Anatoli*, 6, 2015, pp. 263–283.

government, the massacres, ethnic cleansing and death marches suffered by the Greeks occurred over a much longer period (1914–23), often mixed up with warfare between the Greek and Turkish armies (1919–22). Tessa Hofmann calls this "genocide" process a cumulative one relating to Greece's changing position in the World War and the various places where it occurred (the West coast of Ionia, Eastern Thrace, Pontus, Smyrna).[45] This difference largely explains the difficulty the Greek refugees have in obtaining international or even national recognition within Greece of a "genocide" that was comparable only to the Armenian genocide in the case of the Pontic Greeks.

---

45 Tessa HOFMANN, "Genoktonia en roi – Cumulative Genocide: The Massacres and Deportations of the Greek Population of the Ottoman Empire (1912–1923)", in Matthias BJORNLUND, Tessa HOFMANN, Vassileios MEICHANETSIDIS (ed.), *The Genocide of the Ottoman Greeks, op. cit.*, pp. 39–111.

Turkey's Guiding Light and Consolation in Addressing the Loss: Nationalism

Etienne Copeaux
Independent researcher specialized in contemporary Turkey

At the turn of the nineteenth and twentieth centuries, the Ottoman Empire had lost the major part of its territories in Europe and almost all of its Middle Eastern Arabic provinces as a consequence of the Balkan Wars and World War I. As early as 1912, the Bulgarians were at the walls of Istanbul, plunging its Muslim population into fear. After the Empire had been definitely defeated by the Allies, Istanbul and large parts of Anatolia (Asia Minor) were placed under military occupation or foreign mandate. In addition, in the Treaty of Sèvres (1920), East Anatolia was amputated to create newly independent states, Armenia and Kurdistan. The mere mention of this treaty, even today, evokes threat and fear. The "Sèvres syndrome", in Turkish nationalist discourse, refers to the supposedly subversive will of the West to destabilize Turkey by supporting the Kurds, Armenians or Greeks.

The Republican struggle (or Liberation War, *Kurtulus Savası*, 1919–22) led by Mustafa Kemal (Atatürk)[1] succeeded in saving the whole of Anatolia from division and foreign occupation. A new international treaty concluded in Lausanne (1923) declared Sèvres null and void and recognized the Republic of Turkey, established in Anatolia. The Republican Kemalist struggle protected the Turkish nation from completely vanishing, but the loss of the other Ottoman territories, particularly in the Balkans, was heavily felt. The danger of disappearing had been so strong that the national anthem adopted by the Great National Assembly in 1921 begins with the words "Don't be afraid". It is thus not surprising that Turkish nationalism, born when the Empire was

1 Atatürk ('Ata' means 'Father') was the name attributed to Mustafa Kemal by the Great National Assembly in the framework of the Family Surname Law in 1934.

seriously threatened at the end of the nineteenth century, rose after defeat, becoming the prevalent ideology in Turkey until today: nationalism has been felt as the adequate response to fear and loss.

Loss of territories is not the worst event in the history of the Anatolian populations. At the same time, the Armenians were exterminated by a genocide process (1915)[2] and a great majority of the Orthodox population (*Rum*)[3] was deported during the republican struggle. Above all, at the time of the "Great Exchange" (the "Great catastrophe" for the Greeks) in 1923–4, planned by a convention signed by the Greek and Turkish governments at Lausanne (30 January 1923), the entire Muslim population of Macedonia and Epire was "exchanged" with the Orthodox people living in Anatolia. Actually a double mass expulsion, this so-called exchange was compulsory and quickly and dramatically implemented. As this ethnic-cleansing process was over the years completed with the Jewish pogroms in 1934 and the Orthodox pogroms in 1955, followed by the expulsion of most *Rum* from Istanbul, Turkey *de facto* became a republic built for a Muslim population.[4]

"Turkey got rid of its allogenic elements", as favourably wrote the then-famous anthropologist Eugène Pittard, professor, doyen then president of the University of Geneva. And according to a geography textbook published 1929, "Today's Turkey is a land where only Turkish people live. Those who are not Turks, the strangers, stay out of the Fatherland, or have been removed. That is the way the national unity has been built".[5]

---

2 Taner Akçam, *A Shameful Act – The Armenian Genocide and the Question of Turkish Responsibility*, New York, Metropolitan Books, 2006; Raymond Kevorkian, *The Armenian Genocide. A Complete History*, London, IB Tauris, 2011.

3 This word, which is not pejorative, designates the Orthodox population of Istanbul, Turkey and Cyprus. It refers to religious belonging and *not* to a language (a good part of the Anatolian *Rum* was Turkish-speaking), even though they are sometimes designated as 'Greek'.

4 Bruce Clark, *Twice a Stranger. How Mass Expulsion Forged Modern Greece and Turkey*, London, Granta Books, 2006; Anna Theodoridès, *Survivre en contexte minoritaire. Une étude sociologique des résistances des Grecs d'Istanbul (Rûms polites) au lendemain des émeutes de la nuit du 6 au 7 septembre 1955*, Ph.D., Paris, Ecole des Hautes Etudes en Sciences Sociales, 2016.

5 Eugène Pittard, *Le Visage nouveau de la Turquie*, Paris, Société d'Editions Géographiques, Maritimes et Coloniales, 1931, p. 76 [translations by the author]. Faik Sabri Duran, *Türkiye Cografyası, Lise Kitapları III. Sınıf* (Turkey's Geography for High Schools, 3rd level), Istanbul, Devlet Matbaası (State Printings), 1929, pp. 177–178.

The new Republic was imagined and then built on as "Turkish", but the term was and remains ambivalent. Until the founding of the Republic, it hardly had a national or ethnic meaning and was a synonym for "Muslim", in addition to having a meaning of "peasant" or "villager". The Ottoman Empire's society was ruled in the framework of a "*millet*" (nations) system, meaning communities defined by religion (Muslims, Orthodox, Jews, and Armenians faithful to the Apostolic Church). The Muslim community, of course, was politically dominant and included Kurds, Arabs, Albanians, Bosnians, etc., as well as "Turks". The word *millet* remains prevalent today to express the idea of nation and is consequently ambiguous, with some religious overtones.

Thus, the loss of territories was considerably worsened by the loss of population in its demographic, but also in its human, psychological and social, dimensions. For the "exchanged" people, the deportation was so sudden and massive that grief could not easily be erased. These migrants who had lost everything (properties, flocks, friends, neighbours, position in society) arrived in a country they had never seen among people speaking a language they could not understand. After enduring a series of wars lasting twelve years and witnessing genocide and a series of massacres and deportations, in the following years, that part of the population lucky enough to remain at home had to cope with major disruptions in everyday life, in the organization of local government, of regional trades, handicrafts, agriculture, etc. In addition to disorganization and disorientation, there were personal factors such as the loss of Armenian and/or Orthodox friends and neighbours, and, undoubtedly, substantial feelings of guilt.[6]

A reaction of the new state to the loss was to claim that the Republican government was not responsible for what occurred before 1923. The Republic had a vital need to make a revolutionary break with the Ottoman past. In addition to proclaiming the Republic, it implemented a series of reforms such as adopting formal secularism (in fact, close control of Islam by the state), abolishing the Caliphate, and regarding symbols such

---

6 I witnessed the sadness suffered by another exchanged population during research in Northern Cyprus, 1995–2004. Etienne Copeaux, Claire Mauss-Copeaux, *Taksim! Chypre divisée*, Lyon, Aedelsa 2005. See Nergis Canefe, "The Legacy of Forced Migrations in Modern Turkish Society: Remembrance of the Things Past?", *Balkanologie*, Vol. V (1–2), 2001, available at: http://balkanologie.revues.org/709 (accessed 15 February 2017).

as the adoption of the Latin alphabet (creating a radical cultural break) and Western clothing. Nationalism was included in the set of the six "principles of Atatürk" and, *ipso facto*, became an intangible and sacred virtue. Nationalism, under the name of Kemalism, was supposed to give the population some restored pride in being Turkish and it was the first and main remedy to the loss. After all, the Republican struggle was victorious and the reassertion of the state as well as the nation-building process were surprisingly successful.

But nationalism is not an abstraction; it has to be embodied in institutions, signs, behaviours, festivals, celebrations, beliefs and myths. These can all be provided by the education system; an efficient foundation myth can be based upon history as taught at school. What unfolded in Anatolia starting in 1912 was so disastrous that the new elite felt it necessary to build an appropriate national myth in order to erase the humiliation and forget the losses. And, as the Christian part of the population had been erased, the national myth was also built in order to erase their past and history.

This was implemented through an invented history.[7] At the beginning of the 1930s, the state – and Atatürk himself – took over the historical discourse and developed the "Turkish history thesis" (*Türk Tarih Tezi*) first expressed in 1931 as a set of history textbooks for high schools. Then in 1932, an international conference using Stalinist methods and benefiting from the complacency of some European academics approved the new interpretation of the past and the new national history.

According the outline of the new narrative, the Turks were supposed to have developed a high degree of urban civilization along the shores of an inland sea in Central Asia as early as in the 7th millennium BC. Climate change supposedly forced them to migrate towards China, India, the Middle East and Europe. These migrations are said to have introduced a wide-scale civilization process throughout the whole of Eurasia. The "Neolithic revolution", the emergence of high cultures in China, India, Mesopotamia, Egypt, Crete, Greece and Etruria, were explicitly claimed to have been consequences of the alleged Turkish migrations.

7 Etienne Copeaux, *Espaces et temps de la nation turque. Analyse d'une historiographie nationaliste, 1931–1993*, Paris, CNRS-Editions, 1997.

Figure 12: *"The motherland of the Turks and migration routes". The grey spot in the centre is the "motherland of the Turks". The arrows are the migration routes.*

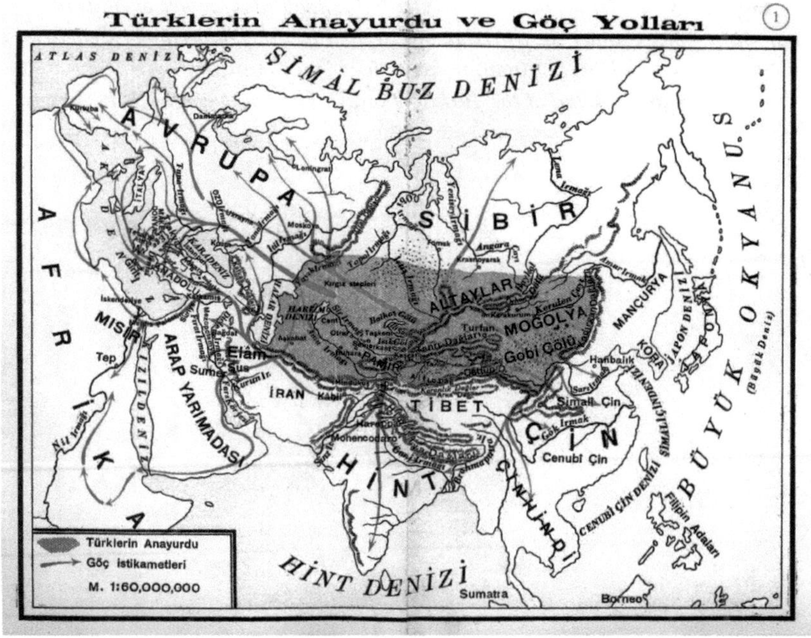

Source: Türk Tarih Tetkik Cemiyeti [Turkish Society for Historical Research, collective work], *Tarih I. Tarihtenevelki Zamanlar ve Eski Zamanlar* (History I. Prehistory and Antiquity), Istanbul, Devlet Matbaası (State Printing Department), 1931, 384 p., 7 colour pl., 22 maps h.t., 136 ill. h.t.

To provide some "proof" of their allegations, the authors of the new narrative (among them well-known intellectuals) hijacked and twisted the results of scholarly research in history and archaeology as far as they could.

While this narrative could offer some pride to the Turks, it was also useful for legitimizing the ethnic-cleansing process of the twentieth century. Since the arrival of Turkish tribes in the Middle East and Anatolia over the 7th millennium was admitted, Sumerians, Assyrians and Hittites were of Turkish origin. Hittite culture was considered the first "Turkish" civilization in Anatolia and the first "Turkish state" in history. "Anatolia, the Land of the Turkish Race", was even the title of a Ph.D. in anthropology by Atatürk's adopted daughter, directed by Eugène Pittard and defended in 1939.[8]

Figure 13: *Cover of the thesis by Afet Inan, adopted daughter of Atatürk, in anthropology under the direction of Eugène Pittard (University of Geneva), 1941:* L'Anatolie, pays de la "race" turque *(Anatolia, Land of the Turkish "Race"). Geneva, Georg, 1941*

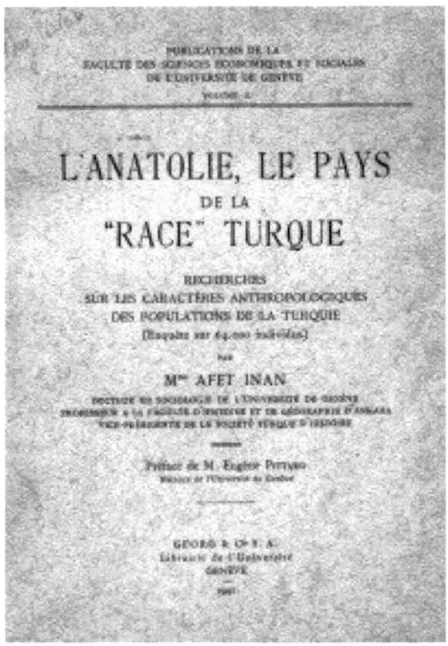
L'ANATOLIE, LE PAYS
DE LA
"RACE" TURQUE
RECHERCHES
SUR LES CARACTÈRES ANTHROPOLOGIQUES
DES POPULATIONS DE LA TURQUIE
Mme AFET INAN

Hijacking history and archaeology was not enough. Some years later, Kemalist intellectuals built another theory, the "Sun-language theory" (*Günes-Dil Teorisi*), stating that the Turks had invented articulated language, and subsequently that all of the world's languages (including America's) were of Turkish origin.

During the second half of the century, these extravagant theories were somewhat distanced, but were never clearly refuted. They still exist today as a set of implicit presuppositions and inferences, and hence are perhaps more

---

8 Afet Inan, *L'Anatolie, le pays de la "race" turque. Recherches sur les caractères anthropologiques des populations de la Turquie (enquête sur 64 000 individus)* (Anatolia, the Land of the Turkish "Race". Research Covering 64,000 Persons on the Anthropological Characters of the Populations of Turkey). Foreword by Eugène Pittard, Genève, Georg, 1941.

insidious, efficient and dangerous as their analysis and deconstruction are more difficult.[9] The consequences are heavy for historical studies in Turkey. History became "a well-established, hegemonic discipline historically allied with the state";[10] the questioning of national and official history and history-writing in a frame of scholarly research emerged as late as the end of the century.[11]

Moreover, the process is not over. The set of allegations, presuppositions, inferences, fake logical arguments and thought processes is still working. Only, the scope is rather different, since history now has to provide arguments in the conflict against the Kurdish movement. During the last third of the twentieth century, the state managed to produce a generation of dedicated historians and academics who try to "prove" using linguistics and history that the Kurds are of Turkish origin, coming from Central Asia as well. This discourse was used at least up until 1998.[12]

---

9 Etienne Copeaux, *Espaces et temps, op. cit.*, pp. 146–177.

10 Leyla Neyzi, "Oral History and Memory Studies in Turkey" in Celia Kerslake et al., *Turkey's Engagement with Modernity: Conflict and Change in the Twentieth Century*, Basingstoke, Palgrave Macmillan, 2010, pp. 443–459.

11 Ismail Besikiçi, *"Türk Tarih Tezi", "Günes-Dil Teorisi" ve Kürt sorunu* ("Turkish History Thesis", "Sun-language Theory" and the Kurdish Question), Ankara, Çaglar Matbaası, 1977; Büsra Ersanli, *Iktidar ve Tarih. Türkiye'de "Resmi Tarih" Tezinin Olusumu (1929–1937)* (Power and History. The Emergence of an Official History in Turkey), Istanbul, Afa Yayınları, 1992; my book *Espaces et temps de la nation turque. Analyse d'une historiographie nationaliste 1931–1993* has been translated into Turkish and published in Turkey in 1998.

12 Etienne Copeaux, "Un discours de vérité de l'Etat sur les Kurdes", 19 January 2013, available at: http://www.susam-sokak.fr/article-esquisse-n-33-un-discours-de-verite-de-l-etat-sur-les-kurdes-114522281.html; Martin Van Bruinessen, "The Kurds as Objects and Subjects of Historiography: Turkish and Kurdish Nationalists Struggling over Identity", in Fabien Richter (ed.), *Identität, Ethnizität und Nationalismus in Kurdistan. Festschrift zum 65. Geburtstag von Prof. Dr. Ferhad Ibrahim Seyder*, Münster, Lit Verlag, 2016, pp. 13–61.

Figure 14: *"The Kurdish tribe and its place in Turkish geography and history".*

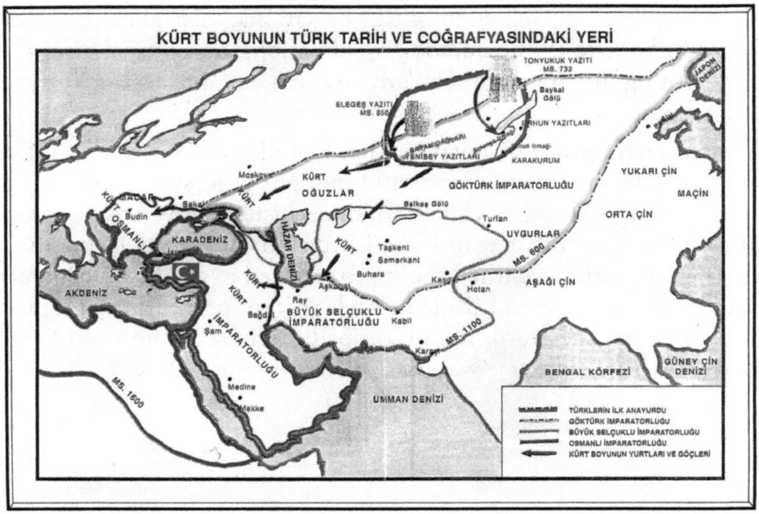

Map published by the Turkish army and distributed as a leaflet in an exhibition on how the PKK deceives the Turkish people. No place or date [1998]. Ringed in red: "The first homeland of the Turks". Ringed in yellow: "The Empire of the Celestial Turks". Ringed in orange: "The Sedjoukid Empire". Ringed in green: "The Ottoman Empire". The arrows indicate the "origin of the Kurdish tribe and their migration routes".

While the loss of territories might easily have been compensated for by a well-implemented nationalist policy, it is more difficult, from a rhetorical viewpoint, to legitimate a loss of population perpetrated by the state itself, which is the producer of the discourse. After having erased the Armenian presence in Anatolia and then evicted the Orthodox, the state has obliterated their history and imposed a narrative to hide everything.

Thus, the state does not explain to its children why there are so many churches spread over the territory of the Republic. Ordinary Turkish citizens are unable to understand the Anatolian architectural and cultural heritage. Amazingly, the historical discourse they have been taught prompts them to consider Greeks and Armenians as enemies who tried to invade Anatolia *after* the arrival of the Turks.

As one can see, the glorious narrative invented by the Kemalist and Atatürk himself is shaky, clumsy and not credible. It does not, of course, concur with the family memories of "exchanged" people of 1923, nor with the Kurdish reality. It has been criticized as well by religious trends over the political spectrum. Thus, later, "The Loss" was offset by another rhetoric that is currently superimposed on the former: the "Turkish–Islamic synthesis". This ideology, enhancing a religious idea of the nation, was already expressed in the early twentieth century by Ziya Gökalp, a famous theoretician of Turkish nationalism.[13] It became increasingly significant during the 1970s, finding resonance and popularity among the population, and eventually was supported by the military authorities after the 1980 coup d'état, becoming official in the 1982 Constitution, labelled "national culture" (*Millî kültür*).

This ideology grew stronger in the late twentieth century and is much more credible than the invented history of the 1930s. The Turks, on the basis of slightly modified historical facts, are presented as the "shields and spearheads of Islam". Without the Turks, Islam would have ossified and Islam's domain would have remained confined to the Arab world. The "national culture" is considered as having synthesized the original Turkish steppe culture with Sunni Islam.

Thanks to the large use, by the nationalist rhetoric, of a historical discourse spreading over large continental areas, and particularly of maps scattered in textbooks and the media, Turks are invited to feel that they belong to greater identities (*identité hypertrophiée*) such as a "Turkish world" stretching "from the Adriatic to the Great Wall of China", to the "Muslim community", to the post-Ottoman world, etc. These enlarged identities still nourish pride.[14]

This discourse, where one can recognize the influence of the old pan-Turkist trend, was very effective at the time of the collapse of the USSR. Among the extreme-rightist press and organizations, the illusion then grew that Turkish hegemony over "the Outside Turks" was at hand. It was a flourishing time for rightist trends and Turkish pride. With Central

---

13 Ziya Gökalp, *Türklesmek, Islamlasmak, Muasırlasmak* (Turkify, Islamize, Modernize), Istanbul, Evkaf-ı İslamiye Matbaası, 1918.

14 Etienne Copeaux, "Les territoires de référence des discours identitaires turcs", in Joël Bonnemaison et al., *Les Territoires de l'identité. Le Territoire, lien ou frontière?*, Paris, L'Harmattan, 1999, Vol. 1, pp. 113–124. Available at: http://horizon.documentation.ird.fr/exl-doc/pleins_textes/divers08-09/010014865-23.pdf. Etienne Copeaux, *Une Vision turque du monde, à travers les cartes*, Paris, CNRS Editions, 2000.

Asia as an economic and cultural influence zone, Turkey would become one of the great powers of the new century: it was a revenge on Sèvres. But the dream did not last. Central Asia is, geographically and culturally, more remote from Turkey than expected. Because of their history, the Turks feel closer to the former Ottoman domains and Balkan countries, even though they are not Turkish-speaking.

Atatürk had tried to stifle Muslim identity and to reject the Ottoman past, but they easily surfaced again. It should be remembered that a significant part of the Turkish population is of Balkan origin: the memory of what they had lost in 1923 was still alive at the end of the century, and perhaps even growing, thanks to civil society and to the Internet.[15] The war in Yugoslavia reopened the wound. The siege of Sarajevo and the Srebrenica massacre (1995) greatly affected the Turks, and these events were fully exploited by the trend of "Turkish–Islamic synthesis". During the 1990s, Muslim Balkan countries like Bosnia, Kosovo and Albania were seen as a Turkish heritage, "a seal affixed by the Turks in Europe" as was said in the mosques at that time.

In addition, an "Ottoman" revival surfaced in Turkey in every field of public life. The Ottoman past was openly prized and used as an implicit criticism of Kemalism and secularism. As an example, the last great sultan, Abdulhamid, was a subject of fierce controversy.[16]

Conclusion

Despite an apparent opposition between two visions of the past, Turkish nationalist discourse, which was precisely generated by the loss, is as glorious as the loss is immense; by invoking glory, heroes and exploits, it actually expresses deep frustration. The continuous ethnic cleansing (1915–74) was so radical, and willingly carried out, that on the one hand the state has chosen to remain silent, and on the other it claims its innocence by constantly evoking its supposed virtues. As we

15 Lisa Deheurles-Montmayeur, *La diplomatie du rapprochement entre villes grecques et turques depuis la fin des années 1980 et ses dynamiques territoriales*, Ph.D., Université de Grenoble-Alpes, 2013.

16 Etienne Copeaux, "Mémoire ottomane, retour du refoulé", 1 March 2013, available at: http://www.susam-sokak.fr/article-esquisse-n-34-memoire-ottomane-retour-du-refoule-115790163.html; "Nous sommes les petits-enfants des Ottomans", 16 March 2013, available at: http://www.susam-sokak.fr/article-esquisse-n-36-les-ottomans-ne-passeront-pas-116237146.html.

know, multiple occurrences of a signifier can underline the absence of the signified: this is the case with the word "tolerance", a qualisign which is very frequently put forward in Turkish historical and political discourse, although Turkey is the only post-Ottoman country to have eliminated almost all non-Muslims.

However, silence and denial, in turn, increase discomfort. The historical narrative has created "a convoluted, tortured and often traumatic relationship to the past";[17] an increasing part of the population feels an immeasurable loss and often guilt. Yet repressed memories are resurfacing, as shown by the huge crowd attending the funeral of Hrant Dink, an Armenian journalist assassinated in Istanbul in January 2007, claiming "We all are Armenians", and by an increasing number of publications.[18]

At the opposite end of the spectrum, discomfort pushes a significant part of the population towards extreme nationalism, whose tough and comforting values apparently help to stifle the feelings of guilt. Moreover, nationalism provides the figure of a charismatic Leader, a Guide, a Father – *ATA*-Türk – who puts to rest and protects.

A comforting and glorious narrative, or a comforting paternal figure (whether Atatürk or Erdoğan), are responses to fear. The threat created the fear of disappearing as a nation, as a society, the fear of a loss of identity. Fear made people insane and criminal, and resulted in genocide. Then, trying to offset the loss and make the country "homogeneous", nationalism implemented mass expulsions (1923, 1955). To cover the crime, an alibi was required: the historical narrative was conceived of as the alibi, and its silences and negations themselves established the reality of the crime.

As the loss is widely unaccepted, nationalist discourse is suffused with a desire for revenge and international power. Many believe that the dream of revenge is coming to life with President Erdoğan, who himself has to deal with personal narcissistic wounds. As a consequence, democracy has little opportunity to be well-established in Turkey as long as the loss is not accepted and the crime not recognized.

---

17 Leyla Neyzi, "Oral History and Memory Studies in Turkey", *op. cit.*

18 Aysegül Altinay and Fethiye Çetin, *The Grandchildren: The Hidden Legacy of "Lost" Armenians in Turkey* (trans. Maureen Freely), 2014; Fethiye Çetin, *My Grandmother: An Armenian–Turkish Memoir*, London, New York, Verso, 2012; Hasan Cemal, *1915: The Armenian Genocide*, London, Gomidas Inst., 2015. (Hasan Cemal, a famous columnist, is the grandson of Cemal Pasha, one of the leaders of the genocide.)

Broken Lives, Silenced Memories and Reappropriations of the Past: The Jews of Egypt and Islamic Countries*

Michèle BAUSSANT
Tenured research fellow at CNRS and member of the Centre de recherche français à Jérusalem

This chapter explores the ways in which the causes and decisions leading to the disappearance of most Jewish communities in Islamic countries have been reframed. Today, some authors regard the history of these communities as reduced to mere fragments of personal memories shared in small family circles. Yet this history has received renewed attention in academic circles, Jewish associations and various national and transnational public spheres. This interest has arisen within social and political contexts that are themselves changing, in particular in France with the immigration of Sephardic Jews to Israel in recent years.

In this study, I will focus on the specific example[1] of the Jews of Egypt in order to understand how representations of the past and memory are constructed, spread and transformed in the present, at the crossroads of

* This research has received financial assistance from the Labex *Les passés dans le présent, Investissement d'avenir*, réf. ANR-11-LABX-0026-01.

1 This chapter is part of an ongoing research project on the forms of patrimonialization of the Jews of Egypt, specifically in France, Egypt, the USA and Israel. The data was collected during an ethnographic survey of Jews born or having grown up in Egypt until the 1960s and having left for other countries, whether regrouped or not into Egyptian Jewish cultural associations, and Jews who remained in Egypt. This study draws on various sources, including over a hundred unstructured and semi-structured interviews, observations, informal discussions, archival documents and autobiographical or semi-fictional works. This research was conducted as part of the ANR project "Religious Circulations and Mediterranean Anchorages" (Cirelanmed) and the PPCARE2 project "Histoires perturbées, passés retrouvés: analyse croisée d'histoires orales et d'histoire dans des contextes post-conflits et postcoloniaux [Disturbed Histories, Recovered Pasts: A Cross-Disciplinary Analysis and Cross-Case Synthesis of Oral Histories and History in Post-Conflict and Postcolonial Contexts.]"

public uses of the past, shared memories and the history of historians.[2] This chapter analyses these reconstructions of the past over the long term in several countries and the ways in which those reconstructions circulated. This research is drawn from a larger project on the links between memory and the recomposition of societies, particularly in cases of postcolonial societies and immigration. Does the fact of having lived through an experience of displacement and loss, which at first seems similar to others, cause homogenized representations of the past to emerge, in which individuals find points of contact with their own, specific memories?

In such a context, does the past serve as a basis for re-creating solidarities among people? Or, on the contrary, does it feed rejection and disaffiliation, in particular, vis-à-vis the group or groups with which individuals identify?[3] And if so, which past is chosen? In this chapter, I will compare two different sets of sources analysed over the long term. The first deals with shaping the narrative of the loss into a political cause demanding refugee status for Jews from Islamic countries, on a national and transnational level and in political, activist and academic spheres. Challenging the "myth" of Ottoman tolerance towards Jews, this corpus of sources reveals the everyday suffering of life in Islamic countries before the European empires and the trauma of expulsion. These discrimination and trauma became experiences shared by all the Jews of Islamic countries. The political cause of fighting for refugee status has been fuelled by an ensemble of new approaches in which the responsibilities of these countries are being reassessed.

The second corpus focuses on Egyptian Jewish associations in France and Israel founded in the wake of the Israel–Egypt peace treaty in April 1979. These organizations seek to reaffirm Egyptian Jews' collective identity and distinct history rooted in their cultural and religious heritage. Each group is also rooted in its own particular local context, sometimes supported by the State of Israel or Zionist institutions and sometimes by private initiatives. Interpretations of departure and loss differ and change over time depending on the historical and social contexts in which those interpretations are made, but all of them reconstruct Egypt a posteriori as an origin, making the Jews of Egypt outside Egypt into a kind of inverted diaspora.[4]

---

2 Marie-Claire Lavabre, *Le fil rouge, sociologie de la mémoire communiste*, Paris, Presses de la Fondation nationale des sciences politiques, 1994.

3 Castel Robert, "Le roman de la désaffiliation. À propos de Tristan et Iseut", *Le Débat*, No. 61, 4, 1990 pp. 155–167.

4 Tom Trier, "Reversed Diaspora: Russian Jewry, the Transition in Russia and the Migration to Israel", *The Anthropology of East Europe Review*, Vol. 14, No. 11, 1996, pp. 34–42.

From "Jewish communities in Egypt" to "Jews from Egypt"

During the second half of the twentieth century, many "Eastern"[5] Jewish communities left or were expelled from countries in which some of them had been established for several centuries. This "mass" emigration has been estimated at around 800,000–900,000 people and affected all social groups, according to authors defending the idea of the "forgotten million".[6] Only a minority has remained in some of these countries.

In Egypt, in the space of two decades (1948 to the end of the 1960s), the majority of so-called "foreign" populations, *mutamassirun*, who belonged to a constellation of local and cosmopolitan communities, left the country. Some had only lived there since the nineteenth century, when their settlement was promoted by the Khedivate of Egypt. Others had been there much longer, as was the case with part of the local Jewish communities. Having prospered in that country, during general decolonization they became regarded as foreigners and were expelled or encouraged to leave on account of the political and social context. This context included the crises that affected Egypt during the first half of the twentieth century[7] and the move to restrict Egyptian nationality at the end of the nineteenth. Egypt's changes to nationality law would gradually lead to the exclusion of many minorities that had been historically rooted in the country.

These Jewish communities had grown significantly in Egypt owing to a wave of immigration (1860–1920). Their composition was heterogeneous, from the point of view of social status as well as origins, nationalities, Jewish rites, languages, and dates of establishment in Egypt. While some of the communities had been established in the country for several centuries, the mythical and historical connection of the Jews to Egypt configured

---

5 'Eastern' Jews refers to the Jews categorized under the terms 'Sephardim' in France and 'Mizrahim' in Israel. About this latter term, see Harvey GOLDBERG and Chen BRAM, "From Sephardi to Mizrahi and Back Again: Changing Meanings of 'Sephardi' in its Social Environments", *Jewish Social Studies*, No. 15, Vol. 1, 2008, pp. 165–188.

6 Malka Hillel SHULEVITZ (ed.), *The Forgotten Millions: The Modern Jewish Exodus from Arab Lands*, Cassell, Bloomsbury Academic, 2000.

7 See Frédéric ABÉCASSIS and Jean-François FAÜ, "Le monde musulman: effacement des communautés juives et nouvelles diasporas depuis 1945", in Antoine GERMA, Benjamin LELLOUCH and Evelyne PATLANGEAN (eds), *Les Juifs dans l'histoire*, Paris, Champ Vallon, 2011, pp. 815–840.

the forms of identification with Egyptian-ness that they developed.[8] The creation of the State of Israel in 1948 had a direct impact on the composition of the Jewish community in Egypt: some would be expelled, others would leave the country in two successive waves (in 1948 and in 1956, with the Suez Crisis, and then in a continuous flow until 1967). They left for Israel or towards Europe, in particular, France, North and South America and Australia. Only a small minority remained in Egypt.

The dispersion of Egyptian Jews in different countries

Faced with the urgent needs of the present, many cut ties with their Egyptian past in order to establish links in the countries they settled in. In Israel, the Egyptian Jewish community[9] are considered "Eastern" Jews, or Mizrahim, a category that includes Jews from Iran, Turkey, the Caucasus and Central Asia. These Mizrahim are estimated at more than 40% of the national Israeli Jewish community. Many of them have long tried to forget their links with the cultures of their countries of origin in order to assimilate, or have adopted strategies of protection[10] or distinction. In Israel, these links to Egypt are often considered a stigma, sometimes by Eastern Jews themselves. They have been marginalized from a spatial, social and cultural[11] point of view, sometimes even called "invisible Jews"[12] depending on their origins, sometimes "blacks" (*shkhorim* in Hebrew, *shvartzes* in Yiddish). The varying origins and diversity of these immigrants as well as of their descendants have been partly obliterated, in different ways, by other common reference points such as the Holocaust or the figure of the Sabra,[13] and masked in the grand official narrative produced in Israel and often in their countries of origin as well.[14] While some groups have attempted to denounce their stigmatization, such as

[8] Michèle Baussant, "Etrangers sans rémission? Etre juif d'Égypte", *Ethnologie française*, Vol. 43, No. 4, 2013, pp. 671–678.

[9] In 1961, the census counted 35,580 Jews born in Egypt or Sudan.

[10] Yoann Morvan, "Juifs d'Istanbul, territorialités d'une communauté entre recompositions et dislocations", *EchoGéo* [online], 16/2011, online 4 July 2011, URL: http://echogeo.revues.org/12419; DOI: 10.4000/echogeo.12419 (accessed 27 February 2016).

[11] Oren Yiftachel, *Ethnocracy: Land and Identity Politics in Israel/Palestine*, Philadelphia, University of Pennsylvania Press, 2006.

[12] W. F. Weiker., *Unseen Israelis: The Jews from Turkey in Israel*, London, The Jerusalem Centre for Public Affairs, Centre for Jewish Community Studies, 1988.

[13] This term refers to Jewish people born before 1948 in the Palestine territory under British rule and their descendants in the Israeli population.

[14] Avner Ben-Amos, *Israël. La fabrique de l'identité nationale*, Paris, CNRS Éditions, 2010.

the Israeli Mizrahi Democratic Rainbow, these movements attract mostly highly educated activists and thus remain marginal even within the circle of so-called Eastern Jews.[15] Among the latter, the Jews of Egypt represent a small, barely visible group. Many of them arrived in Israel without a nationality. Many belonged to a multilingual, urban middle class and were traditionalist Jews. Some of them blended into Israeli urban life in Be'ersheba, Haïfa, or Tel Aviv and its nearby suburbs where they found jobs, particularly in the banking and retail sales industry.

In France, the 240,000 Jews who arrived from North Africa (primarily Algeria) in the 1950s and 1960s made up the majority of the Jews in France, with the French Jewish diaspora (Ashkenazi) becoming a "national minority".[16] Among this population of immigrants categorized as "Sephardic",[17] the Jews of Egypt amounted to around 10,000 people[18] who arrived in France between 1948 and the 1960s. Their socio-economic profiles are diverse, but most of them specifically chose to come to France instead of other destinations for exile. Some arrived with only a secondary-school diploma; many of them continued their university studies while working. Some had French nationality, others were stateless. They came for a variety of reasons: some had been expelled from Egypt because they belonged to Zionist and/or communist movements, some because of their French nationality during the Suez crisis in 1956. Some followed their families, while others came before 1956 for school. Starting a new life in France was often difficult. They tended to reconstruct Egyptian Jewish sociability in fairly closed networks made up of others like themselves. Thus, they concentrated settlement in central Paris and in certain cities South and North of Paris.

---

15 See Nissim Mizrachi and Hanna Herzog, "Participatory Destigmatization Strategies among Palestinian Citizens, Ethiopian Jews and Mizrahi Jews in Israel", *Ethnic and Racial studies*, 35/3, 2012, pp. 418–435.

16 Estimated at around 550,000 people. Jacques Taïeb, "Immigrés d'Afrique du Nord: combien? Quand? Pourquoi?", in Colette Zytnicki (ed.), *Terres d'exil, terre d'asile: migrations juives en France aux 19eme et 20eme siècles*, Villefranche de Rouergue, Eclat, 2010, pp. 148–154.

17 This term remains controversial. See Benjamin Lellouch, "Les Juifs dans le monde musulman XVème siècle-milieu XIXème siècle", Antoine Germa, Benjamin Lellouch, Evelyne Patlagean (dir.), *Les Juifs dans l'histoire*, Paris, Champ Vallon, 2011, pp. 261–290.

18 There are no precise statistics on the number of Jews in Egypt. According to Gudrun Krämer, the Jewish community in Egypt was estimated at 3,000 to 4,000 people in 1840 and more than 60,000 people in 1920. Gudrun Krämer, *The Jews in Modern Egypt*, Seattle, University of Washington Press, 1989.

From *dhimmi* to refugee: the emergence of a "unified" narrative about the Jewish past(s) in Islamic countries

The histories of the Jews in Islamic countries, the disappearance of those communities from those countries, and ways in which they integrated into European countries like France, Great Britain and Italy, or in other connected countries such as Israel and the USA, have long remained at the margins of national narratives. In recent years, there has been a shift in academic and association circles and in different national and transnational public spheres. Today, the uses of these histories break down into at least two types. First, in France and other countries, there has been a movement to preserve the local material heritage of Jewish communities in Islamic countries since the 1990s.[19] This has occurred along with the development of community museums (Libyan, Iraqi, Egyptian, etc.), particularly in Israel. Sometimes, this movement has also sought to re-establish connections with the countries of origin in order to preserve the traces of Jewish history *in situ*. Among the younger generations in Israel, Mizrahi identity is gradually being reclaimed through movements that combine art and politics, although this is less observable in France. Several related literary works and films have been produced.

The second use of history, in Israel and elsewhere, particularly the USA and Canada, invests this past with a new political (and legal) purpose: to recognize Jews from Islamic countries as refugees. This has led to a certain rewriting of national history, especially in Israel, which must be re-examined with the notions of *Aliyah* (ascent, immigration) and the Palestinian *nakba*. These political uses, which have gained unequal press in societal debates in France, Israel and the USA, have been fuelled by academic research that sees the daily living conditions of these communities and their departure as having been the same over the long term and throughout the ensemble of Islamic countries. Certain reference points have been mobilized – such as the Holocaust[20] or the Algerian War – to reinterpret the present general situation of the Jews in the Diaspora and in Israel in light of this "unified" past, and even to announce their possible future confronted with the new/old Arab (and/or Muslim) persecutor. This reinterpretation differs from previous historical

19 Frédéric Abecassis and Jean-François Faü, "Le monde musulman", *op. cit.*

20 Bat Ye'or, "En islam, il n'y a pas de distinction entre politique, loi civile et religion", http://ripostelaique.com/Bat-Ye-Or-en-islam-il-n-y-a-pas-de.html, 2008 (accessed 12 March 2013).

and socio-anthropological work done in France around the singular histories of each of these varied populations. It also differs from research in Israel emphasizing the differences among these communities that have been "united" through their shared social marginalization in Israel.

In the shadow of the Holocaust: the "forgotten" Exodus

How did these seemingly shared discourses emerge? What are the stakes involved and the differences linked to national and historical contexts? How were this unity of historical and sociological condition and this unity of the future of Jews from Islamic countries elaborated? The writing of this history has as its object the departure and disappearance of "Eastern" Jewish communities, referred to as the "Forgotten Exodus".[21] These authors do not really seek to re-situate this disappearance within the framework of the profound transformations affecting the societies of the Muslim world as a whole. Rather, they follow the thread of history back from the present, stressing successive dramatic episodes that make up the main plot of that history, in order to obtain an overall vision of the whole and of elements of continuity. The modes of integration and the status of the Jews were unified under the neologism of *dhimmitude* (dhimma servitude) and their story was made to resemble that of the Jews of Europe.[22] This vision has sometimes been accompanied by a unitary rewriting of the history of the Arab-Muslim world, understood through the prism of evolutions in the history of the Jews. In this narrative, two opposing "units of civilization" clashed. The departure of the Jews was ultimately attributed to these clashes, which became one of the sources of the Israeli–Palestinian conflict and even the cause of the creation of the State of Israel.

This rise in generality can be observed among certain historians, essayists and activists, especially within the Jewish Diaspora.[23] Also present

---

21 This 'forgetting' contrasts with the increase of works in Arabic on Judaism and the Jews since the end of the Six-Day War. Michel Abitbol, *Les Amnésiques – Juifs et Arabes depuis 1967*, Paris, Perrin, 2005.

22 Georges Bensoussan, who uses the terms of ethnic cleansing and of Nuremberg-type laws. Georges Bensoussan, "L'exode des Juifs des pays arabes, un véritable nettoyage ethnique par la peur" http://www.crif.org/fr/revuedepresse/georges-bensoussan-%C2%AB-lexode-des-juifs-des-pays-arabes-un-v%C3%A9ritable-nettoyage-ethnique-par-la-peur-%C2%BB/58159 (accessed 3 October 2016); Georges Bensoussan, *Juifs en pays arabes, le grand déracinement, 1850–1975*, Paris, Tallandier, 2012.

23 See especially Maurice Roumani, *The Case of the Jews from Arab Countries: A Neglected Issue*, Tel Aviv, World Organization of Jews from Arab Countries (WOJAC), 1978;

in Israel, this trend is part of a political agenda in the Middle East and the USA.[24] Some dates sketch out the chronology of this agenda, which leads to claiming recognition of the legal status of these Jews as "refugees from the Arab countries" – a recognition joined to the Palestinians-in-diaspora's right of return and compensation and recognition demanded from the Arab countries.[25] The memories of the migrations and their consequences are used in this unifying narrative to support a broader policy towards the Islamic countries surrounding Israel and as part of the stakes related to the Israeli–Palestinian space.

Figure 15: *Internet screenshot. September 2012 campaign "I am a Refugee" spearheaded by Foreign Minister Daniel Ayalon*

In 1957-8, the Central Registry of Jewish Losses in Egypt was established in Paris, under the aegis of the *Alliance Israelite Universelle*, the World Jewish Congress, the American Jewish Committee and the Jewish Agency. In 1958, the organization of the victims of anti-Jewish

Itamar Levin, *Locked Doors: The Seizure of Jewish Property in Arab Countries*, Westport, Greenwood Publishing Group, 2001; Shmuel Trigano (ed.), *La Fin du judaïsme en terres d'Islam*, Denoël, 2009; Paul Fenton et Daniel Littman, *L'Exil au Maghreb. La condition juive sous l'Islam, 1148–1912*, Paris, PUPS, 2010.

24 Such as Justice for Jews from Arab Countries (JJAC), the World Organization of Jews from Arab Countries, The Jews Indigenous to the Middle East and North Africa, etc.

25 The JJAC thus estimates that 350 billion USD of Jews' property were destroyed or seized by so-called Arab countries.

persecution in Egypt was founded in Israel by a businessman from Alexandria to record and document the claims of Jews who had lost their property in Egypt, making a parallel between their experiences and those of the Jews of Europe.[26] In 1969, the Israeli State opened a Department for Rights of Jews from Arab Countries. Then in 1975 in Paris, the WOJAC (World Organization of Jews from Arab Countries) was founded. Nevertheless, after the peace accords with Anwar Sadat, compensation claims slowed. In the 1990s, the subject of compensation returned with books and documentaries on the subject and two conferences organized by the World Jewish Congress.[27] In September 2000, after the stalemate in Israeli–Palestinian negotiations, the outbreak of the second intifada highlighted the key question of refugees, susceptible of threatening the balance of the Israeli state. During the Camp David negotiations, Bill Clinton suggested setting up an international fund for Israelis[28] who had had to flee the Arab world. In 2003, Israel recognized the rights of Jews who had left Arab countries as refugees[29] and set up a campaign to collect information. The Organization for Justice for Jews from Arab Countries, which succeeded WOJAC and is headquartered in New York, was created in 2002. In 2008, the US Congress adopted Resolution 185 extending recognition of refugee status to Jews and Christians from Arab countries. This resolution was followed by a bill introduced in the Knesset by Nessim Zeev of the Shas party, adopted on 22 February 2010. It states that a peace agreement cannot be signed with an Arab country unless that accord includes compensation for Jewish refugees from the country.[30] In this case, refugee status refers only to Israeli citizens who have left an Arab country or Iran because of religious discrimination.

---

[26] Joel Beinin, *The Dispersion of Egyptian Jewry: Culture, Politics, and the Formation of a Modern Diaspora*, Contraversions 11, Berkeley: University of California Press, 1998.

[27] Bill Clinton is attributed with recognizing 'Eastern' Jews as refugees during discussions at Camp David. See Justice for Jews from Arab Countries, http://www.jewishrefugees.org/JusticeForJews.htm.

[28] In the USA, the first lawsuit against an Arab country was filed by Jews from Egypt whose property was confiscated by the Egyptian government.

[29] Decision 1250 of the Israeli government on 28 December 2003. http://israel.francophones.narkive.com/UZacyT6w/900-000-refugies-juifs (accessed 15 September 2016).

[30] On the calculation of property lost or confiscated, see Maxime Perez, "Séfarade blues: Israël et la question des réparations pour les Juifs chassés du monde arabe", *Jeune Afrique*, 28 March 2014, http://www.jeuneafrique.com/134094/politique/s-farade-blues-isra-l-et-la-question-des-r-parations-pour-les-juifs-chass-s-du-monde-arabe/ (accessed 25 March 2015).

A day of commemoration was set for 30 November in Israel and other countries, such as Canada and the USA, starting in 2014. The choice of 30 November as the official day of commemoration is linked to the anniversary of the 1947 United Nations vote (29 November) that terminated the British Mandate for Palestine and the partition of the land into two independent states – Arab and Jewish.

Palestinian Nakba versus Jewish Nakba

These political and historiographical uses of history are based, on the one hand, on comparing Jewish refugees from Arab countries with Palestinian refugees; and on the other, on using the term "Jewish Nakba"[31] to describe the persecutions, departures and/or expulsion of Jewish communities to oppose a counter-narrative to the Palestinian version. These usages have emerged in a context in which the figure of the victim has evolved, with that notion becoming increasingly polysemic and referring to distinct experiences. The two registers used here are that of experiences of the past over the long term, part of the "ordinary" course of life, and the register of an extraordinary event or period. Nevertheless, the goal of these uses is not to achieve reconciliation, nor to depoliticize the demands of justice and of history for the Jews of Islamic countries. On the contrary: their politicization is presented as a means of strengthening a union and a social consensus within Israeli society and beyond. This law adopted by the government does not evidence the degree of peace desired, but rather the status quo sought through recognition, which effectively blocks any negotiation treaty with Arab countries. In fact, does this law mean recognizing the historical connections between the dispossession of the Jews of Arab countries and the Palestinians? Or rather, does it respond to a political objective to put an end to the Palestinian question?

Concerning the use of the term "Jewish Nakba" or its rejection, the reasons diverge. For some, the Jewish Nakba was worse than the Palestinian Nakba[32] and only one category of refugees exists: the Jews driven out of

---

31 The Arabic term *nakba* (catastrophe) is used by the Palestinians to designate the exodus of the Arabic Palestinian population in 1948 during the Palestinian war and the commemorations of that event. It also refers to being forbidden to return.

32 The Jewish Nakba: expulsions, massacres and forced conversions, *Maariv*. http://www.nrg.co.il/online/1/ART1/891/209.html, 2009 (accessed 20 May 2012) [in Hebrew].

Islamic countries and "welcomed" by Israel. For others, the Jewish Nakba is not merely a response to the Palestinian Nakba, but should serve to highlight historical injustice and promote better awareness of the history of Jews in Islamic countries.[33] Some reject the very idea of the existence of two comparable Nakbas because it tarnishes Zionist history and agents who led the *Aliyah* of the Jews in the countries of Islam. Others reject the term because it refers to two different situations: for Zionist Jews immigration was the fulfilment of a national dream, while for the Palestinians it was an unwanted catastrophe. Others reject the Jewish Nakba because it compares what some consider to be ethnic cleansing of the Jews by Islamic countries with the departure of the Palestinians. Finally, some refuse the term because it creates injustice by making the Palestinians pay for acts committed by other countries.

This debate reveals the contradictions and the stakes involved in the return of the Palestinians and the place of the Jews from Islamic countries in Israeli society, in historiography, and more widely in the Diaspora. Consequently, use of the term does not refer, or not only, to the "reality" of the history around the events of 1948. Rather, this debate brings up many conflicts between the duty of historical objectivity, the context of intra-diasporic competition, the positioning vis-à-vis Israel or within Israeli society, and defending the Zionist programme.

The unified narrative and the diversity of memories: denouncing the marginalization of Jews from Islamic countries in national histories: a comparison

In referring to the exile of the Jews, more than the term "Nakba", "exodus" is more readily used in certain writings both in Israel and in the Diaspora. For the Jews of Egypt in particular, Passover, which commemorates the Exodus of the Hebrews from Egypt, is thus linked to what some call now the Second Exodus (*Yetzi'at Misrayim Hashenia*), which is not contradictory with the idea of *Aliyah*.[34]

---

[33] Ada Aharoni, 2009, "What about Jewish Nakba? Publicizing story of Jewish refugees could facilitate genuine peace process", http://www.ynetnews.com/articles/0,7340,L-3743829,00.html (accessed 12 March 2013).

[34] Levana Zamir, *The Golden Era of the Jews of Egypt in Modern Times and the Mediterranean Option for a United Middle East*, Tel-Aviv, Keness Hafakot, 2006.

Figure 16: *"To Zion, to mark the day of the exit and expulsion of Jews from Arab countries", photo taken at the University of Bar-Ilan on 3 December 2017, for the day-conference of commemoration, 26 November 2017*

© Michèle Baussant

If one follows only the political chronology and the narratives that seek to unify the histories of the Jews of Islamic countries and smooth over the contradictions, what becomes clear is the great plasticity of Eastern Jewish memory and its public uses. Grafting their individual life stories onto the tragic experiences of European Jews creates perspectives that can be shared and discussed and makes their suffering intelligible for other audiences, both Jewish and Christian. While specifying the uniqueness of Jewish history in the land of Islam, this unifying chronology also converges with the history of Christians of the Near East, seen as likely to raise public awareness in "predominantly Christian" Western countries.[35] Today, they are supported by the group Evangelical Christians United for Israel, founded in 2006, the largest pro-Israel organization in the USA. This organization has launched its "Mizrahi Project", collecting the story of the Mizrahi Jews in a series of video clips and recorded testimonies.

However, beyond the sometimes divergent issues that are unique to each national context, this narrative is also based on common interests

---

35 For example, this was the case with the *Réfugiés Oubliés* project in France in 2011 carried out by the B'nai B'rith. See http://www.bbfrance.org/le-projet-refugies-oublies-mene-par-le-b-nai-b-rith-france_a116.html (accessed 20 March 2012).

since there is a consensus about the silence and marginalization of the history of Jews from Islamic countries, both in Israel and in the countries where they settled. This silence seems to be the fruit of a triple alienation in the narratives of the countries of Islam, of Western countries and of Ashkenazi Judaism. In this context, Jewish–Islamic organizations, as well as certain actors from the academic and/or political world, have come together to take up these stories in a heterogeneous way. Public history sites have thus emerged such as Sephardi Voices, whose stated goal is "to ensure that the testimonies and stories of the Jews from North Africa, the Middle East, and Iran who came to the UK in different waves of emigration will be recorded and documented and that they will become an integral part of the history of British Jewish settlement in the UK. The mission of Sephardi Voices UK is to preserve the memories of Sephardi and Mizrahi Jews and to make them digitally accessible."[36] This site is now working in partnership with the Hebrew University of Jerusalem and the University of Miami.

Contradictions: nostalgia for Egypt in France

Yet is memory really that malleable? How and at what level is this unified model of memory reworked, reinvested and reappropriated, or rejected, as it originates in a country in which the stakes, the social and political goals, and even the very meaning given to this rewriting differ? What are the convergences and contradictions with the memories recounted by individuals?

It is difficult to know the weight of this issue outside circles of activists, organizations and academics in France, in Israel and elsewhere. Among the Egyptian Jews in France, when mentioning the past, they first privilege links with Egypt as well as relations with the West as cosmopolitanism. The ambiguities that ran through inter- and intra-community relations are not hidden, but people mostly paint a portrait of a golden age in which differences were minimized. The memory of anti-Semitism is rarely mentioned spontaneously, although it is not totally absent. What brings these people together is a common past (and not shared misfortune) in a country that they consider their homeland.

This is reflected in the work carried out by the *Association pour la Sauvegarde du Patrimoine Culturel des Juifs d'Egypte* (ASPCJE), founded

---

[36] http://www.sephardivoices.org.uk/ (accessed 12 October 2015).

in 1979 in Paris because of its founders'[37] desire to examine their plural identity and to reconnect Jewish and Egyptian culture. The association protects the non-material cultural heritage and knowledge about the Jews in Egypt. This association is closely linked to another, more recent, organization that protects Egyptian Jewish heritage *in situ*.[38] Together, they work to preserve the traces of Jewish communities in Egypt, in particular in Cairo and Alexandria. They are driven by the desire for the Egyptian state to recognize the Jews' contribution to Egyptian culture and history. Their purpose is thus twofold: to work both on identity and on knowledge of the past. They do so by emphasizing the long history of the Jews in Egypt, the incorporation of Egypt into a sacred geography of Jewish tradition,[39] and the processes of exchange between various religious and ethnic communities, in particular Jews and Muslims.

Among the people interviewed in France, whether or not they belong to such organizations, few agreed with the claim that Jews should be considered as refugees, even though a certain number of them came to France stateless. Some, however, noted that it had become difficult to talk publicly about a "golden age" of relations between Jews and Muslims as they once did. Others feel that the often tragic conditions of departure, for which they blame Egypt and its political leaders, have been minimized:

> In Egypt, I think we were integrated, in the sense that we spoke Arabic. We did not live on handouts. We produced something in that country … We were good, integrated citizens, but the circumstances changed. It became restricted, you had to be Egyptian, you more or less had to be Muslim … So we found ourselves outside the box. We were given to understand that we

37 Some of them are former childhood friends from Alexandria, who often went to the same schools and sometimes were imprisoned in Egypt for being Jews or communists, then expelled from the country.

38 In 2003, the international association *Nebi Daniel* was created, in reference to Nebi Daniel Street where the Great Synagogue was located in Alexandria, the *Eliahou Hanabi*. In the association's statutes, its goal is "The preservation and continuous management, in accordance with Jewish traditions, of the religious and cultural heritage, the financial and real-estate assets and the civil and religious registers of the Jewish Community of Alexandria and, by extension, the Jewish Community of Egypt".

39 This representation was based on the prior movement to draw up the history of the Jews in Egypt, which occurred at about the same time as the *Al-Nahda*. See Dario Miccoli, "Moses and Faruq. The Jews and the study of history in interwar Egypt 1920s–1940s", *Quest. Issues in Contemporary Jewish History. Journal of Fondazione CDEC*, No. 4, November 2012. url: www.quest-cdecjournal.it/focus.php?id=319.

> did not have what was needed, that we did not respect the fairly restrictive standards of the good citizen ... we were, you could say, the occupiers.[40]

Those interviewed pointed to the end of a world in which the situation of the Jews, like those of other groups, was increasingly marked by uncertainty. This uncertainty was reinforced both by political events that opposed Egypt to other countries and by the gradual collapse of the organization of their socio-ethnic community and their cosmopolitan circles. Their loyalty and attachment to Egypt had been challenged starting in 1948 and they were doubly suspect: often perceived as agents of Western imperialism, they were now also potential Zionist spies. When leaving, those who had Egyptian nationality obtained a laissez-passer "valid for a single trip without return" and had to sign a document renouncing their nationality.

Others interviewed sought broader causes of the break with Egypt: the creation of Israel, as if that state were "embedded in the body [of the community] ... around which the flesh would slowly become gangrenous and dig in ever deeper until it tore the flesh [of the community] apart".[41] Others thought the cause was the failure of Egyptian Jews' political involvement in the struggle for Egypt's independence, linked to forms of Pan-Arab national struggles and to the integration of minorities, who felt they were Egyptians and not Arabs. Others felt the cause had been their choice of a European way of life in Egypt, which eventually sealed their fate and condemned them to leave the country:

> That was their home, but they were not Egyptians ... In fact, what started to be a problem is that when you are born in Egypt, you had a residence certificate that was renewable every 10 years, and after a certain time, after Nasser, when you went to renew the card, they kept your passport and they gave you an Egyptian passport or an Egyptian identity card. And that, for the people who lived in Egypt who had kept their original nationality, for

40 "En Égypte, je pense que nous étions intégrés. Dans le sens où nous parlions l'arabe. Qu'on ne vivait pas sur le dos des gens. Mais on produisait quelque chose dans le pays ... Nous étions de bons citoyens intégrés, mais le cadre a changé. Il s'est rétréci, il fallait être égyptien, il fallait être plutôt musulman ... Alors on s'est retrouvé qu'on était hors du cadre. Ils nous ont fait comprendre qu'on n'avait pas, qu'on ne respectait pas les normes assez restrictives du bon citoyen ... nous étions, disons, des occupants." Statement (translated above) by Johann, born 1938 in Alexandria, whose father had Italian and whose mother had French nationality. A retired executive manager, he now lives in Switzerland.

41 Translated here. Carole Naggar, *Egypte. Retour*, Paris, Editions Nahar Misraïm, 2007, p. 38.

them, becoming Egyptian was out of the question. Egypt was our home, but we were not Egyptians.[42]

Thus the issue was not only the departure of the Jews of Egypt and the historical and geopolitical circumstances in which they were caught up, but this process of deculturation of the Egyptian Jews. Some of them described this loss of Egyptian ways of life as the founding moment of the future community of Jews outside Egypt – the factor that sealed their future disappearance from the country.

In Israel: knowing the past to denounce discrimination in the present

In Israel, the disappearance of Jewish communities from Islamic countries has been recognized from an institutional point of view, notably through commemorative activities and the desire to introduce the history and the "heritage of Jews from Arab countries and Iran" into education.[43] Focused more on symbolic politics than on concrete action to redress past and current discriminations experienced by Jews from Islamic countries in Israel, these various initiatives seek to generate shared values, symbols and identity by writing a common narrative, modelling their experiences on those of European Jews. Since 2009, the Ministry for Social Equality has been documenting the lost property and rights of communities originating from Islamic countries and Iran. However, by 2014, few actions had apparently been undertaken by the Ministry for Pensioners' Affairs to identify candidates eligible for restitution.[44]

---

42 "Ils étaient chez eux, mais ils n'étaient pas Egyptiens … Et en fait, ce qui a commencé à poser problème, c'est que quand on était né en Égypte, on avait un certificat de résidence renouvelable tous les 10 ans, et à partir d'un certain moment, après Nasser, quand on allait pour renouveler, ils gardaient le passeport et ils donnaient un passeport égyptien ou une carte d'identité égyptienne. Et ça, les gens qui vivaient en Égypte, qui avaient gardé leur nationalité d'origine, pour eux, il n'était pas question de devenir Egyptien. L'Égypte c'était chez eux, mais ils n'étaient pas Egyptiens" [our translation]. Woman born in Alexandria in 1945, a Catholic and mid-level manager. Her father was from Sicily and her mother from Greece. She left Egypt in 1962 for France.

43 See "Israël commémore l'exode des Juifs des pays arabes", http://fr.timesofisrael.com/israel-commemore-lexode-des-juifs-des-pays-arabes/ (accessed 2 December 2015).

44 See M. Perez, "Sefarades", *op. cit.*

Such recognition seems to have support from some of the Jews of Egypt, at least those who belong to organizations. According to J. Beinin,[45] these association members highlighted two aspects of their experience that allowed them to fit into the values of Israeli society: (1) they remained silent about their memories of life in Egypt, incompatible with the discourse of fitting into Israeli society in a political context shaped by a consensus on the relations between Jews and Muslims, past and present; and (2) they were considered to have been Zionists in Egypt and victims of anti-Semitic persecutions similar to those of Jews in Europe.[46] This can be partially explained by the fact that Egypt had long been presented as one of Israel's main military opponents. The peace negotiated between Egypt and Israel[47] partially changed the situation; afterwards, publicly expressing their memories of their former life in that country no longer meant they were viewed as sympathetic to the enemy. The creation of organizations[48] after the peace allowed them to reveal their presence, without, however, creating a consensus in nationalist Zionist and Egyptian historiographies. Some of these associations initially centred on depoliticized forms of evoking the past, around culinary culture for example. But they then actively campaigned for the repatriation of their heritage and belongings out of Egypt, in particular civil status documents and artefacts like the Sifrei Torah, and for the recognition of the history of "Jewish refugees from Arab countries". This shift shows that which representations of the past actors chose to follow resulted more from their positions within a given social sphere than their support or rejection of the narratives proposed or imposed by institutions.

This discourse also highlights the experience of dispossession and refugee status through the memory of *Ma'abarot*, the camps established in the 1950s to house Jews arriving in Israel. Moreover, some of the Egyptian Jews interviewed did not recognize themselves in a history that was debated in "European Jewish terminology". Some wanted the differences in the cultures of Jews from different Islamic countries to be recognized.

---

45 Joel Benein, *The Dispersion*, *op. cit.*

46 See the bulletin of the "Association des ex-victimes des persécutions anti-juives en Egypte/Irgun nifgaey ha-radifot ha-anti-yehudiot be-Mizrayim".

47 In April 1979.

48 Such as the Association pour l'Amitié Israël–Egypte, founded by Levana Zamir, which became the Union des Juifs en Israël, l'Union des Juifs d'Egypte in Haifa and which published the bulletin Goshen: alon Moreshet Yahadut Mitzrayim, IFLAC at Haifa.

For others, nostalgia for the country they had left behind, the experience of being uprooted and their marginal position in their new country gave them reservations about the idea of "restoring" the unity of the Jewish people. For them, being granted the title of refugee was paradoxically a way of being identified as a legitimate part of the memory of the Arab world. It was also, for others, to see their place in the development of Israel being recognized.

Conclusion

In Europe, the process of integration and reconciliation efforts around various painful historical events, including the Holocaust, only marginally concerns Jewish minorities from Islamic countries, who have nevertheless swelled the ranks of Jewish communities in Europe. These Jews from Islamic countries have not really been included in the various national narratives of the countries in which they have settled. Therefore, they have written their own histories inspired by websites or projects to collect stories such as the USC Shoah Foundation Institute of S. Spielberg. In connection with academic, activist and/or political circles, they have worked to invigorate national narratives, particularly in Israel, and to circulate accounts about the disappearance of Jewish communities from Islamic countries, which are unified to varying degrees.

Some Egyptian Jews work for a better understanding of the history of Jewish communities in Islamic countries as a means of achieving peace and mutual recognition. Others mobilize traces of the past and memories of lived experience to debate current relations between Jewish and Muslim populations, in countries where the question of coexistence involves different treatment, representations and practices for the two groups. The stakes involved with these shared discourses, their evolutions with younger generations, and the slow implementation of memorial or educational policies are all organized around the construction of a nation, and the losses of territory and society linked to those constructions. The hypothesis of discrimination, whether religious or political, is put forward in these shared discourses, supported by a triple appeal to emotion, to a historical model and to law. In the process, the fate of the Palestinians is redefined along with the chronology of their history in light of the history of the Jews from Islamic countries, at the end of a complex chain of responsibility.

These political uses of the past, both normative and conflictual, find their limits in the traces left by, and the weight of, lived experiences in the Israeli–Palestinian space, in the countries of Islam where Jewish minorities were (or are) rooted, and in other places. But if these political uses of the past are effective to a certain extent, it is perhaps because they intersect with a very long history which, at least in Europe, is made up of conflicts and reconciliations between the two communities. In that history, the place of the Jews, as well as that of Muslims, continues to challenge the always heterogeneous and often incompatible values of the social imperative of living together in harmony.[49]

Translated from French by Cynthia J. Johnson

[49] On this, see Jacques Derrida, *Le dernier des Juifs*, Paris, Galilée, 2014.

List of Abbreviations

AKP – Adalet ve Kalkınma Partisi (Justice and Development Party)

ASPCJE – Association pour la sauvegarde du patrimoine culturel des Juifs d'Egypte (Association for the Safeguarding of the Cultural Heritage of Egyptian Jews)

CUP – Committee for Union and Progress

EU – European Union

FYROM – Former Yugoslav Republic of Macedonia

MA – Master of Arts

MSI – Movimento Sociale Italiano (Italian Socialist Movement)

NATO – North Atlantic Treaty Organization

NGO – Non Governmental Organization

NKVD – Narodniï Komissariate Vnoutrennikh Diel (People's Commissariat for Internal Affairs)

PCI – Partito Comunista Italiano (Italian Communist Party)

Ph.D. – Doctor of Philosophy

PiS – Prawo i Sprawiedliwość (Law and Justice)

UK – United Kingdom

UN – United Nations

UNESCO – United Nations Educational, Scientific and Cultural Organization

USA – United States of America

USSR – Union of Soviet Socialist Republics

WOJAC – World Organization of Jews from Arab Countries

List of Tables and List of Figures

List of Tables

Table 1: Overview of the population of Eastern Central Europe in the 1920s 42

List of Figures

Figure 1: Monument situated at the entrance of the Burghalden cemetery in Sindelfingen, Germany 30

Figure 2: Reverse side of the monument 31

Figure 3: Germany's Eastern borders in 1945 40

Figure 4: Borders of Trieste / Istria (1937-1954) 72

Figure 5: Karelian territories attributed to the Soviet Union by the Paris Peace Treaty (1947) 82

Figure 6: Poland (1918-1945) 110

Figure 7: Expulsions and displacement of minorities in Turkey and surrounding lands (1830-1924) 137

Figure 8: Refugees in Greece (1928) 139

Figure 9: "Pontic Greek genocide", commemorative monument in Kastoria 148

Figure 10: Monuments to the memory of Hellenism of Asia Minor (Ionia, Cappadocia, Eastern Thrace) (1936-2004) 149

Figure 11: Annual 19 May commemorative demonstration for the recognition of the "Pontic Greek genocide" in the centre of Thessaloniki (2008) 153

Figure 12: "The motherland of the Turks and migration routes" (map) ... 171

Figure 13: Cover of the thesis by Afet Inan, adopted daughter of Atatürk, *L'Anatolie, pays de la "race" turque* ... 172

Figure 14: "The Kurdish tribe and its place in Turkish geography and history". Map published by the Turkish army and distributed as a leaflet in an exhibition on how the PKK deceives the Turkish people ... 174

Figure 15: Internet screenshot. September 2012 campaign "I am a Refugee" spearheaded by Foreign Minister Daniel Ayalon ... 186

Figure 16: "To Zion, to mark the day of the exit and expulsion of Jews from Arab countries", photo taken at the University of Bar-Ilan on 3 December 2017, for the day-conference of commemoration, 26 November 2017 ... 190

Index

Places, countries, regions, towns, cities, rivers, borders, monuments

A

Adriatic Sea, 60
Aegean Basin, 142
Aegean islands, 136
Aegean Sea, 163–165
Aeolia, 142
Agia Sofia, Trebizond (Saint Sophia, Trebizond), 144, 164
Albania, 176
Allenstein (Olsztyn), 131
Alsace, 33
Anatolia, 150, 163–164, 167–168, 170–171, 174
Ancient Greece, 36, 136
Arbe (Rab), 63
Armenia, 167
Armenian East, 45
Asia, 23, 46, 173, 176
Asia Minor, 29, 135–136, 138, 140, 142, 146, 149–150, 152–155, 158–159, 161, 163, 167
Athens, 140, 149
Atlantis, 131
Australia, 77, 145–146, 182
Austria, 20
Austrian Galicia, 115
Austrian Silesia, 39
Austro-Hungarian Empire, 115
Autonomous Region Friuli-Venezia Giulia, 75
Ayvalik, 160

B

Bay of Edremit, 160
Bafra, 140
Balkan, 167, 176
Baltic Sea
Baltic States, 104
Banat, 67
Basovizza, 80
Bavaria, 21
Belarus, 111, 130
Berkeley, 129
Berlin, 27, 40, 56, 93, 110, 118, 144
Bithynia, 138, 142
Black Sea (*Pontus Euxinus*), 41, 43, 140, 142
Black Sea Coast, 140
Bloodlands, 122, 133
Bohemia, 39, 110
Bosnia, 176
Boston, 145
Breslau (Wrocław), 120
Brest-Litovsk, 49
Bulgaria, 43, 154–155
Bursa, 155
Byzantium, 99, 136

C

Canada, 145–146, 184, 188
Capodistria (Koper), 71
Cappadocia, 138, 140, 142, 149–152, 158
Caucasus, 34, 140, 142, 182
Central Anatolia, 142
Central Asia, 176, 182
Chania, 159
Cologne, 46
Colonies, 33, 53, 60–61
Constantinople, 140
Crete, 159–160, 170
Cunda (Moschonisi), 160
Curzon Line, 110, 118, 120
Czech Republic, 20, 27, 39
Czechoslovakia, 42–44, 54

D

Dalmatia, 12, 29, 62–63, 68, 74, 79
Dalmatian Coast, 62–63
Danzig, 43
Deutscher Osten,
Deutz, 46
Didymoteicho, 154
Dodecanese, 61
Dresden, 93

E

East Prussia, 39–40
Eastern Border, 39–40, 49, 60, 65, 73, 76–79, 83, 90, 98, 102–103, 105, 113, 116, 123–126, 131
East(ern) Central Europe, 41–44, 54–55, 111, 114, 122, 132–133
Eastern Coast of the Adriatic Sea, 60
Eastern Europe, 12, 19, 23–24, 27, 33, 41, 43–46, 51–53, 55–56, 118
Eastern Finland, 100
Eastern Karelia, 89, 91, 94
Eastern March, 39
Eastern Polish borderlands, 111
Eastern Thrace, 135–136, 138, 142, 145, 149–150, 152, 154, 155, 163, 165
Egypt, 32, 61, 170, 180–183, 186–187, 189, 191–195
Elbe, 40, 50, 110
England, 55
Estia Neas Smyrnis, 154
Estonia, 42, 111
Ethiopia, 61
Euboea, 151
European North, the, 97
European Union, 13, 105

F

Farther Pomerania, 39
Federal (Republic of) Germany, 38–39, 43, 45, 55
Finland, 34, 81, 83–85, 87, 89–96, 98–107
Finnish State, 85–86, 91
Finnish Eastern border, 83, 90, 98, 105
Finnish–Russian border, 104, 106
Fiume (Rijeka), 69
Former Yugoslav Republic of Macedonia (FYROM), 155
France, 14, 36, 110, 179, 180, 182–185, 191–194
Frankfurt/Main, 47
Frankfurt/Oder, 37

G

Galicia, 39, 115, 120
Gelveri (Güzelyurt), 151–152, 158
German East, 15, 37–39, 41, 43–48, 51–53, 55–57
German Eastern border, 39

German Reich, 41, 44, 50, 53
German–Polish border region, 50
Germany, 14–15, 20, 27, 29, 34, 37–41, 43–44, 49–51, 54, 56, 60, 63, 84, 91, 106, 110, 118, 120–121, 130, 158
Gorica (Gorizia), 62, 65
Gorizia (Gorica), 62, 65
Grand Duchy of Finland, 87, 91, 103
Grand Duchy of Lithuania, 113, 115, 129
Greater Finland, 89, 96
Greece, 33–34, 60, 62, 135, 136, 138–143, 145–146, 150–153, 155–165, 170
Gulf of Bothnia, 97
Gulf of Trieste, 62
Güzelyurt (Gelveri), 151–152, 158

H

Heraklion, 159
Hermannstadt, 39
Hungary, 20, 42, 110

I

India, 23, 55, 170
Imera, 143
Ionia, 138, 142, 145, 149, 165
Islamic countries, 12, 32, 179–180, 184–186, 188–190, 194–196
Isonzo River, 65
Israel, 34, 179, 180, 182–191, 193–196
Istanbul, 155, 164, 167–168, 171, 177
Istria, 12, 29, 62, 64–65, 68, 70–72, 74, 79
Istrian peninsula, 68
Italy, 14, 34, 50, 59–65, 68, 70–71, 73–76, 78, 80, 184

J

Jewish East, 45
Joensuu, 100

K

Karelia, 81–89, 91–108
Karelia ceded areas (territories), 95, 104
Karelian Isthmus, 89–90, 94
Karvali, 151
Kastania, 144
Katyń, 119, 133
Katyń Forest, 119
Kaunas, 115
Kavala, 151
Kingdom of Poland, 112–113
Koper (Capodistria), 71
Kosovo, 176
Kozani, 158
Kozelsk, 119
Kresy, 12, 29, 47, 111–133
Kromni, 143
Kurdistan, 167

L

Lake Ladoga, 90
Lappeenranta, 100
Latvia, 42, 111
Lefki, 151
Lemberg (Lviv, Lwów, Lvov, Leopol), 39
Libya, 60–61
Lithuania, 40, 42, 110–111, 113, 115–117, 129–130
Livera, 143
Ljubljana, 64
London, 119, 126, 128
Lublin, 110, 119
Lviv (Lwów, Lvov, Leopol, Lemberg), 39, 110

Lwów (Lviv, Lvov, Leopol, Lemberg), 39, 110
Lychakiv Cemetery (Lwów), 117
Lower Silesia, 40, 124

M

Macedonia, 29, 143, 151, 155, 158, 168
Memel Territory, 43
Middle East, 23, 167, 170–171, 186, 191
Monastery of Ferres Evros, 154
Monastery of Panagia Soumela, 143–144, 150, 154, 161
Monastery of Saint George Peristereota, 143
Monastery of Saint John Vazelon, 143
Monastery of Saint Theodore Gavras, 143
Monfalcone, 65, 68
Montenegro, 63
Moravia, 39
Moschonisi (Cunda), 160
Moscow, 68, 76, 118
Mytilene, 160

N

Namibia, 54
Nea Karvali, 151–152, 158
Nea Prokopi, 151–152
Nea Smyrni, 149–150
Neisse, 120
Novgorod, 102
North-East Asia Minor, 142
North-Eastern Europe, 14
Northern Europe, 46
North Karelia, 100
North Karelia (County of)

O

Oder, 37, 120
Oder and Neisse Rivers, 120
Oder–Neisse line, 38, 40
Old Finland, 90–91, 101–102
Olonets, 89, 91
Olsztyn (Allenstein), 131
Oriental Africa, 60
Ostashkov, 119
Ottoman Empire, 33–34, 135, 155–156, 159, 163, 167, 169, 174
Overseas colonies, 33, 53–54

P

Pakistan, 23
Panagia Goumera, 143
Panagia Kosmosoteira, 154
Panagia Soumela, 143–144, 150, 154, 161
Pazin (Pisino), 70
Paris, 68–69, 105, 110, 113, 119, 127–128, 130, 183, 186–187, 192
Pirin Macedonia, 155
Pisino (Pazin), 70
Pola (Pula), 65, 69
Poland, 27, 29, 34, 40, 42, 44, 46–47, 50, 53–54, 109–113, 115–123, 125–133
Polish–German border, 120
Polish-Lithuanian Commonwealth, 111–117, 122
Polish Republic, 116, 118
Pontus, 138, 140, 142–143, 145, 161, 165
Potsdam, 120, 126
Poznań, 123
Principality of Novgorod, 102
Province of Ljubljana, 63
Pula (Pola), 65, 69

R

Rab (Arbe), 63
Region of Istanbul, 155
Region of Marmara, 155
Rethymnon, 159
Rijeka (Fiume), 69
Rhône, 50
Romania, 42, 54, 110
Rome, 76, 127
Russia, 23, 34, 56, 87, 89–92, 96, 99, 111, 113, 115–116, 119, 125, 133, 158
Russian Empire, 112, 115, 129, 142
Russian Federation, 104
Russian Karelia, 89, 91, 93, 101

S

Saint Sophia, Trebizond (Agia Sofia), 162, 164
Salonica Vilayet, 155–157
Salonica, 140
San River, 121
Sanda, 143
Sarajevo, 176
Savo, 86
Sejny, 131
Siberia, 118, 121
Silesia, 39
Smyrna, 140, 149, 154, 165
Smolensk, 111
Smolensk Military Air Base, 133
Sortavala, 101
South Caucasus, 33
South-Eastern Europe, 22, 33
South Karelia (County of)
South-West Africa, 54
Soviet Arctic region, 118
Soviet Central Asia, 118
Soviet Karelia, 98, 103
Soviet Union (USSR), 11, 33, 43, 105, 119, 175
Spain, 36
Srebrenica, 176
Stalingrad, 94
Starobelsk, 119
Stettin (Szczecin), 120
Sweden, 85, 89–90, 93, 101, 146
Szczecin (Stettin), 120
Szetejnie, 129

T

Thessaloniki (Salonica), 140, 145, 149–150, 153
Thessaly, 151
Thuringian Saale, 50
Tomb of the Unknown Soldier (Warsaw), 117
Toronto, 145
Transylvania, 39
Trabzon (Trebizond), 144, 162
Trebizond (Trabzon), 144, 162
Trentino–Alto Adige, 29, 77
Tripoli, 143
Tunisia, 61
Turkey, 31, 34, 135, 137, 145, 150, 154–155, 157–158, 160–162, 164, 167–168, 173, 176–177, 182
Turkish West, 45

U

Ukraine, 46, 111, 113, 117, 119, 127, 130
Upper Franconia, 50
USA, 23, 65, 145–146, 184, 186, 188, 190
USSR (Soviet Union), 11, 33, 43, 105, 119, 175

V

Venezia Giulia, 63, 65–66
Vermio Mountains, 144
Vienna, 39, 112, 144

Vilnius (Wilno), 115, 117–118, 120–121, 129
Virgin of Sumela, 144
Virolahti, 101
Vojvodina, 67
Volhynia, 120
Vyborg, 89

W

Weichsel, 50
Western Asia Minor, 140, 142, 149, 154
Western Europe, 29, 36, 76, 84, 112, 126–128
Western Poland, 29, 123
Western Ukraine, 119
Western Ukrainian SSR, 125
White Sea, Karelia, 89, 91
Wilno (Vilnius), 115, 117–118, 120–121, 129

Y

Yalta, 120, 126
Yugoslavia, 24, 61, 63, 65–68, 69, 73, 75–77, 176

Z

Zadar (Zara), 62, 68–69
Zara (Zadar), 62, 68–69

Persons

A

Abdülhamid II, 176
Agtzidis, Vassis, 145
Ahtiainen, Pekka, 96
Akçam, Taner, 146
Akritas (Akrita tou Pontou), 148
Alapuro, Risto, 100
Anartis
Apih, Elio, 63
Arndt, Ernst Moritz, 49
Atatürk, Mustafa Kemal, 136, 156, 164, 167, 170, 172, 175–177
Auer, Väinö, 93

B

Bartholomew I (Ecumenical Patriarch), 161
Baussant, Michèle, 12, 32, 33, 179, 190
Bayindir, Gökçe, 158
Bazin, Anne, 11
Beauvois, Daniel, 132
Bell-Fialkoff, Andrew, 25, 32
Berlusconi, Silvio, 78–79
Blomstedt, Yrjö, 88
Boehm, Max Hildebert, 51
Bohdan Chmielnzykyi, 114
Broz, Josip (Tito), 61, 65, 67–68, 76
Bruneau, Michel, 12, 32, 135
Bülow, Bernhard von, 52–53

C

Chmielnzykyi, Bohdan, 114
Chrysostomos (last Metropolitan of Smyrna), 149
Copeaux, Etienne, 12, 31, 32, 167
Corni, Gustavo, 12, 59
Czapski, Józef, 127
Czyżewski, Krzysztof, 131

D

Danielson-Kalmari, Johan Richard, 86
Dink, Hrant, 177
Dmowski, Roman, 117
Dündar, Fuat, 146

E

Enepekidis, Polychronis, 144
Engels, Friedrich, 46
Erdoğan, Recep Tayyip, 164, 177

F

Ferrara, Antonio, 12
Ficker, Julius, 52
Forsman, Georg Zakarias, 86
Fotiadis, Kostas, 144–145
Freytag, Gustav, 49

G

Gaddafi, Muammar, 61
Gallén, Jarl, 98–99, 102–103
Giedroyć, Jerzy, 127
Gökalp, Ziya, 175
Gombrowicz, Witold, 127, 130
Grass, Günter, 27
Grönhagen, Yrjö von, 93

H

Hadaczek, Bolesław, 128
Hahn, Eva, 12, 15, 37
Hahn, Hans Henning, 12, 15, 37, 41
Halicka, Beata, 12, 31, 109
Herling-Grudziński, Gustaw, 127
Hitler, Adolf, 51–52, 54–55, 84, 106, 118
Hofmann, Jerzy, 126
Hofmann, Tessa, 165

I

Inan, Afet, 172
Iosifidis, Koplanis, 151
Iwaszkiewicz, Jarosław, 125

J

Jaakkola, Jalmari, 89, 92, 97
Jordan, Wilhelm, 46, 50
Julku, Kyösti, 102
Jutikkala, Eino, 93
Juva, Einar W., 92

K

Kaczyński, Jarosław, 133
Kaczyński, Lech, 133
Katajala, Kimmo, 12, 81
Kekkonen, Urho, 97–98, 104
Kemal, Mustafa (Atatürk), 136, 156, 164, 167, 170, 172, 175–177
Kirkinen, Heikki, 99, 102–103
Kjellén, Rudolf, 88
Kolbuszewski, Jacek, 132
Kopaliński, Władysław, 125
Korhonen, Arvi, 90, 99
Koskinen, Yrjö, 85–86
Kulczycki, Jerzy, 128
Kulischer, Eugene, 23, 25
Kyriakidis, Tassos, 153

L

Leggewie, Claus, 13–14
Lemkin, Raphael, 145
Lieberman, Benjamin, 14
Liikanen, Ilkka, 12, 81
Lind, John, 102–103

M

Mandeville, John de, 47
Medvedev, Dmitry, 119
Merlié, Melpō, 140
Mesić, Stjepan, 80
Metropolitan of Trebizond, 140
Mickiewicz, Adam, 109, 113, 125

Mieroszewski, Julian, 127, 130
Miłosz, Czesław, 117–118, 127, 129
Mniszkówna, Helena, 126
Moniuszko, Stefan, 125
Montesquieu, Charles-Louis de Secondat, Baron de La Brède de, 47
Montmayeur, Lisa, 158
Mustafa Kemal (Atatürk), 136, 156, 164, 167, 170, 172, 175–177

N

Napoleon (Bonaparte), 112–113
Napolitano, Giorgio, 80
Nissilä, Viljo, 95

O

Okkonen, Onni, 95

P

Palacký, František, 15
Papadopoulou-Simeonidou, Parysatis, 162
Pasha, Talaat (Ottoman Minister of the Interior), 144
Pavelić, Ante, 63
Penck, Albrecht, 52
Perron, Catherine, 11, 30–31
Philippidis, Chrysanthos, 140
Piast dynasty, 122
Piłsudski, Józef, 117
Pittard, Eugène, 168, 172
Pupo, Raoul, 63, 66
Putin, Vladimir, 56

R

Ranta, Raimo, 101
Ratzel, Friedrich, 88
Renan, Ernest, 18
Rodogno, Davide, 64
Rosenberg, Alfred, 51
Rosoux, Valérie, 19
Ruchniewicz, Krzysztof, 12
Ryti, Risto, 92

S

Santin, Antonio (Archbishop of Trieste and Koper), 71
Schechtman, Joseph, 23, 25
Schlögel, Karl, 37–38, 44, 56
Schulze, Hagen, 38–39
Schwarz, Michael, 17
Schwarzenberg, Karel, 56
Sienkiewicz, Henryk, 113–114, 125–126
Sihvo, Hannes, 100
Słowacki, Juliusz, 125
Snyder, Timothy, 111, 122, 132
Stalin, Josef, 67–68, 84, 106, 118–120, 122
Stasiuk, Andrzej, 132
Steinbach, Erika, 55
Straszewicz, Czesław, 127
Struck, Bernhard, 50
Suckdorff, Victor, 88
Sultan, the, 159
Sybel, Heinrich von, 52, 54
Szymanowski, Karol, 125

T

Tervonen, Jukka, 96, 107
Tito (Josip Broz), 61, 65, 67–68, 76
Theophylaktou, Theophylakto, 140
Ther, Philipp, 16
Thum, Gregor, 44–45
Togliatti, Palmiro, 65
Tommila, Päiviö, 106
Topelius, Zacharias, 87
Tourkosporoi (Turkish seeds), 160
Traverso, Enzo, 21

Tsar, the, 112
Tsirkinidis, Charalambos, 144
Turks, 142, 154, 156–157, 161–163, 168–172, 174–176, 226

U

Üngör, Uğur Umit, 146

V

Venizelos, Elestherios, 164
Vilkuna, Kustaa, 93, 95–97
Voionmaa, Väinö, 88
Voltaire, François-Marie Arouet, 47

W

Waris, Heikki, 94–95
Wehler, Hans-Ulrich, 38
Winkler, Heinrich August, 38
Wippermann, Wolfgang, 45
Wittlin, Józef, 128
Wolfrum, Edgar, 21

Institutions, treaties, wars, norms, regimes, actors, groups, associations and political parties

A

Academic Karelia Society, 100
Academy of Finland, 106, 220
Adriatic Littoral Operational Zone (*Operationszone Adriatisches Küstenland*), 64
AKP (*Adalet ve Kalkınma Partisi*), 162
Alleanza Nazionale (National Alliance), 79
Alliance Israelite Universelle, 186
Allied Control Committee, 83, 105
Allies, the, 54, 60, 64, 69, 94, 126, 167
American Jewish Committee, 186
Anatolians, 138
Antemuralis (Christianitatis), 113
Arab refugees, 23
Armenian genocide (1915), 14, 136, 164–165
Armenians, 45, 145, 154, 161–162, 164, 167–169, 174, 177
Armistice
Italian Armistice (08/09/1943), 64
Moscow Armistice (19/09/1944), 81
Asia Minor Catastrophe (1922), 136, 159
Association of Friends of Lwów, 131
Association of Friends of Wilno, 131
Association of Greek refugees from Asia Minor and Eastern Thrace, 150
Association of the "Borussia" Cultural Community (*Stowarzyszenie Wspólnota Kulturowa "Borussia"*) in Olsztyn, 131
Association of Lausanne exchangees (*Lozan Mübadilleri Vakfi*), 157
Association pour la Sauvegarde du Patrimoine Culturel des Juifs d'Egypte (ASPCJE), 191
Associazone dei Giuliani nel mondo (Association of the Julians of the World), 74
Associazone Nazionale Venezia Giulia e Dalmazia (National Association for Julia Venezia and Dalmatia), 74
Axis powers, 63

B

Balkan Wars (1912–13), 135, 156, 167
Battle of Stalingrad (1942–3), 94
Battle of Warsaw (1920), 118
Belarussian, 111, 116, 121, 127, 130, 132
Beneš Decrees, 20
Berlusconi era, 76
Bolshevik Revolution, 115
Bulgarians, 142, 154, 167
Bund der Vertriebenen (Federation of the Expellees), 27
Byzantine Empire, 136, 148

C

Cappadocians, 138, 141–142, 150–155, 163
Catholic,59, 112, 114, 117
Catholic Church, 112
Central Registry of Jewish Losses in Egypt, 186
Centre against Expulsions (*Zentrum gegen Vertreibungen*), 27, 29
Centre "Borderland of Arts, Cultures and Nations" (*Ośrodek Pogranicze – sztuk, kultur, narodów*) in Sejny, 131
Centre for Asia Minor Studies (*Kentro Mikrasiatikon Spondon*), 140
Christians, 135, 155, 163, 187, 190
Christian minorities, 136
Cold war, 11, 24, 29, 35, 59, 65, 84, 104–106, 127, 137
Colonial war, 224, 53–55
Commemorative law, 145, 153
Commission (European), 20
Committee for Union and Progress (CUP), 136
Communist regimes, 24, 31
Communist Yugoslavia, 61, 65, 67, 77
Congress of Vienna (1815), 112
Continuation war (1941–4), 91–93, 94, 98, 103
Convention concerning the Exchange of Greek and Turkish Populations (Lausanne, January 1923), 157
Communist partisans, 69, 76
Communists, 65, 68, 71, 76, 78–79, 119, 122–124
Constantinopolitans, 138
Cossack leaders, 114
Cretan Turks, 159–161
Crimes against humanity, 17
Croats, 63–64, 71
Croatian clergy, 63

D

Day of National Memory of the Genocide of the Greeks of Asia Minor by the Turkish Authorities, 146
Dayton Peace Agreement (1995), 17
Department for Rights of Jews from Arab Countries, 187
Diaspora, 141, 143, 145, 151, 153–154, 163, 180, 184, 186, 189
Displaced Person, 20, 23
Domobrani, 66
Duty of remembrance, 36

E

Eaglets, 117
Ethnic cleansing, 12, 14, 17, 24, 33, 55, 73, 80, 136, 154, 165, 168, 171, 176, 189
European colonial powers, 33

European heritage label, 34
European integration, 17, 19–20, 34–35, 104, 108
European museums, 34
European Parliament, 20
Evangelical Christians *United for Israel*, 190
Exchangees, 155, 156, 157, 164
Exodus, 12, 61–62, 64, 66–74, 77–78
Exodus of the Istrians and Dalmatians, 62
Expulsion, 12–13, 19, 31, 39, 78–79, 120, 124, 168, 177, 180, 188

F

Fascists, 62, 71, 76
Fascist Italy, 62
Fascist regime, 60, 63
Federal Statistical Office of Germany, 43
Finns, 12, 81–82, 87, 89, 91–94, 98, 103
Finnish Army Information Office in Berlin, 93
Finnish Party, 86
Finno-Ugric (tribes), 86
Flight, 12, 120, 124
Foibe, 64–66, 70, 78–80
Forced migrations, 16–24, 28, 30, 32–35

G

Gavur Fidani (infidel saplings), 160
Genocide, 14, 18, 54, 66, 73, 78, 119, 135–136, 144–146, 150, 153–154, 161–165, 168–169, 177
German government, 39, 145
German (civilian) victims of the war, 27
German-speaking minority, 29
Giorno del Ricordo, 79–80
Government of the Republic of Poland in exile, 126
Great Exchange agreement (Lausanne, 30 January 1923), 168
Great National Assembly (1921), 167
Great War, the, 115–116
Greeks, 136, 138, 140–147, 149–150, 153–155, 157–158, 159–165, 167–168, 174
Greek Army, 145, 163
Greek government, 145–147, 153, 161
Greek Ministry of Education and of Local Authorities, 162
Greek Orthodox, 135, 142–143, 151–152, 163
Greek refugees from Asia Minor, 29, 138, 150, 154, 161
Greek-speaking (Muslim) minority, 161–162
Greek–Turkish friendship Treaty (1930), 15, 137
Greek–Turkish population exchange, 22, 32–33

H

Heimat, 15, 27, 47
Heimatrecht (right of return), 16, 31, 186
Holocaust, 13, 36, 80, 120–122, 182, 184–188, 196
Human rights, 16–19, 34
Hasidic (movement), 112

I

Iconography, 141, 143–146, 152–153, 158, 164
Imperial Alexander University of Helsinki, 86

Indian partition, 33
Inönü–Venizelos Greek–Turkish friendship Treaty (1930), 137
International Criminal Court (Rome Statute of the), 17
International Holocaust Remembrance Day, 80
Islamists, 162
Istituto regionale per la cultura istriano-fiumano-dalmata (Regional Institute for Istrian, Fiumian and Dalmatian culture), 75
Israeli Ministry for Social Equality, 194
Israeli Mizrahi Democratic Rainbow, the, 183
Italians, 12, 29, 33, 59–71, 73–80
Italian minority, 67
Italian Social Republic, 60

J

Jews, 23, 45, 80, 116, 118, 121, 145, 169, 185
Jews from Muslim countries, 12, 33, 180, 184–185, 188–191, 196
Jews of Egypt, 32, 179, 180–183, 191–195
Jewish Agency, 186
Jewish diaspora, 129, 185
Jewish pogroms, 168
Jewish refugees from Arab countries, 186–188

K

Kalevala, the, 88
Kalevala Society, 96, 99
Karelians, 12, 81, 86–87, 91–94, 97, 172, 175
Kemalist (Turkish) Republic, 136, 158–159
Kinship wars (1918–22), 98, 103
Kritiki, 160
Kultura, 127
Kurds, 167, 169, 173

L

Landsmannschaft, 20
Lausanne (Great Exchange agreement of, 30 January 1923), 168
Lausanne (Treaty of, 24 July 1923), 15–16, 135–136, 141, 154–155, 157, 159–160, 163, 167–168
Lausanne exchanges, 154, 157–159, 164
Liberation War, *Kurtulus Savası*, 1919–22, 167
Literary Institute (*Instytut Literacki*), Paris, 127
Lithuanian, 111–118, 121–122, 127, 130, 132

M

Megali Idea (Great Idea), 136
Megali Katastrofi (Great Catastrophe), 136–137, 154, 168
Mikrasiates, 140–141, 144, 149
Mikrasiates associations, 140
Millet – Ottoman millet system, 138
Mizrahim, 182
Mizrahi Project, 190
Molotov–Ribbentrop Pact (Moscow, 23 August 1939), 126
Movimento Sociale Italiano (Italian Social Movement), 78
Muslim, 135–136, 142, 151, 155, 158–159, 161, 163, 169, 192, 195, 197
Muslim exchanges, 136, 155–159, 164
Muslims from Greece, 155

N

Nakba (Palestinian), 33, 184, 188–189
National Committee for a Free Europe, 128
National Socialist Germany, 60
Nazis, 51, 54–55, 84, 106, 119–120
NKVD, 119–120
Non-aggression Pact (Molotov–Ribbentrop Pact, Moscow, 23 August 1939), 118
Novgorodian State, 102

O

Odnowa Press (London), 128
Official Day to remember Jewish refugees from Arab countries (30 November), 188
Operation Barbarossa (June 1941), 84, 106
Orbis Books, 128
Organization for Justice for Jews from Arab Countries, 187
Organization of the victims of anti-Jewish persecution in Egypt, 186–187
Orthodox, 112, 135, 138, 168–169, 174
Orthodox Church, 112
Orthodox Greeks, 135, 142–143, 151–152, 163
Orthodox pogroms, 168
Organization of Ukrainian Nationalists (*Orhabizacja Ukarinskych Naionalistiv*), 120–121
Ottoman, 33–34, 135, 138, 167, 169, 176
Ottoman Greek refugees, 144–146, 164

P

Palestinian people, 16
Paris Peace Conference (July–October 1946), 68, 70
Paris Peace Treaty (February 1947), 69, 79, 81–83, 105
Partisan movement, 59–61, 63, 65
Partito Comunista Italiano (Italian Communist Party), 65, 76
Partito Democratico Cristiano (Christian Democratic Party), 76–77
Patriots, 112, 156
Paulskirche, 47, 49–50
Piast dynasty, 122
Pilgrimage, 135, 138, 143–144, 150–152, 154, 157, 161
Poles, 12, 29, 45, 109, 111–121, 123–124, 126–127, 130, 132–133
Polish Army, 115, 119
Polish Committee for National Liberation (*Polski Komitet Wyzwolenia Narodowego*), 119
Polish émigrés, 126–128
Polish–Soviet War (February 1919–March 1921), 115, 117–118
Polish–Soviet Brotherhood, 125
Polish–Ukrainian (Civil) War (1918–19), 115, 117, 120–121, 123
Pomaks, 156
Pontians, 140–141, 149–150, 153–154, 158, 161–163
Pontic Greeks, 138, 140–146, 150, 153, 161, 164–165
Pontic Greek (cultural) associations, 146, 162
Pontic Greek-speaking Muslims, 161
Pontic hero, 148

Population transfer, 12–14, 16–17, 20, 23–24, 31, 35, 66
Potsdam Agreement (August 1945), 16
Prawo i Sprawiedliwość (PiS), 133
Protestant, 112

R

Recovered Territories, 122
Red Army, 118–119
Red Finns, 103
Reich (German), 41, 44, 49–51, 53–54, 65
Repatriates, 13, 121, 130
Repatriation, 12, 28, 121, 195
Republic of Pontus, 161
Resistance movement, the, 59
Resolution 185 (US Congress), 187
Right of return/*Heimatrecht*, 16, 31, 186
Robert Bosch-Stiftung, 56
Roma, 156
Russian State Duma, 119
Ruthenian, 114

S

Salonicans (*Selaniki*), 155–158
Sarmatism, 114
Seljuks, the, 142
Sèvres (Treaty of, 1920), 167
Sèvres syndrome, 167
Sephardi Voices, 191
Slavic-speaking populations, 29
Slavic minorities, 63
Slovenes, 63–64, 71
Slovenian clergy, 63
Socialist partisans, 59
Soviet occupation, 124
Soviet Socialist Republics, 121, 127
Sudeten Germans, 20
Swedes, 87

T

Thracians, 138, 140–141, 144, 152–155
Thracian associations,
Third Reich, 23, 54
Titoist regime, 66
Tourkosporoi (Turkish seeds), 160
Treaty of Brest-Litovsk (3 March 1918), 49
Treaty of Nöteborg (1323),
Treaty of Osimo (10 November 1975), 75
Treaty of Riga (18 March 1921), 115–116, 118
Treaty of Stolbovo (1617), 90
Treaty of Tartu (1920), 90
Turks, 142, 154, 156–157, 161–163, 168–172, 174–176, 226
Turkish Army, 145
Turkish history thesis (*Türk Tarih Tezi*) (1931), 170
Turkish Directorate General of (Population) Exchange, Development and Settlement, 155
Turkish government, 145, 161–162, 168
Turkish–Islamic synthesis, 175–176

U

Ukrainian, 45, 111–112, 114–117, 120–121, 123, 125, 127, 130, 132
Unione degli Istriani (Union of Istrians), 74
United Church, 112
United Nations, 80, 84, 105, 145, 188
UN Resolution (3236), 16
University of California, Berkeley, 129
Ustaša, 63

V

Valachs, 156
Versailles (disgrace of), 50
Versailles (post-war order), 118
Vertriebene, 16, 23

W

Warsaw Confederation Act (1573), 112
Western Institute (*Instytut Zachodni*), Poznań, 123
Winter War (1939–40), 90–92, 94
WOJAC (World Organization of Jews from Arab Countries), 187
World Jewish Congress, 186–187

Y

Young Turks, 136, 161
Yugoslav wars (of the 1990s), 16–17, 33

Z

Zentrum gegen Vertreibungen (Centre against Expulsions), 27, 29

List of contributors

Michèle Baussant is a tenured research fellow in anthropology at CNRS, a member of the Centre de recherche français de Jérusalem and an associated member of the Laboratoire d'Ethnologie et de Sociologie Comparative (LESC). Her research focuses on the processes of acculturation and social conditions that inform the dynamics of memory and heritage through a comparative study of minorities in Islamic countries that have been expelled en masse. It explores the cross-cutting themes of memory, migration and exile, with a particular interest in claims for financial compensations. Her latest publications are, together with Marina Chauliac, Irène Dos Santos, Evelyne Ribert and Nancy Venel, "Des passés déplacés. Mémoires des migrations (Dossier)", *Communications*, 2017/1, No. 100, and "Living in permanent exile, Egyptian born Jews in France", *Ethnologie française*, Vol. 43, 2013/14.

Anne Bazin is Associate Professor of Political Sciences at Sciences Po Lille, where she is director of the Master's programme in Advanced European and International Studies. She also teaches at Sciences Po Paris and NYU (Paris). She is a researcher at the Centre for European Research on Administration, Politics and Society (CERAPS), University of Lille – CNRS, and an associate researcher at the Institute of Social and Political Sciences (ISP), University of West-Paris – CNRS. She is a member of the editorial board of the journal *Revue d'Etudes Comparatives Est-Ouest*.

Professor Bazin works on post-conflict reconciliation as well as on transitional justice. Her work initially focused on the process of reconciliation in Central and Eastern Europe, post-Cold War. Among her recent publications are: Anne Bazin and Charles Tenenbaum (eds), *L'Union européenne et la paix. L'invention d'un modèle européen de gestion des conflits*, Paris, Presses de Sciences Po, 2017; "Reue, Vergebung und Sühne: der Beitrag der symbolischen Gesten zu Verständigung und Versöhnung", in U. Pfleil, C. Defrance (eds), *Verständigung und Versöhnung: Deutschland nach dem Zivilisationsbruch,*

Brussels, Peter Lang, 2016; "La question des expulsés dans les relations entre l'Allemagne et ses voisins après 1989", in C. Hähnel-Mesnard and D. Herbet (dir.), *Fuite et expulsions des Allemands: transnationalité et représentations 19ème–21ème siècle*, Villeneuve d'Ascq, Presses Universitaires du Septentrion, 2016, pp. 53–64; "Les prémisses d'une justice transitionnelle transnationale? La politique de rapprochement et de réconciliation de l'Allemagne avec ses voisins à l'Est après 1989", in K. Andrieu and G. Lauvau (dir.), *Quelle justice pour les peuples en transition? Études de justice transitionnelle*, Paris, Presses Universitaires de Paris-Sorbonne, 2014, pp. 65–90; and "Les acteurs publics de la réconciliation en Europe depuis la fin de la Seconde Guerre mondiale", *Les Cahiers Sirice*, No. 15, 2016/1, pp. 41–51.

Michel Bruneau, geographer, is Director of Research Emeritus at CNRS and Bordeaux University. He is currently working on diasporas and transnational spaces with a trans-disciplinary approach (*Diasporas et espaces transnationaux*, Paris, Economica, 2004, 249 p.). He has published numerous articles in international scientific journals, as well as chapters in books related to this research subject in French, English and Greek, in particular "Diasporas, Transnational Spaces and Communities" in R. Bauböck, T. Faist (eds), *Diaspora and Transnationalism: Concepts, Theories and Methods*, Amsterdam University Press, 2010, pp. 35–49. He recently published a geo-historical essay, *De l'Asie Mineure à la Turquie: minorités, homogénéisation ethno-nationale, diasporas*, Paris, CNRS-Editions, 2015, 412 p.

Etienne Copeaux is a specialist in contemporary Turkey. Formerly *attaché de recherches* (CNRS), he is currently an independent researcher, publishing articles and analyses on his own blog, susam-sokak.fr, devoted entirely to Turkey and Cyprus. His publications include: "A la recherche d'un 'miracle turc'", in O. Polychronopoulou, R. Treuil, *Nous avons rêvé la Grèce. Représentations et idéalisations de l'héritage hellénique*, Paris, Editions de Boccard, 2016, pp. 219–244; "The Research Topic as a Guideline", in I. Brandell, M. Carlson, Ö. Çetrez, *Borders and the Changing Boundaries of Knowledge*, Swedish Research Institute in Istanbul, 2015, pp. 78–88; "Laïcité et tolérance: deux mythes politiques turcs contemporains", *Cahiers de la Méditerranée*, 86/2013, pp. 319–329; "Geschichtsunterricht zwischen Affekt und Intellekt", in A. M. Nohl, B. Pusch, *Bildung und gesellschaftlicher Wandel in der Türkei – Historische und aktuelle Aspekte*, Würzburg, Ergon Verlag, pp. 110–120; "Le nationalisme d'Etat en

Turquie: ambiguïté des mots, enracinement dans le passé", in A. Dieckhoff, R. Kastoryano (dir.), *Nationalismes en mutation en Méditerranée orientale*, Paris, CNRS-Editions, 2002, pp. 23–40; and "Le consensus obligatoire", in I. Rigoni (ed.), *Turquie: Les mille visages. Politique, religion, femmes, immigration*, Paris, Syllepse, 2000, pp. 89–104. Most of his papers are published on the independent site https://independent.academia.edu/EtienneCopeaux/Articles-publi%C3%A9s-Published-papers

Gustavo Corni is Professor of Contemporary History at the University of Trento. His main fields of interest are the history of Germany in the twentieth century, the comparative study of dictatorships and the social history of wars, with particular interest in military occupations. His most recent publications are: *Storia della Germania. Da Bismarck a Merkel*, Il Saggiatore, Milan, 2017 (revised and updated edition), *Breve storia del nazismo 1920–1945*, Il Mulino, Bologna, 2015 (Spanish translation, Madrid, 2017), *Raccontare la guerra. La memoria organizzata*, Bruno Mondadori, Milano, 2012; with Katja Hrobat Virloget, Catherine Klein-Gousseff (eds), *At Home But Foreigners: Population Transfers in 20th Century Istria*, University of Primorska, Science and Research Centre, Annales University Press, 2015; and with Pertti Ahonen, Jerzy Kochanowski, Tamàs Stark, Rainer Schulze and Barbara Stelzl-Marx, *People on the Move: Forced Population Movement in Europe in the Second World War and its Aftermath*, Oxford, Berg Books, 2008.

Eva Hahn (in Czech: Hahnová), Dr, was born in Prague. She has lived in Germany since 1968 and in England in 1975–81 (Ph.D. 1981, LSE). In 1981–99 she was a researcher at the Collegium Carolinum in Munich, and later an independent historian and author in Oldenburg. She specializes in Czech history and Czech–German relations, expulsions after World War II, collective memory and research on stereotypes. Her major publications are: *Sudetoněmecký problém: obtížné loučení s minulostí*, Praha, Prago Media, 1995; and with Hans Henning Hahn, *Sudetoněmecká vzpomínání a zapomínání*, Praha, Votobia, 2002, and *Die Vertreibung im deutschen Erinnern. Legenden, Mythos, Geschichte*, Paderborn, Ferdinand Schöningh, 2010. *Od Palackého k Benešovi. Německé texty o Češích, Němcích a českých zemích*, Praha, Akademia, 2016; *Dlouhé stíny předsudků. Německé a anglické stereotypy o Češích v dějinách 20. Století*, Praha, Akademia 2015.

Hans Henning Hahn is Professor Emeritus. Born in 1947, he defended his Ph.D. in 1976 and his habilitation in 1986 at the University of Cologne. Between 1992 and 2016 he was Professor of Modern East European History at the University of Oldenburg, specialized in Polish and East Central European history, research on stereotypes and collective memory. In 1990 and 2000 he was Guest Professor at the universities of Warsaw and Cracow. In 2010 he was awarded the Medal of Gratitude of the European Solidarity Centre, and 2011 the Grand Cross of the Order of Merit of the Republic of Poland. From 2006 to 2017 he was president of the Societas Jablonoviana Leipzig, Member of the German Polish Textbook Commission. His major publications are (together with Eva Hahn): *Die Vertreibung im deutschen Erinnern. Legenden, Mythos, Geschichte*, Paderborn, Ferdinand Schöningh, 2010. *Stereotypy–tożsamość–konteksty. Studia nad polską i europejską historię*, Poznań, Wydawnictwo Poznańskie, 2011; Hans Henning Hahn, Robert Traba: *Deutsch–Polnische Erinnerungsorte*, vols 1–5, Paderborn, Ferdinand Schöningh, 2012–2015 (also in Polish, Warszawa, Scholar 2012–2015).

Beata Halicka is Professor of Cultural History of East Central Europe at the Adam Mickiewicz University in Poznań (Poland). She lectured at the European University Viadrina in Frankfurt/Oder between 2006 and 2014 and was a visiting professor at the universities in Calgary (2014) and Chicago (2015), and in 2016 in El Paso (USA). She is the author of five books and numerous articles and the editor of many collective publications. For her study *Poland's Wild West: Forced Migration and Cultural Appropriation of the Oder Region 1945–1948* (Paderborn, Ferdinand Schöningh, 2013, 393p.) she received the Identities Prize 2016 for the best historical book in Poland. Her research interests are: nationalism, forced migrations, constructions of identities in border regions, German–Polish relations, and issues relating to the culture and politics of remembrance. See: www.beatahalicka.pl/home/

Kimmo Katajala is Professor of History at the Department of Geographical and Historical Studies, University of Eastern Finland. He is a Docent (Adjunct Professor) in History at the University of Tampere, Finland. Professor Katajala is a member of the editorial board in the journals *Scandia* (Sweden) and *Kirchliche Zeitgeschichte* (Germany) and a full member of the Academy of Sciences and Letters in Finland. He has published a number of books and articles about the history of Karelia, the history of borders, historical cartography and the history of peasant revolts. His recent works are the edited book *Meanings of an Urban Space. Understanding the historical layers of Vyborg* (Lit Verlag 2016) and the chapter "Did the Rich Lead the Poor to Rebel in the Finnish Peasant Revolts of the 15th–17th–Centuries?" in *Aggressive and Violent Peasant Elites in the Nordic Countries, c. 1500–1700*, Ulla Koskinen (ed.) (Palgrave Macmillan 2016).

Ilkka Liikanen is Professor and the director of the VERA Centre for Russian and Border Studies at the Karelian Institute, University of Eastern Finland. He is a Docent in Political History at the University of Helsinki. He has functioned as director of the Karelian Institute (2002–2008) and as head of the Finnish Graduate School in Border Studies (2006–2013). He has published widely on nationalism and nation-building, post-Soviet politics, European borders and EU external relations. He is the co-editor and co-author of *The European Neighbourhood through Civil Society Networks? Policies, Practices and Perceptions*, London and New York, Routledge 2011, *EU–Russia Borderland: New Contexts for Regional Co-operation*, London and New York, Routledge 2013, and *The EU's Eastern Neighbourhood. Migration, Borders and Regional Stability*, London and New York, Routledge 2016.

Catherine Perron is Assistant research Professor with tenure at Sciences Po, Centre for International Studies (CERI) in Paris. She is a politologist and is member of the editorial board of the journal *Critique internationale*. Her current research focuses on politics of history and memory in Germany and in Central and Eastern Europe in relation to forced migrations and migrations in general. Her latest publications are "§96 Bundesvertriebenengesetz. Ein Instrument der Versöhnung Deutschlands mit seinen mittel- und osteuropäischen Nachbarn?", in C. Defrance, U. Pfeil (eds) *Verständigung und Versöhnung nach dem "Zivilisationsbruch". Deutschland und Europa nach 1945*, Brussels, Peter Lang, 2016, pp. 499–518; "'*Schaffen wir das?* Un enchevêtrement complexe de mémoires migratoires difficiles à concilier", in Christophe Bertossi (dir.) *L'Europe et ses réfugiés en 2015. Une crise de la mémoire*, IFRI-Paris, 2016, pp. 31–41 (web publication: https://www.ifri.org/sites/default/files/atoms/files/europe_refugies_2015_cmc_2016.pdf); and "§96 Museums" Against Forgetting?: The Museum as a Key Tool for the Diffusion of Knowledge about the Past German Presence in Eastern Europe", *Revue d'études comparatives Est–Ouest*, Vol. 47, Nos 1–2, March 2016, pp. 53–90,

Abstracts

Anne Bazin and Catherine Perron

Methodological Considerations in Addressing the Issue of Forced Migrations, Lost Territories and the Related Politics of History: A Comparative Approach

The introductory chapter presents methodological considerations concerning how to address the issue of forced migrations associated with the loss of territories. Starting with definitions, the chapter attempts to explain why the issue of forced migrations has not been addressed at a pan-European level, from a methodological point of view. It examines academic literature dealing with the issue of the loss associated with forced migrations and underlines the fact that in the last two decades, the research framework has considerably evolved in an attempt to overcome national-centredness. The authors introduce the concept of "politics of history", which constitutes the core research material of the following chapters focusing on case studies, in an attempt to analyse the legacy of past experiences of the loss in societies and public memory as well as domestic and external policies.

Eva Hahn and Hans Henning Hahn

The "German East": Myth? Reality? Lost Land of Dreams?

Starting from the expression the "German East", still in use – even among leading historians – in Germany today, this chapter critically addresses the following questions. What is the "German East", where is it, and how can it be located concretely? And, related to the idea of a loss, what is this loss exactly, and who lost what? Is this loss an overwhelming disaster for German existence as some claim? And if yes, does it have a special relevance for German identity? This last question induces two more questions, namely: when was the "German East" constructed as having a bearing on German national identity; and can this identity still claim to be relevant today in the first decades of the twenty-first century?

After having demonstrated the existence of a myth of the "German East", built up in discourse especially in the first half of the twentieth century, a true colonial myth, which differs from the other Eastern myths in that it claims ownership in addition to the aspect of duty and civilizing mission, the chapter concentrates on four aspects, the open border, the myth of loss, images of history and Eastern Europe, and colonial war, showing that the attempts to raise expulsion to a cornerstone of national memory and thus of German national identity have an influence on drafting and realizing German foreign policy vis-à-vis Eastern Europe.

Gustavo Corni

Private versus Public: The Memorialization of the Exodus of the Istro-Dalmatians, 1945–2015

Between 1945 and 1956, as a consequence of war events (the Italian occupation of Yugoslavia, the rise of a partisan movement) as well as in the context of the initial phase of the cold war, around 250,000 Italians were victims of an exodus from the areas of the Eastern border (Istria and Dalmatia) under the pressure of the newly communist Yugoslavia. This was the major event in the forced dislocations of Italians from former colonies, such as the Dodecanese and Libya. The exodus provoked strong remembrance in the families and the associations of refugees. But in the larger field of Italian politics it was for a long time obliterated, for opposing political reasons. Only after the political change of the 1990s, when the so-called "First Republic" collapsed opening the way to a new political system, was the exodus instrumentally presented to the public in order to legitimize the centre-right government of Silvio Berlusconi, culminating in the law on the National Memorial Day issued by the Parliament in March 2004. The contrast between a deeply rooted private memorialization and a weak public memory, largely instrumentalized for political reasons, characterizes the heritage of this dramatic population drive.

Kimmo Katajala and Ilkka Liikanen

The Politics of History of the Lost Land: Shifting European, National and Regional Approaches to the History of Karelia

The history of Karelia has been a vital element not only in addressing the loss of the region ceded to the USSR after World War II but also in addressing the national trauma of the lost war and legitimizing Finnish wartime political choices. This chapter examines the changing European, national and regional contextualization of the history of Karelia and analyses how paradigmatic shifts have been related to political circumstances. It studies the main trends in writing Karelia's history during the nation-building and inter-war periods and, importantly, its political use during the war. Its main focus is on the narratives and hidden meta-histories that were central for addressing the Karelian issue after the war. Finally, it discusses the renewal of historical writing on and perspectives on Karelia's history since the 1960s. Before the war, historical approaches to Karelia were profoundly influenced by grand narratives of Finnish national and European history. After the lost war, the most common publications were local histories, memoirs and studies of everyday life cherishing the memory of the lost land. From the 1960s onwards, political themes and perspectives on European and national history have returned and new critical approaches have given rise to more open discussion of the politics of history.

Beata Halicka

The Kresy *in Polish Memory: Between a Lost Arcadia and the Bloodlands of East-Central Europe*

Territorial losses and forced migrations are, next to war and occupation, the most traumatic experiences suffered by the Polish people in the twentieth century. Poland was apportioned by Nazi Germany and the Soviet Union in 1939, and shifted to the West in 1945. In particular, the loss of the huge territory in the East of the country – the so-called *kresy* – has an important place in the memory of the Poles and became one of the main topics in the politics of history. This chapter analyses how the losses have been dealt with over time, showing many different interpretations of the historical facts and different actors in Poland and in exile. Next to nostalgic narratives about a lost Arcadia, we have a great example of attempts to overcome the nostalgia and to look for reconciliation and dialogue with the neighbours in the East. The history of the territory named by Timothy Snyder "the Bloodlands" has been the subject of diverse debates, not only among historians. Unfortunately, it seems that the current politics of history in Poland takes a new development, in which the main narrative about *kresy* is not a dialogue of equal partners, but much more a defence of national interests.

Michel Bruneau

The Ties of Greek and Turkish Refugees and "Exchangees" to their Lost Homelands: An Asymmetry of Memory

The differences in the relationship with the memory of the "lost homelands" by the Greeks and the Turks can only be understood against the historical background of the events that led to the uprooting of these communities, how their forced exile occurred, and the societies in the two nation-states that emerged from the fall of the Ottoman Empire. The Greek Orthodox refugees were brutally driven from their lands and homes in Asia Minor between 1914 and 1924, and in Eastern Thrace by massacres and the rout of the Greek army in 1922. The Turkish Muslim refugees from Greece left in 1923–4 under a negotiated population exchange as part of the Treaty of Lausanne (1923), organized by the newly created Turkish Republic of Mustafa Kemal.

The population exchange on the basis of religion was a determining factor in the organization of two ethnically homogeneous nation-states living in peace, but at the cost of denying or not recognizing the memory of the refugees and exchangees on both sides. In Greece, the strength of their assertion of identity and right to, or even duty of, memory eventually took shape in townscapes (memorials, sanctuaries) and achieved official recognition by the Government in the 1990s, whereas in Turkey, the descendants of the Lausanne exchangees only tardily and shyly began to express their ties of memory. Official policy to forget was more effective and lasting in Turkey than in Greece, and it was not until the 1990s that memory began to show itself, whereas in Greece it had always been present and had grown from the 1970s on, because of the larger number of victims whose descendants felt a duty of memory.

For the Greeks, religion, their close attachment to Orthodoxy, was crucial to their constructing a collective memory so as to maintain links with "lost homelands" never to be forgotten. They used their religious faith to put together an "iconography" supporting their identity and the memory of their origins. The difficult question of the recognition of the "genocide" of the Pontic Greeks and of the Ottoman Greeks in general has become a central theme in the refugees' memory. The Muslim exchangees had no religious faith as a basis for a collective memory of their homelands like the Ottoman Greek refugees. On the contrary: most of them abandoned their special religious practices (*bektashi*, *alevi*) so as to melt into the dominant Sunni Islam of the new Turkish nation-state.

Etienne Copeaux

Turkey's Guiding Light and Consolation in Addressing the Loss: Nationalism

In considering the losses sustained by the Ottoman Empire after World War I, one generally thinks of territorial amputations. But it was even more so, since the period of transition between the empire and the republic was characterized by a genocide, and mass expulsions based on religious criteria, which were carried on during the Republic until 1974. The result was mourning, disorientation and a feeling of guilt.

Since the policy of ethnic-religious cleansing cannot be overtly acknowledged, the Republic of Atatürk has set up a new historical narrative, taught since 1931, which erases the history of the victims and glorifies the Turkish race, then, from the seventies onwards, a Muslim national identity. The discomfort and anxiety caused by the losses and crimes was compensated by a virulent, xenophobic and revanchist nationalism based on religion as much as on "race", and the cult of a reassuring Father (whether Atatürk or Erdoğan), who acts, up to the present, as a compass and a solace for the Turkish-Muslim population. As a result, Turkey will not experience democracy, and will remain guided by a nationalist ideology, until the loss is acknowledged and the crime confessed.

Michèle Baussant

Broken Lives, Silenced Memories and Reappropriations of the Past: The Jews of Egypt and Islamic Countries

This chapter explores the ways in which the causes and decisions leading to the disappearance of most Jewish communities in Islamic countries have been reframed. Focusing on the case of the Jews of Egypt, it intends to grasp the reconstructions of the past over the long term and the ways in which those reconstructions are spread and transformed in the present. Two different sets of sources are compared here. The first set deals with shaping the narrative around loss into a political cause, on a national and transnational level and in the political, activist and academic spheres, which demands refugee status for Jews from Islamic countries. The second corpus focuses on Egyptian Jewish associations in France and Israel founded in the wake of the Israel–Egypt peace treaty in April 1979. They are dedicated to the reaffirmation of Egyptian Jews' collective identity and distinct history rooted in their cultural and religious heritage.

L'Allemagne dans les relations internationales

Située au cœur de l'Europe, l'Allemagne occupe une position clé sur la scène internationale et représente un enjeu majeur pour ses voisins. C'est pourquoi cette collection entend rassembler des études portant sur la ou les Allemagnes dans ses rapports aux Autres du début du XXe siècle à aujourd'hui. Collection d'histoire et de relations internationales ouvertes aux disciplines proches à démarche historique, elle rassemble des ouvrages analysant les évolutions inter- et transnationales entre les États et les sociétés. Elle est ouverte aux approches comparées, croisées, connectées et aux processus d'échanges dans les champs politique, culturel, économique, scientifique, sociétal ou mémoriel. La collection s'articule principalement autour de monographies et d'ouvrages collectifs, éventuellement de l'édition scientifique de documents. Une attention spéciale sera accordée aux travaux des jeunes chercheurs et aux projets menés dans le cadre de coopérations franco-allemandes ou multilatérales. Les ouvrages s'adressent aux enseignants, chercheurs et étudiants, mais aussi à toutes celles et ceux qui s'intéressent à l'Allemagne contemporaine.

Directeurs de la collection

Comité scientifique / Wissenschaftlicher Beirat

Titres parus dans la collection

Vol. 15. Anne Bazin, Catherine Perron (eds.), *How to address the Loss? Forced Migrations, Lost Territories, and the Politics of History. A Comparative Approach in Europe and at its Margins in the XXth century*, 2018

Vol. 14. Mathieu Dubois, *Les conséquences économiques de mai 68. Du désordre social français à l'ordre monétaire franco-allemand*, 2018.

Vol. 13. Axelle Fariat (dir.), *La vie artistique en Allemagne après 1945. Analyses et réflexions sur l'enseignement et ses répercussions dans l'art*, 2018.

Vol. 12. Fabien Théofilakis (dir.), *Die Höhe 108 bei Berry-au-Bac im Ersten Weltkrieg. Die Front an der Aisne aus deutscher und französischer Sicht*, 2018.

Vol. 11. Fabien Théofilakis (dir.), *Cote à côte : Berry-au-Bac dans la Première Guerre mondiale. Perspectives franco-allemandes sur les fronts de l'Aisne*, 2017.

Vol. 10. Nicole Colin, Corine Defrance, Ulrich Pfeil, Joachim Umlauf (dir.), *Le Mur de Berlin. Histoire, mémoires, représentations*, 2016.

Vol. 9. Corine Defrance, Ulrich Pfeil (Hg.), *Verständigung und Versöhnung nach dem « Zivilisationsbruch »? Deutschland in Europa nach 1945*, 2016.

Vol. 8. Corine Defrance, Romain Faure, Eckhardt Fuchs (Hg.), *Bildung in Deutschland nach 1945. Transnationale Perspektiven*, 2015.

Vol. 7. Corine Defrance, Juliette Denis, Julia Maspero (dir.), *Personnes déplacées et guerre froide en Allemagne occupée*, 2015.

Vol. 6. Corine Defrance, Michael Kißener, Jan Kusber, Pia Nordblom (Hg.), *Deutschland – Frankreich – Polen seit 1945. Transfer und Zivilization*, 2014.

Vol. 5. Christin Niemeyer, Ulrich Pfeil (Hg.), *Der deutsche Film im Kalten Krieg. Mit einem Vorwort von Hans Helmut Prinzler*, 2014.

Vol. 4. Anne Kwaschik, Ulrich Pfeil (Hg.), *Die DDR in den deutsch-französischen Beziehungen*, 2013.

Vol. 3. Corine Defrance, Ulrich Pfeil (dir.), *La construction d'un espace scientifique commun ? La France, la RFA et l'Europe après le « choc du Spoutnik »*, 2012.

Vol. 2. Andreas Wilkens (dir.), *Willy Brandt et l'unité de l'Europe. De l'objectif de la paix aux solidarités nécessaires*, 2011.

Vol. 1. Bernard Ludwig, Andreas Linsenmann (dir./Hg.), *Frontières et réconciliation / Grenzen und Aussöhnung. L'Allemagne et ses voisins depuis 1945 / Deutschland und seine Nachbarn seit 1945*, 2011.

www.peterlang.com